EXAMINING
RELIGIONS

Judaism

Arye Forta

Heinemann

Heinemann Educational Publishers
Halley Court, Jordan Hill, Oxford OX2 8EJ
A Division of Reed Educational & Professional Publishing Ltd

OXFORD MELBOURNE AUCKLAND
JOHANNESBURG BLANTYRE GABORONE
IBADAN PORTSMOUTH (NH) USA CHICAGO

© Arye Forta 1989, 1995

First published 1989

New edition 1995

99 98
10 9 8 7 6 5 4

British Library Cataloguing in Publication Data

A catalogue record for this book is available from the
British Library.

ISBN 0 435 30321 X

Designed and typeset by Gecko Ltd, Bicester, Oxon
Illustrated by Barry Rowe and Gill Bishop
Printed and bound in Spain by Mateu Cromo

Acknowledgements

I wish to acknowledge my gratitude to Rabbi Zvi
Telsner of Finchley Central Synagogue, who read the
original draft of this text to check its accuracy; to the
various rabbis, ministers, teachers, historians and
other scholars who gave me invaluable help – in
particular Roger Butler, Doreen Fine, Moshe Golomb,
Bernard Hooker, Ezra Kahn, Michael Leigh, Sydney
Leperer, Naftali Loewenthal, Pinchas Toledano, Faige
Rabin, Chaim Weinreb and Jonathan Wittenberg, as
well as the many teachers up and down the British
Isles who piloted various chapters of the original
draft of this book in their classrooms. I thank them
all for their freely given assistance; responsibility for
any errors remains mine alone.

Thanks are due to religious studies consultant
W. Owen Cole and Keith Wicks for commenting on
the manuscript.

The publishers would like to thank the following for
permission to reproduce copyright material.
Lis Harris for the extracts from *Holy Days*, published
by Summit Books, a division of Simon & Schuster
Inc, on p. 109; Jewish Publication Society of America,
for the extract from *Judaism and Modern Man* by W.
Herberg on p. 142; Yigael Yadin for the extract from
Bar-Kokhba, reproduced with permission of the
publishers, Weidenfeld and Nicolson Ltd, on p. 5.

The publishers would like to thank the following for
permission to reproduce photographs.
The Ancient Art & Architecture Collection pp. 8, 14,
60; Peter Arkell/Impact Photos p. 117; Stephen
Bolsom p. 81; Werner Braun pp. 32, 90, 108, 129;
Hans-Jurgen Brurkard/Network Photographers
p. 126; Circa Photo Library pp. 4 (bottom left), 50;
Charles Green p. 82; The Hutchison Library p. 62;
Illustrated London News p. 79; Yehudis Ives p. 113;
Rabbi Louis Jacobs p. 142; The Jewish Education
Bureau p. 84; The Jewish National & University
Library p. 10; The London Museum of Jewish Life
p. 140; Marisa & Gerard Photographers p. 75;
Microscopix p. 96 (bottom left & right); Sidney
Moulds/Science Photo Library p. 97; Peter Osborne
pp. 4 (middle & bottom right), 27, 31, 36, 37, 38, 40,
44, 45, 46, 49, 54, 57, 64 (both), 66 (right), 70, 71, 88,
92, 95; Raissa Page/Format Partners p. 25;
Z. Radovan, Jerusalem pp. 23, 63, 132, 136, 145, 148;
John Rifkin p. 120; John Rifkin/Jewish Care p. 118;
Anat Rotem-Braun pp. 4 (top right), 102, 135; Royal
Observatory, Edinburgh/Science Photo Library p. 18;
RSPCA p. 124; Rachel Rietman pp. 43, 98; Science
Photo Library p. 96 (top right); R. Shymansky p. 76;
E. Simanor/Robert Harding Picture Library p.29;
Juliette Soester pp. 53, 59, 66 (left), 72, 78, 87; Frank
Spooner Pictures pp. 4 (top left), 107; Andrew
Syred/Science Photo Library p. 96 (top left); Topham
Picturepoint pp. 16, 100, 115, 147; B. Weinbraum
p. 130; Zefa Pictures pp. 122, 151.

Cover photographs by: David Richardson (top);
Hutchison Library (middle); David Harris (bottom).

The publishers have made every effort to trace
copyright holders. However, if any material has been
incorrectly acknowledged, we would be pleased to
correct this at the earliest opportunity.

CONTENTS

1 WHO ARE THE JEWS?

Look at the pictures below. The people you see do not look alike. They come from different parts of the world, speak different languages and represent different racial groups. Yet they all have one thing in common – they are Jews. The British schoolgirls and the American actress are **Ashkenazim**, Western Jews. The Indian secretary is an Oriental Jew. Oriental Jews are known as **Sephardim**. Ashkenazim and Sephardim form the largest two groups of Jews and this book will be mainly about them.

The Jews are one of the world's most ancient peoples. Their history goes back nearly 4,000 years. During that time they have been free people and slaves, rulers of kingdoms and homeless refugees,

American actress

Yemenite couple

British schoolgirls

Ethiopian boy

Indian secretary

settled in their own land and scattered throughout the world. There is hardly a country where Jews have not lived at some time.

Jews make up only 0.27 per cent of the world's population. In other words, if 10,000 people from different parts of the world were to gather in a big field, you could expect 27 of them to be Jews. However, their influence on human history has far outweighed their numbers. Many of the world's most accomplished musicians, writers, scientists, business people and politicians have been Jews. Not only this, but the religious beliefs and moral values of millions of people the world over have their origins in Jewish teachings about God and morality.

This book is not just about the Jewish people; it is also about Judaism, the religion of the Jews. Judaism is much more than a religion, it is a way of life. Not all Jews live this way of life to the same degree. Many Jews today have not had the chance to learn much about Judaism. They may keep some Jewish practices and hold certain Jewish beliefs, while ignoring or disagreeing with others.

However if you are going to study Judaism properly, you must look at where it is lived to the full. To enable you to do so, this book deals mainly with the beliefs, practices and institutions of observant Jews.

THE JEWS AS A FAMILY

Scientists interested in the origins of human society have thought of Jews in different ways. Some have described them as a race or a nation, but you can see from the pictures that neither of these terms is suitable. Jews belong to different races and nations. Others have thought of Jews as a religious group. This, too, is inappropriate since religious and irreligious Jews are just as Jewish as each other. So who are the Jews?

Most Jews do not choose to be Jewish – they are born so. Because of this, they tend to think of themselves as having a special relationship with other Jews, even with those they have never seen or heard of. Most Jews also feel a sense of kinship with Jews of the past, and take it for granted that they are descended from the ancient Israelites of the Bible. Of course, it is doubtful whether anyone today could actually trace their family history back that far, and over the centuries there has been marriage out of Judaism and conversion into it (p. 22). However, most Jews today are descended from Jewish parents and grandparents, and those grandparents were themselves descended from Jewish grandparents

and so on. The term which best sums up how Jews see themselves is 'family'.

It is because they think of themselves as a very large, widely scattered family that Jews in one part of the world have always tried to help Jews elsewhere who might have been in difficulties. In recent years, Jews in Britain or the USA have campaigned on behalf of oppressed Jews in the former Soviet Union and those in Israel have arranged airlifts to rescue Jews living under impossible conditions in Yemen and Ethiopia. You can now begin to understand why they do this.

FIND OUT

▶ Find out the names of some famous people who are Jews (there is one on the opposite page). A Jewish newspaper might be a good place to start. Make a list of the things they are famous for.

FOR YOUR FOLDERS

▶ Some years ago Professor Yigael Yadin, an Israeli archaeologist, discovered some household goods in a cave near the Dead Sea in Israel. They had been left there by a Jewish family running away from the Romans. Professor Yadin wrote about it:

'Archaeologists are also human beings, and as human beings, they are often emotionally attached to the history of their own people. Here were we, living in tents erected by the Israel Defence Forces, walking every day through the ruins of a Roman camp which caused the death of our forefathers. Nothing remains here today of the Romans save a heap of stones on the face of the desert, but here the descendants of the besieged were returning to salvage their ancestors' precious belongings.'

What do you think he meant?

'Remember the days of old, consider the years of each passing generation; ask your father and he will inform you, your elders and they will tell you.'

(Deuteronomy 32:7)

Jews are proud of being an ancient people and have a strong sense of their own history. It is necessary to know something of this history to understand how Jews think about themselves.

THE PATRIARCHAL AGE

Abraham and Sarah, Isaac and Rebecca, Jacob and his four wives Rachel, Leah, Bilhah and Zilpah are the three generations of Patriarchs (fathers) and Matriarchs (mothers) of the Jewish people. Jews today still speak of **Avraham Avinu** (our father Abraham) and **Sarah Imenu** (our mother Sarah).

The Patriarchs and their families were semi nomads who wandered over what is now Syria, Israel and Egypt about 38 centuries ago, grazing their herds as they went and camping within easy reach of cities. They were different from their neighbours because they believed in one God (p. 18)

and served Him not only through prayer and sacrifice, but also through acts of kindness and hospitality. The Bible tells how God promised the Patriarchs that the land of Canaan (now called Israel) would one day belong to their descendants.

Owing to a severe famine, Jacob and his family went to Egypt, where food was available. They settled there. A century later, they numbered many thousands. A revolt brought a new king to the Egyptian throne. He saw the Israelites as a convenient scapegoat on whom he could blame Egypt's economic and political problems (p. 48) and decided to make them slaves.

After several generations, God wanted to fulfil His promise to the Patriarchs and bring the Israelites back to Canaan. He called a man named Moses to set the Israelites free and lead them across the desert towards the Promised Land. The Bible describes how, seven weeks after leaving Egypt, they came to Mount Sinai (p. 52). There Moses received God's **Torah** (instructions about how Jews should live) and taught it to the people as he led them on their journey. Jews regard Moses as the greatest of the prophets and still refer to him as **Moshe Rabbenu**

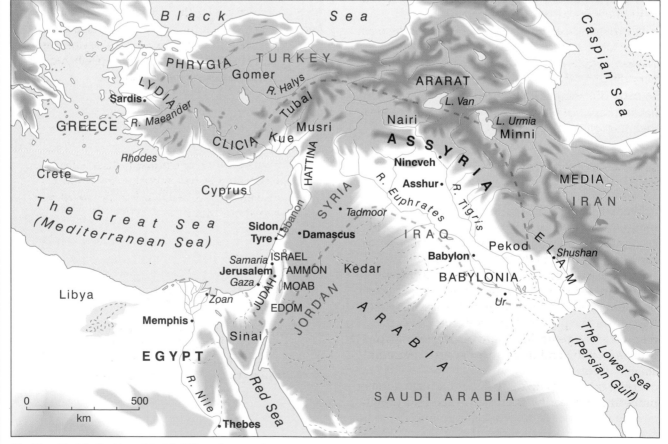

The Near East in the time of Isaiah (8th century BCE)

(our teacher Moses). God commanded Moses to have the Israelites build a Sanctuary, a portable temple which they could take with them as they travelled. This became the model for all Jewish places of worship, even to the present day (p. 84).

After 40 years, the Israelites reached the land of Canaan. Moses died within sight of the Promised Land, and his successor, Joshua, led the Israelites in.

THE TRIBAL CONFEDERACY (c. 1500–1000 BCE)

The Israelites entered Canaan and, after several years of warfare, conquered it. They divided the land among the twelve Israelite tribes. Each had its own territory and was ruled by its own elders. The most important leaders were the Judges, great prophets who were respected by all the tribes. Each tribe also had its high place, a raised point where people came to worship and priests offered sacrifices to God. The Sanctuary, which was set up in a number of places, was the most important place of worship.

Throughout this period, hostile neighbours came to rob and plunder. The Judges tried to raise armies to fight off the invaders, though usually only those tribes that were actually threatened would take part. By the late eleventh century BCE, the Philistines, a warlike people who lived in the south west, posed a very different threat. They aimed at total conquest. To meet this danger the people asked Samuel, the last Judge, to give them a king. A brave and pious man named Saul was chosen.

THE MONARCHY AND THE PROPHETS (c. 1100–586 BCE)

A king brought the Israelites together in a way that the Judges could not, and Saul took the field with an army raised from all the tribes. He fought several battles against the Philistines. After some initial success, he suffered a crushing defeat and was killed. He had reigned for barely two years.

Saul's son-in-law David, who became king after him, broke the power of the Philistines. David reigned for 40 years. Most of this time was spent at war, and by the end of his reign he had created a small empire.

The reign of David's son Solomon was a time of peace and prosperity. Trade flourished and wealth poured in from the empire and beyond. By now, the simple Sanctuary seemed inappropriate alongside the magnificent buildings which Israelite architects were designing. Solomon replaced it with a Temple which took seven years to build.

After Solomon died, some people did not want his son to be king. The northern tribes rebelled and set up their own kingdom, which they called Israel. The southern tribes remained loyal to Solomon's son and formed the kingdom of Judah. The people of Judah became known as Jews. The two kingdoms existed side by side for 200 years.

During the latter part of this period, a class of wealthy Israelites emerged. They robbed and oppressed their poorer brethren, and corrupt judges did nothing to stop them. Great prophets arose – men like Hosea, Amos, Isaiah, Jeremiah – who fearlessly denounced the most powerful people, even kings. Their teachings about justice and compassion have influenced Jewish moral thinking to the present day.

In 722 BCE Assyria, the superpower of the day, conquered the northern kingdom and led the Israelites into exile. They became lost to Jewish history. Just over a century later, by which time Assyria was no longer a major power, the tiny kingdom of Judah became caught up in the conflict between Babylon (now Iraq) and Egypt. In 586 BCE the Babylonians destroyed Jerusalem and the Temple (p. 60) and led the people of Judah to exile in Babylon.

FIND OUT

▶ Some of the best-known Judges were Deborah, Gideon, Jephthah and Samson. Use an encyclopedia to find out what you can about them.

THINGS TO DO

▶ How did the worship of the Patriarchs and Matriarchs differ from that of the people around them? What significance might this have for Jews today?

UNDER PERSIAN RULE (538–333 BCE)

Some time before the Temple was destroyed, Jews began settling outside the Holy Land. These settlements became known collectively as the Diaspora, the dispersion of the Jews. Babylon was the largest centre of the Diaspora.

In 538 BCE Cyrus the Great, King of Persia, conquered Babylon. He granted permission to all the nations exiled by the Babylonians to return to their native soil. Among them were the Jews. Some returned to Judah to begin rebuilding the Temple. Most chose to stay in Babylon, where large Jewish communities were thriving. After a number of setbacks, the Temple was finally rebuilt and more Jews returned to repopulate the Holy Land.

THE HELLENISTIC PERIOD (323–63 BCE)

By 323 BCE Alexander the Great had conquered the Persian Empire. Alexander and his successors wanted to introduce Greek culture to Asia. New forms of art, literature, philosophy and government emerged. All this is known to us as Hellenism. Many Jews became attracted to Hellenism and abandoned their traditional way of life. Tensions began to develop between hellenized and traditional Jews. These came to a head when a Greek–Syrian king Antiochus IV (175–163 BCE) tried to force the Jews of his empire to hellenize. This led to the Maccabean Revolt (p. 56) when the Jews rebelled and set up their own monarchy. It lasted until the Romans dissolved it.

THE RULE OF ROME (63 BCE–c. 300 CE)

The Jews of the Holy Land were brought under Roman rule in 63 BCE. The Romans were very harsh rulers and the Jews were divided as to how they should respond to them. Some wanted to rebel, others wanted to live in peace.

During this period a number of Jewish sects were formed. These were groups of Jews who differed as to how they thought Judaism should be practised. Most of them expected the immediate coming of a Messiah (anointed one), though they had different ideas about what he would do. Some thought the Messiah would drive the Romans out, others expected him to be a great teacher. They all believed, however, that when he came a new age of universal peace would begin. There were several Jews in that period who claimed to be the Messiah. The best known is Jesus of Nazareth. His followers, a small group of Jews known as Nazarenes, later grew into the Christian Church.

Sacred objects plundered from the Temple. Arch of Titus, Rome

In 66 CE, one of the sects, the Zealots, led a revolt against the Romans. Four years later Jerusalem and the Temple were destroyed (p. 60). Roman rule now became very severe and, during the years that followed, the Jews became more and more desperate. In 132 CE, under the leadership of Simon bar Koziba, known as Bar Kokhba (son of a star), the Jews rebelled. Bar Kokhba drove the Romans out of Jerusalem and ruled it for three years. In 135 CE he was defeated and Jewish life in the Holy Land was reduced to its lowest ebb. Many Jews left the country to find homes in the Diaspora. It was to be nearly 2,000 years before Jews would once again establish a sovereign state on the soil of their ancient homeland.

THE JEWS OF BABYLON (c. 200–1040 CE)

By about 200 CE Jews were living in many countries. Apart from the Holy Land, there were very large communities in Rome, Egypt and Persia. The largest Jewish settlement was in Babylon. There, the descendants of those Jews exiled after the destruction of the first Temple were flourishing. In some areas, they were so powerful that they formed independent principalities, and Jewish troops helped the local kings in their wars against the Romans. Jewish learning reached a high standard in Babylon. The **Talmud**, one of the most important works of Judaism (p. 31), was written in this period. The heads of the major academies were known as **gaonim** (singular **gaon**, meaning excellency). Jews all over the world consulted them on questions of Jewish law (p. 32). The last gaon was assassinated in 1040 CE, by which time Jewish life in Babylon was already in decline.

THE EUROPEAN MIDDLE AGES (c. 8TH – 15TH CENTURIES)

During the Middle Ages, Europe was Christendom. The church and aristocracy ruled, and of the two the church was usually the more powerful. This was a difficult time for Jews; at best they were merely tolerated, at worst massacred. Mediaeval Christians regarded Jews as the killers of Christ, (p. 14) and harsh laws were often passed to restrict or humiliate them. At times they were forced to live in ghettos, walled off parts of towns where they could be locked in at night, or were made to wear special clothes. They were seldom allowed to enter the more honourable professions and in some places they had to step into the gutter to allow Christians to pass.

The Jews were accused of almost anything – from poisoning wells to desecrating the wafers used by Christians in worship, even of killing Christian children to use the blood in their rituals (blood libels). They were often at the mercy of angry mobs. Towns and even countries sometimes expelled their entire Jewish populations. England expelled its Jews in 1290.

In spite of all this, Jewish learning reached new heights both in Europe and in Arab lands. Jewish scholars were mainly concerned with explaining the Talmud. Their writings were so profound that they became the basis for all later Talmud study, even to the present day. They were also engaged in Bible commentary and the development of Hebrew grammar. One of the most famous Jewish scholars of this period was Rabbi Shlomo ben Yitzhak (1040–1105), known as Rashi. Rashi wrote very important commentaries on the Bible and Talmud (p. 31).

In 1492 the Jews were expelled from Spain. Some settled in Holland, others made the difficult journey to the Holy Land. One group of scholars established a major centre of Jewish learning in Safed. The most important was Rabbi Joseph Caro. In 1555 he published a Code of Law called the **Shulchan Aruch**, the Prepared Table (p. 32). Others began explaining the Jewish mystical teachings (p. 33), which dealt with the individual's relationship with God.

THE JEWS UNDER ISLAM

Islam was more tolerant of other religions than Christianity, and Jews in the east were generally better off than their brethren in Europe. They were allowed to enter the professions and some rose to high governmental positions. Some Jews migrated from Christian to Islamic countries; seldom the other way.

However, there were also times when they were treated harshly. Muslims never really forgave the Jews for not accepting Muhammad, and Jews were subject to occasional humiliations and expulsions. Under the Almohads, who conquered North Africa and Spain in the twelfth century, Jews were made to wear distinctive clothing and their trading was restricted. At times, the humiliations were particularly severe. For example, in one Iraqi town Jews were neither allowed to wear shoes nor touch fruit and vegetables. Their homes could not have balconies jutting out over the street so that Muslims would not have to walk under them. This continued until the twentieth century.

As in Europe, Jewish scholarship flourished during this period. One of the most influential Jewish scholars was Rabbi Moses ben Maimon (1135–1204) known as Maimonides. He wrote an important code of Jewish Law (p. 32) and philosophical works.

$\diamond$

FIND OUT

▶ Look up Hellenism in an encyclopedia. Why might some Jews have found it attractive? Why do you think other Jews opposed it?

▶ The Pharisees, Sadducees and Essenes were important Jewish sects during the first century CE. Find out what their main teachings were.

THINGS TO DO

▶ Who were the gaonim? What did they contribute to Jewish scholarship?

▶ What were Jewish scholars mainly concerned with during the Middle Ages?

▶ What was the importance of Safed?

▶ Why were Jews punished (a) by Christians, (b) by Muslims?

THE EUROPEAN ENLIGHTENMENT

Throughout the Middle Ages, most people in Europe took it for granted that God was watching them from heaven above their heads, hell was somewhere beneath their feet and Christianity was the only route to salvation. During the latter half of the seventeenth century, all this began to fall apart. The English scientist Isaac Newton showed that the motions of the planets could be explained mathematically, without reference to God; Europeans discovered China, an ancient civilization that was thriving without Christianity; the translation of the Qur'an into French and English showed Christians that there was spirituality in a religion other than their own. Ideas such as these began to weaken the Church's hold on people's minds and opened the door to new ways of thinking.

The new thinking became associated with the Enlightenment, a movement that arose in western Europe during the early eighteenth century. Previously, people had taken the teachings of religion for granted. Now Enlightenment thinkers were attacking the accepted traditions of the past; for them the supreme human value was reason. The age of secularism (living without religion) was about to dawn, and it was to have far reaching effects on Jewish life.

Another Englishman, John Locke, wrote that people are largely what their environment makes them and that no human being is innately inferior to another. As far as the Jews were concerned, this and similar writings made people question the age-old Christian view that the Jews were an accursed race. Some people began to think that if the Jews were given the same educational and social opportunities as everyone else, they could become good citizens. Others even began speaking of emancipating the Jews, i.e. granting them civic rights.

THE RISE OF HASKALAH

At that time, in most of Europe, the Jews were very much a people apart. They dressed differently from the people among whom they lived and spoke a different language. The laws in Christian countries kept them out of the higher professions and humiliated them in many ways. People took this as proof that the Jews were inferior and that they were under a divine curse.

Here and there, individual Jews did learn the language of their gentile neighbours and studied mathematics or philosophy. They were usually self-taught. One of these was Moses Mendelssohn, a fashionable figure in Berlin in the mid-eighteenth century. He did gain acceptance into German society due to his powerful intellect and philosophical writings, which people respected.

Mendelssohn believed that the Jews would be emancipated if they changed their lifestyle. He and his followers tried to persuade other Jews to study secular subjects as well as Bible and Talmud, to use European languages, stop writing their business records in Hebrew and train for agricultural and craft work. This move to make Jewish life resemble that of the non-Jewish world became known as the

Napoleon's 'Sanhedrin'

Haskalah (Jewish Enlightenment). Those who followed its ideals were known as **maskilim**.

The maskilim themselves varied in outlook. Some merely wanted to change the way other Jews dressed, spoke and traded. Others wanted to change the Jewish religion to make it more acceptable to gentiles. These maskilim laid the foundation for the Reform movement that emerged in Germany in the early nineteenth century (p. 136).

EMANCIPATION

Some governments in western and central Europe saw emancipation as a prize to be given to Jews for shedding those elements of their religion which made them different from others. The French Revolution of 1789 proclaimed 'liberty, equality, fraternity' for everyone in France, including the Jews. But it was only to be granted them if they started thinking of themselves as Frenchmen. Soon after coming to power, Napoleon declared that 'within ten years there will be no difference between a Jew and a Frenchman'. In 1807 he set up a Sanhedrin (supreme Jewish council) because, among other things, he wanted the rabbis to pass a law permitting Jews to marry non-Jews. The rabbis compromised by agreeing that mixed marriages were to be valid according to the laws of France but not according to Jewish law.

THE JEWS OF RUSSIA

As elsewhere, the Jews of Russia were under pressure to become like everyone else. Jewish men had to serve 20 years in the Tsar's army. This was to weaken their ties with their communities so that they could be converted to Christianity. Crown schools were set up to make the Jews more Russian, and the government formed a society to persuade Jews to accept Christianity. Maskilim who went to Russia received government support for their plans to introduce secular studies into Jewish schools and reduce the time spent on Talmud. In spite of all this, most Jews remained loyal to their people, if not always loyal to their religion.

The Jews of Russia were persecuted for a long time and harsh laws were often passed against them. This drove thousands of Jews away from eastern Europe. From about 1880 onwards, they began leaving Russia, Poland and the Ukraine. Most went to the USA. Others settled in Palestine (now Israel), Britain, South Africa and Australia.

THE RISE OF RELIGIOUS AND POLITICAL MOVEMENTS

During the nineteenth century, Haskalah, emancipation and persecution led to enormous changes in Jewish life in Europe. In Germany, the Reform movement began trying to adapt Judaism to the needs of assimilated Jews. In eastern and central Europe, the Zionist movement sought to gain for the Jews a country of their own. In Russia, the Bund, a Jewish socialist movement, wanted Jews to shed their Judaism and become accepted as loyal Russians.

At the same time, traditional Jews were beginning to make their own responses to the new conditions. The **Hasidic movement**, which had begun during the late seventeenth century in Poland, the **Musar movement** in Russia and neo-Orthodoxy in Germany all became powerful forces in strengthening traditional Jewish values in a changing world. These movements will be discussed in detail on pp. 128–35.

FIND OUT

▶ Some of the most important enlightenment thinkers were the Frenchmen Diderot and Voltaire. Find out what their contributions were and what they said about Jews.

THINGS TO DO

▶ What was the Enlightenment? How did it affect the Jews?

▶ In what ways did Moses Mendelssohn want the Jews to change? What did he hope to accomplish? Who were the maskilim?

▶ How did the French Revolution benefit the Jews of France? How did it threaten their survival?

▶ How did many Russian Jews respond to persecution?

▶ What is the difference between a religious movement and a political one? Which of the movements mentioned in this unit are mainly political?

By the early years of the twentieth century, thousands of Jews had left eastern Europe, mainly for the United States. In Britain, too, large numbers settled near the docklands of London, Merseyside and Tyneside, as well as Manchester, Hull and Bradford. These Jewish refugees were poor, working-class people, who struggled to make a living and provide their children with an education.

Many of these immigrants were deeply religious. In Britain, they found that no one would employ them unless they worked on Saturday (the Jewish Sabbath) and festivals. In those days, there was no welfare state and if a man did not work, his family starved. They agonized over working on the holy days. Some worked on Sabbath mornings, then went to synagogue in the afternoon and wept. However, as time went on, religious observance began to decline. The new generation had other concerns and were not committed to Judaism in the same way that their immigrant parents had been.

Young Jews growing up in Britain in the 1920s and 1930s wanted, above all else, to be accepted into British society. They felt uncomfortable that their parents spoke English with east European accents. Many changed their foreign names to English-sounding ones; some married non-Jewish partners (known as 'marrying out'). Only a minority of Jews in London, Manchester and Gateshead remained loyal to their faith and its teachings. The majority wanted to cast off their refugee past – and that usually meant casting off Judaism, too.

THE HOLOCAUST

In 1933, in Germany, the National Socialist (Nazi) Party was elected to power with Adolf Hitler as its leader. The Nazis had two objectives. First, they would produce arms, train men for war and restore Germany to greatness by armed conquest. Second, by blaming all the country's problems on the Jews (p. 16) they would provide an outlet for German anger and frustration.

Nazi propaganda claimed that the Jews controlled the banks, had a monopoly on the professions and universities and were plotting with the communists to take over the country. As they gradually stripped the Jews of their citizen's rights, other Germans began to feel that they were doing the right thing. This paved the way for the Nazis' 'final solution to the Jewish problem' – wiping out the Jews entirely. Concentration camps were built and the Jews were collected into them. Throughout the Second World War these camps were set up in almost all the countries which the Germans conquered. Six million Jews perished in these camps; 1.5 million of them were children. This destruction is known as the Holocaust.

THE STATE OF ISRAEL

Between 1945 and 1948 many Holocaust survivors were kept in Displaced Persons' Camps. Gradually, they were allowed to resettle in Palestine, then

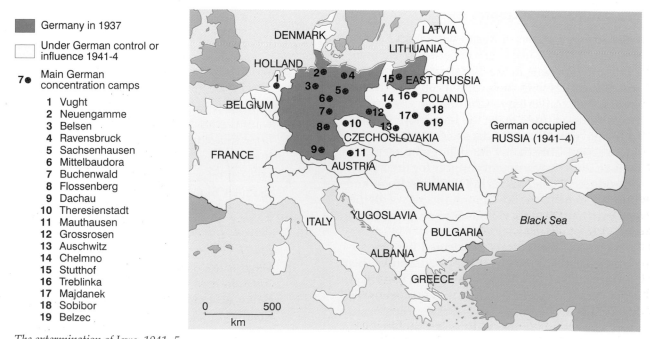

Germany in 1937

Under German control or influence 1941-4

7● Main German concentration camps

1 Vught
2 Neuengamme
3 Belsen
4 Ravensbruck
5 Sachsenhausen
6 Mittelbaudora
7 Buchenwald
8 Flossenberg
9 Dachau
10 Theresienstadt
11 Mauthausen
12 Grossrosen
13 Auschwitz
14 Chelmno
15 Stutthof
16 Treblinka
17 Majdanek
18 Sobibor
19 Belzec

The extermination of Jews, 1941–5

under British control (p. 147). However, the resettlement programme was very slow and the Arab governments strongly opposed it. This sparked off hostilities between the Jews of Palestine and the British authorities. In May 1948, Britain withdrew its forces. On the day before they left, the Jews of Palestine declared the State of Israel (p. 63).

Almost immediately, Israel was attacked by the armies of the surrounding Arab countries, who did not want a Jewish state to exist. The Jews fought back in what has become known as the War of Independence and defeated the Arab armies.

THE POST-WAR PERIOD

In 1945, the allied armies entered the concentration camps and the world saw the full horror of the Nazi Holocaust. Jews in many countries felt angry, frustrated, guilty that they had not been able to help and determined that it should never happen again.

The establishment of the State of Israel in 1948 brought a new sense of pride and hope to Jews all over the world. Being Jewish suddenly began to mean something once more. Whereas the pre-war generation had tried to cast off its Judaism, that of the post-war period felt a growing desire to find it again.

From the 1950s onwards, there was a steady growth of new Jewish schools, community centres, youth movements, yeshivot and seminaries (places of higher Jewish learning, p. 89). This has continued until the present day.

JEWS TODAY

It would be wrong to think of Jews today as all thinking the same way or believing the same things. This brief history has shown that the Jewish experience has been very varied, in particular during the last century. Some Jews are religious; many are not. Some have strong political feelings; others do not.

Most Jews feel supportive of Israel. They have helped Israel with funds and personnel over the years, in particular during the wars with its Arab neighbours (p. 17). Israel, in turn, has become a haven for Jews living under persecution. Those living under terrible conditions in Yemen and Ethiopia were airlifted to Israel; after the collapse of the Soviet Union thousands of Jews who had never been allowed to leave, settled in Israel.

In Britain, as in other countries, Jewish life is a complex web of religious, communal and political movements. Sometimes their aims coincide; at others they contradict. There is also widespread apathy. Jews are meeting non-Jews on equal terms in the universities, in the professions and in the business world, and more are marrying out than at any time in the past. Many Jews are worried about this.

On the other hand, there are signs of healthy growth. Nearly a third of Jewish children in the UK attend Jewish schools with many more involved in Jewish youth organizations. Jews today are generally more conscious of their Jewishness than their parents or grandparents were. Young people in particular are taking an interest in their Jewish heritage in a way that would have been unthinkable two generations ago.

THINGS TO DO

▶ What dilemmas did young Jews face in the 1920s and 1930s? How do you think this might have affected family relationships?

▶ What was the result of Nazi propaganda?

▶ How did the establishment of the State of Israel change the way many Jews felt about being Jewish?

▶ Draw a time chart tracing Jewish history from the earliest times to the present day. You might try using a scale of 2 cm to a century. Draw your time scale down the centre of the page so that you can set down Jewish history on one side and events from world history on the other. In this way you will be able to see how they relate. Use the events described on pp. 6–17, and include the following as well: the reign of Tutankhamun, the rise of the Assyrian Empire, the assassination of Julius Caesar, the building of Hadrian's Wall, Alfred the Great, the Battle of Hastings, Marco Polo's voyages, the voyage of Columbus, the Great Fire of London, the French Revolution, the Battle of Trafalgar, the First World War, the Russian Revolution, the Second World War, the assassination of President Kennedy and the collapse of the Soviet Union (use an encyclopedia to help you). Add in any other events you wish.

Alongside the Jews' own history, and interwoven with it, is the history of how other people have thought about them and treated them. Some people have admired the Jews so much that they have converted to Judaism and joined them; others have hated them to the point of trying to exterminate them. Sadly, for much of their history, Jews have suffered the hostility of others. This is known as **anti-semitism**.

Many people have suggested reasons for anti-semitism. Jews have been hated for being too rich and for being too poor; for being communists and for being capitalists; the alleged misdeeds of individual Jews have erupted into wholesale anti-Jewish riots. Some forms of anti-semitism have originated in religion, such as the Christian belief that Jesus is God and that the Jews killed him or the Muslim belief that Muhammad was God's final prophet whom the Jews rejected. Yet even this is not clear cut, for there are many Christians and Muslims who get on very well with Jews.

In some countries (e.g. Poland and Germany) anti-semitism seems deeply ingrained in people's thoughts and feelings. In others (e.g. Britain and the United States) it is usually uncommon, except at a very subtle level. Yet Jews are still spat on and called obscene names, even in the UK today, and Jewish cemeteries are still desecrated. No one has ever provided a satisfactory explanation for anti-semitism.

THE ANCIENT WORLD

For most of their early history, Jews were accepted by others on equal terms. There were times when their neighbours were at peace with them and times of hostility (p. 7). There was also occasional resentment among the pagan population of the Holy Land because the Jews would not intermarry with them or eat their food.

Now and then, special measures were taken against the Jews. For example, in the Persian period (p. 8), a Grand Vizier, insulted when a Jew refused to bow to him, tried to kill thousands of Jews (p. 58). Later, the Romans suspected Jews of disloyalty when they refused to worship the emperor. But apart from such instances, the Jews were not objects of continued hostility. Under the Roman Empire they even enjoyed certain privileges denied to others. Some Roman nobles adopted certain Jewish practices believing them to be expressions of a higher morality. Only in late antiquity did slanderous stories about Jews begin to circulate – including tales that they were descended from a race of lepers or that they worshipped an ass.

CHRISTIAN TREATMENT OF JEWS

Anti-semitism, in the sense of regarding the Jews as a people set apart for special contempt or hatred, began with the rise of Christianity. In Christian eyes, Jews had committed the worst possible crime – they had rejected Jesus. Since Christians believed that Jesus was God in human form come to save the world, rejecting Jesus was the same as rejecting God. From the earliest times, therefore, Christians believed that God hated the Jews. Their literature described Jews as descendants of the devil (e.g. *John 8:44*). The Jews' only hope was to accept Christ and convert.

Throughout the Middle Ages, Christian thinkers preached and wrote appalling things about Jews. Small children were taught that the Jews were the murderers of Jesus, rulers passed humiliating laws against them, crusaders massacred them. Martin Luther, the father of the Protestant Reformation wrote:

'. . . their synagogues should be set on fire, and whatever does not burn up should be covered or spread over with dirt so that no one may ever be able to see a cinder or stone of it. And this ought to be done for the honour of God and of Christianity . . . their homes should likewise be broken down and destroyed . . . they should be deprived of their prayer books and Talmuds in which such idolatry, lies, cursing and blasphemy are taught . . . . all their cash and valuables ought to be taken form them . . . this money should be used in the case where the Jew has honestly become a Christian . . . . God's rage is so great against them that they only become worse and worse through mild mercy, and not much better through severe mercy. Therefore away with them . . . .'

Jews being burned alive. Medieval woodcut

A Jew could always change his or her situation by becoming a Christian though, in fact, very few did. However, in the fifteenth century when Jews in Spain were forced to convert, this began to change. People mistrusted the 'New Christians', as they were called because they doubted their sincerity (p. 46). Christians refused to have anything to do with them and would only marry other Christians of 'pure blood'. 'Purity of blood' could be carried through several generations. This sowed the seeds of the racial anti-semitism that was to have horrific results five centuries later (p. 16).

THE ENLIGHTENMENT

The Enlightenment thinkers (*philosophes*) believed firmly in justice. They also opposed the authority of the Church (p. 10). These two strands of thinking led some of them to support the Jews, who had suffered centuries of injustice at Christian hands. Other *philosophes*, believing that the Jews were superstitious and backward, regarded them as the enemies of the modern, secular state. This gave birth to the *Judenfrage* (Jewish question), which was raised every time the emancipation of the Jews (p. 10) was discussed. Basically, the 'Jewish question' was this: Can Jews really become full Germans or French if they are, at the same time, a people with a distinct and different web of relationships and loyalties living by their own laws? Indeed, people began to suspect that Jews had sinister motives for retaining their separate peoplehood. Some even came to see Napoleon's Sanhedrin (p. 11) as a Jewish secret society. This was the beginning of the myth of the 'Elders of Zion' plotting to take over the world (see below).

At the same time, German nationalism was reviving, drawing upon ancient Teutonic mythology in which Jews had no part. The Germans' growing awareness of their own peoplehood was fuelled with prejudice carried over from the Christian centuries. However German they appeared to be, Jews were really aliens. In the mid-nineteenth century, a German historian wrote that the emancipated Jews of his day, who thought themselves thoroughly German, would never really be so until their Jewishness disappeared.

Yet, even in France, where the Enlightenment was most successful, anti-semitism remained deeply ingrained. In 1894, Alfred Dreyfus, the first Jew to become an officer in the French army, was accused of spying (p. 146). He was found guilty and sent to Devil's Island (he was later proved innocent and pardoned). The anti-semitic rumblings the trial provoked continued for about ten years.

THE RUSSIAN EMPIRE

From the end of the fifteenth century, Jews were not allowed to live in Russia. In 1772, the Russians annexed part of Poland and found that they had suddenly acquired thousands of Jews. They dealt with the first Jewish village by taking the inhabitants to the nearest river and drowning them. However, the numbers were too large to deal with in this manner. In 1791 it was decided to permit Jews to live in a clearly defined area (later known as the Pale of Settlement) stretching from Kovno near the Baltic Sea to Odessa on the coast of the Black Sea. In this way, the Tsarist government sought to restrict the influence of the Jews and not have them defile 'Holy Russia'.

During the years that followed, Jews in the Pale were kept in abject poverty. Many of the younger generation joined the growing revolutionary movements. In 1881, Tsar Alexander II was assassinated. Among those responsible was a Jewish girl (a fact which the Russian press made much of) and, one month later, pogroms (anti-Jewish riots) broke out. During the following years, the pogroms spread to 160 towns and villages. The police did nothing as Jews were killed and plundered. When a Russian minister, sickened by the carnage, raised the matter with Tsar Nikolai II, he responded, 'But they shed the precious blood of our saviour'.

In 1905, the Tsar's secret police produced the 'Protocols of the Elders of Zion', a document supposed to contain the Jews' plans for taking over the world. This has been used in anti-Jewish propaganda to the present day.

THINGS TO DO

▶ What is anti-semitism? What forms has it taken? Why do you think it is so difficult to find a satisfactory explanation for anti-semitism?

▶ What was the 'Jewish question'? How did it arise?

▶ What is a pogrom? What justification was given for the pogroms of 1881? What were the real reasons? What were the 'Protocols of the Elders of Zion'?

THE SOVIET UNION

The revolution of October 1917 brought the Tsarist regime to an end. With it, anti-semitism was officially over and Lenin condemned those who had carried out pogroms as enemies of the revolution. As long as Jews lived as loyal citizens of the communist state, they were unharmed.

By the end of the 1920s, this began to change. The official Communist Party policy was that anti-semitism only belonged in morally backward capitalist countries. However, Stalin actively encouraged anti-semitism so that he could use it for his own advantage and remove Jews from positions of authority. In his later years, Stalin condemned the State of Israel as a US-backed, anti-Soviet entity. Jews with relatives in the USA or Israel were suspected of anti-Soviet activities. During Stalin's rule, thousands were either murdered by the secret police or sent to labour camps in Siberia and Jewish organizations were closed down. A handful of synagogues were left (and placed under surveillance) to impress the world with the tolerance of the Soviet regime.

After Stalin's death in 1953, state-backed anti-semitism continued. Under Khrushchev, Judaism was declared culturally backward. Synagogues were closed, Jews were not allowed to gather in private homes for prayer, nor to bake **matzot** for Passover (p. 48). Those wanting to emigrate to Israel automatically lost their jobs. This continued until the collapse of the Soviet Union. Under Boris Yeltsin, Russian Jews began to enjoy freedom. Many thousands left to settle in Israel.

NAZI GERMANY

In November 1918 the First World War ended. Under the terms of the Treaty of Versailles, Germany lost 12 per cent of its territory, most of its coal and steel industries and was forced to pay the cost of the war. Disbanding the armed forces led to massive unemployment. During the 1920s, various political parties emerged in Germany, each offering a way of solving these problems. In 1933 the National Socialist German Workers' Party (Nazi Party) was elected to power.

The Nazi Party had been formed in 1920. It blamed the Jews for Germany's defeat in the First World War. From the time they came to power, the Nazis began a systematic campaign to rid Germany of Jews. They began stripping Jews of their citizens' rights, removing them from public office and imposing increasing restraints on their freedom of movement. Jewish businesses were closed down,

Nazis calling for Germans to boycott Jewish shops

Jewish lecturers removed from the universities, Jewish judges from the courts. Everywhere Jews were humiliated and subjected to sudden outbreaks of violence. Swimming pools, libraries, sports stadia, even park benches, were forbidden to Jews.

The purpose behind all this was to force the Jews to emigrate. The Nazis wanted Germany to be *Judenrein*, free of Jews. There was even a plan to resettle Germany's Jews in Madagascar and use them for slave labour.

In 1937 the Nazis began sending Jews to concentration camps. In these camps, able-bodied Jews were forced to work as slaves; when they could no longer do so, they were killed. Some were used for medical experiments. Young Jewish girls were sterilized and then forced to become prostitutes for the entertainment of German soldiers. Old and disabled people were sent straight to the gas chambers. By 1945 when the war ended, six million Jews had been murdered; a quarter of them were children. Jews call this the **Shoah**, catastrophe or **Hurban**, destruction. It is commonly known as the Holocaust.

The Nazis based their treatment of the Jews on the theory that Semites were an inferior race to Aryans (a name the Germans called themselves). In Nazi philosophy, Germans were the *Herrenvolk*, the master race; the highest form of Aryans; Jews were sub-human. The Nazis even made absurd devices for measuring the shape and dimensions of people's heads to determine whether they were Aryans or Semites.

Many ordinary Germans, including most of the Protestant and Catholic Christian churches, were seduced by Nazi propaganda and came to accept that the Jews really were an inferior race. The only resistance came from the Confessing Church (a

German Protestant Church that opposed Nazism) and as a result, 700 of its priests were arrested. Anti-semitic Poles and Ukrainians used the German occupation of their countries to massacre their Jews. The Danes and Norwegians made heroic efforts to save theirs. Sweden was exceptional in opening its doors to Jewish refugees. There were also high-minded individuals who risked their lives to hide Jews or help them escape. One outstanding personality was Cardinal Angelo Roncalli who saved thousands of Jewish lives. Later, when he became Pope John XXIII, he had anti-Jewish references removed from the Catholic prayer book. During the post war years, many more clergy have tried to make amends for the Church's silence.

In recent years, neo-Nazi groups have began springing up in Germany. These consist mainly of young thugs who hold rallies, regard Hitler as their hero and carry out sporadic acts of violence against non-Germans and disabled people.

THE MIDDLE EAST

In 633, the year after Muhammad died, the Muslim Arabs began their conquest of the Holy Land. Five years later, with the capture of Jerusalem, it was complete. Muslims believe that Muhammad ascended to heaven from the spot that was once the Holy of Holies in King Solomon's Temple (p. 7) so Jerusalem has special significance for them.

During the centuries that followed, Arab and Jewish communities lived alongside one another. In the nineteenth century, when the Jews began making their way back to their homeland (by then called Palestine), they found an established Arab population who, not unnaturally, believed that the land really belonged to them. As Jewish immigration increased, Palestinian Arabs began thinking that the Jews intended to dispossess them of the country they lived in.

Throughout the early years of the twentieth century, relations between Jews and Arabs were tense and there were sporadic riots. Since the establishment of Israel, some Arab governments have pursued a consistent policy of trying to destroy the Jewish state. Since the 1950s, they have launched three major wars against Israel. Arab propaganda proclaimed Zionism as evil and claimed that the establishment of Israel was just the first stage towards world Jewish domination. The 'Protocols of the Elders of Zion' (p. 15) was translated into Arabic and taught in Arab secondary schools.

During the same period, Arab terrorist organizations attacked Jewish targets in Israel and abroad. Israeli civilian aircraft were hijacked, Israeli athletes murdered at the Olympic Games, synagogues and other Jewish institutions bombed in Rome, Paris, Buenos Aires, London and other places.

In 1979 Israel signed a peace agreement with Egypt. In 1993 and 1994 similar agreements were reached with the Palestine Liberation Organization (PLO) and the neighbouring Kingdom of Jordan. These agreements reflect the fact that most Arabs, like most Jews, are tired of the long enmity and want peaceful relations. However, several Arab terrorist groups, all of whom have sworn to destroy Israel, continue to operate. They plant bombs around the world, kill and maim innocent civilians and do their utmost to disrupt the peace processes.

THINGS TO DO

▶ How were Jews treated after the Russian Revolution? What happened to them during the Stalinist era?

▶ Why do you think thousands of Jews left Russia after the collapse of the Soviet Union?

▶ How did Nazi anti-semitism differ from that of earlier centuries?

▶ How did the Christian churches respond to Nazi propaganda?

▶ Why have the Arabs wanted to destroy the Jewish state?

FIND OUT

▶ Find out what you can about the following.

   a   the Hebron massacre of 1929

   b   *Kristallnacht* in 1938

   c   Soviet 'show trials' in the 1960s

   d   Hizbollah terrorist organization.

The next four units look at some of the things Judaism teaches about God, life and the world as a whole. Although Jews differ from one another and do not all have the same views, those who are committed to Judaism share these beliefs.

BELIEF IN ONE GOD

'Hear O Israel, the Lord is our God, the Lord is One.'

(Deuteronomy 6:4)

This is the opening sentence of the **Shema** (rhymes with 'bazaar'), a prayer which Jews recite every morning and evening (p. 86). It declares the most basic teaching of Judaism – belief in one God (monotheism). In ancient times this belief set the Jews apart from their neighbours who believed that the crops, rainfall, illness, childbirth and death were controlled by different gods. Today, many people besides Jews are monotheists.

Monotheism is more than just a belief. It is a way of thinking about the world and everything in it. As monotheists, Jews think of people, trees, flowers, rock formations and the rest of nature as creatures of the one God. This belief turns everything one sees, hears or experiences into an encounter with God. Monotheism brings an overall unity to life.

GOD AS CREATOR

'In the beginning, God created heaven and earth.'

(Genesis 1:1)

'I see your heavens, the work of your hands; the moon and stars which you have placed there' (Psalm 8:4)

Jews believe that God created the universe out of nothing. This belief leads them to regard the world as designed by God precisely to suit His plan. If God had started with raw materials, He would not have been able to make the kind of world He wanted. His work would have been hampered by any defects in His materials. By creating the world out of nothing, He made it exactly the way He wanted it.

We humans cannot hope to understand fully creating something out of nothing. But we can grasp a little of its meaning with an analogy. Imagine that you had the power to project your thoughts outwards and make them real. You could think about a donkey and suddenly there would be a real donkey standing in front of you. Everyone would be able to see it, touch it and smell it. You could feed it and ride it. It would be real in every way. However, if you stopped thinking about it, it would cease to exist. It is only there because your thoughts are pouring into it.

Jews think of creation in a similar way. Our world is real, but it only exists while God's creative energies are pouring into it. Creation, therefore, is not a one-off event, it is continuous. This is why, in their prayers, Jews praise God who 'in His goodness, renews the work of creation each day, continually'.

OMNIPOTENCE, OMNISCIENCE AND OMNIPRESENCE

Although we cannot imagine what God is like, Jews believe Him to be omnipotent (all powerful), omniscient (all knowing) and omnipresent (existing everywhere at the same time). According to an ancient Jewish teaching, 'Wherever you find God's greatness, there you will find His humility'. This is a way of expressing an important Jewish idea – that although God has the power to do whatever He wishes, He usually holds back His power and allows people freedom to choose whether they will do good or evil (p. 20). Sometimes, He does use His power to intervene in human affairs. Jews call such intervention miracles. However, Jews believe that God remains mostly, as it were, behind the scenes trying to coax people to turn to Him by sending blessings or suffering, or in other ways.

God is also thought of as knowing everything. However, His knowledge is very different from ours. Our knowledge of things around us comes from the way our brains interpret messages received from the senses. Of God, an ancient Jewish teaching says, 'by knowing Himself He knows all things'. Since all created things exist only because He is constantly pouring His creative energies into them (see opposite), by knowing Himself, He knows whatever derives from His will, i.e. all of creation.

Jews also believe God to be omnipresent. He fills the entire cosmos and beyond; He is present in every atom. Although people, animals, plants and mountains occupy space, God is there too.

We can partly understand this too with an analogy. We all think. Yet when we do, our brains do not move to one side to make room for our thoughts. Our thoughts exist in the same space occupied by our brains because our brains are physical objects but our thoughts are not. In a similar way, Jews believe that God exists in the same space occupied by trees, houses and people because He is not a physical object. This is what Jews refer to in their prayers when they say to God, 'You are as You were before the world was created; You are as You are after it is created,' i.e. the presence of the world and everything in it has not brought about any change in God.

CONCERN FOR HUMANITY

Since Jews believe that God created the universe out of nothing, is omnipotent, omniscient and omnipresent, this means that they believe that God is very different from us. However, Jews also believe that God is deeply concerned with human affairs, that He is holy, completely good, merciful and just, and that He expects people to strive to be the same – as far as human beings can be. 'You must be holy because I, the Lord your God, am holy,' says the Torah, the Jewish holy book (*Leviticus 19:2*). Jews believe that God is the one to whom people can turn in prayer and that He always hears prayers, although He may not always answer in the way people imagine.

ADDRESSING GOD

In prayer, Jews address God as 'You'. This expresses the direct relationship Jews believe that all people can have with God. They might also address Him by one of the names He is called in the Torah. However, while feeling close to God, they believe it is right for humans to maintain a sense of deep respect. For this reason, they only ever pronounce God's names in worship. There is one name they never pronounce at all. When speaking about God, they often refer to Him as 'Hashem', a word meaning 'the name', i.e. the One whose name we treat respectfully and do not pronounce unnecessarily.

In their prayers, Jews also refer to God variously as father, king, helper, healer, protector, sustainer and similar terms.

THINGS TO DO

▶ How might believing in one God affect a person's view of the world?

▶ What is monotheism?

▶ Before Jews eat they recite a special blessing to thank God for creating the food. The word 'creating' is always in the present tense. Why is this so?

▶ What does it mean to say that God is omnipotent and omniscient? How might this belief affect the way a person lives?

▶ The **Midrash** (a collection of ancient Jewish teachings, p. 33) says, 'Just as the soul fills the body, so God fills the world.' What do you think this means?

▶ Why do Jews not pronounce God's name unnecessarily?

▶ 'It's impossible to have any sort of relationship with God because He is so very different from us.' How might a Jew respond to this view?

'The righteous of all nations have a share in the world to come.'

(Tosefta)

Judaism teaches that God is the God of all humankind and that He wants all people to serve Him by living their lives the way He wants. The guidelines for this lifestyle are set down in the **Noachide Laws**, so called because they were given to Noah after the flood (*Genesis 9*). Jews regard the Noachide Laws as the basic framework for a moral and spiritual life.

THE NOACHIDE LAWS

The Noachide Laws consist of seven principles. First, they forbid (1) idolatry and (2) blasphemy. Literally, idolatry means worshipping an image. Jews use the term to mean worshipping anything other than God – the sun and moon, mountains, animals, a person or a process (e.g. fire). In Jewish thinking, worshipping creatures instead of the One who created them is a terrible insult to God. Idolatry is forbidden to Jews and non-Jews alike. Jews also regard it as idolatrous even to try to represent the one God as an image. God is different from anything we can imagine (p. 18) and so far beyond our understanding that He could never be portrayed as an image. At best, images can only represent God in some limited form and are therefore a barrier to real worship.

Judaism also forbids blasphemy, i.e. cursing God. Some people might do this in time of great suffering. At a deeper level, however, Judaism expects people to develop a respectful and sensitive attitude toward Godly matters.

The Noachide Laws also forbid (3) murder, (4) theft, (5) sexual malpractice (which, in Jewish thinking, includes adultery, incest, homosexuality and sexual relations with animals) and (6) cruelty to animals. Finally, it demands (7) promoting justice. A system of justice, with law courts to enforce it, ensures that people live together in harmony. In Jewish teaching, setting up a legal system is fulfilling God's will since it leads to **tikkun olam**, the betterment of the world.

These seven principles do not make up a total code of practice, but are the basis upon which an individual can build an ethical and spiritual life. Judaism teaches that it is the duty of all people – Jews and non-Jews – to observe them. In Jewish thinking, someone who violates any one of these principles has no right to be called a civilized human being.

FREEDOM OF CHOICE

'I have set before you today life and death, the blessing and the curse: therefore choose life.'

(Deuteronomy 30:19)

The first chapter of the Torah (p. 26) describes how God created the first human pair, Adam and Eve, 'in His (i.e. God's) image' (*Genesis 1:4*). Jews have always understood this to mean that just as God is completely free to do as He wishes, so are humans (that is, within the limitations of being human). This means that every person is completely free to choose whether to do good or evil. Certain things are decided by God, i.e. whether a person will be healthy or sick, clever or dull, rich or poor. Jews believe that God makes those decisions each New Year (p. 44). But within each situation, a person is entirely free to make moral choices. This means that Jews think of each individual as responsible for his or her actions.

OTHER RELIGIONS

Jews regard any religion which upholds the Noachide Laws as an acceptable way for non-Jews to serve God. This does not mean that they agree with everything that other religions teach, but that they

The Jewish view of an ideal world – all humankind living under God's law

can recognize some religions as pointing out a path to God. For this reason, Jews do not see the need to convert other people to their religion (p. 23).

In particular, Jews recognize that Islam teaches pure monotheism and that Muslims have a strict morality that upholds the principles of the Noachide Laws. The same may be said of the Sikh religion.

Jews have always been less certain about Christianity. Although they acknowledge Christianity's high moral principles, they feel uneasy about the Christian belief that Jesus is God. During the Middle Ages, Jewish scholars debated the question of whether Christians were committing idolatry by worshipping Jesus. Although they decided that such worship is not idolatrous, Jews do not regard Christians as pure monotheists. Jews are also unhappy about the use of images and icons in Catholic and Orthodox worship. They feel that this comes rather close to idolatry.

Nonetheless, Jews have always recognized a special relationship with Christianity and Islam. Rabbi Judah Halevi, a twelfth-century scholar, described Judaism as the seed of the tree and Christianity and Islam as the branches, since through these religions, millions of people have come to worship the one God.

Jews find Hinduism difficult to generalize about. While some Hindus live by moral principles Judaism would approve of, others have moral beliefs with which it could never agree. Also, whereas Hindus claim to believe in one god, Jews find this difficult to see in practice. Jews regard the use of images in worship, even where they are discarded afterwards, as idolatrous.

Buddhism encourages people to strive for moral virtue and Jews can respect that. On the other hand, Buddhism does not have a clear belief in one God, which is incompatible with Jewish teaching that all people are put into the world to serve Him. Jews regard the use of statues in Buddhist worship as idolatrous.

Jews look forward to a future time when all people will recognize and serve the one God. In the **Aleinu** prayer, with which Jews conclude each of their daily services, they ask:

'. . . may all the inhabitants of the world recognize and know that every knee should bend to You, every tongue swear by your Name. Before You, Lord our God, may they bow and prostrate themselves and give honour to the glory of Your Name, and may they all accept upon themselves the yoke of Your Kingship . . . .'

THINGS TO DO

▶ Look up 'idolatry' in the dictionary. What does the word mean? How do Jews use this word? Why do Jews regard idolatry as a barrier to a real relationship with God?

▶ Make a list of ten different crimes in the news recently. Do you think any of these crimes would have been committed if everybody lived according to the Noachide Laws?

▶ How might Jews use the Noachide Laws as a way of knowing how to respond to other religions?

▶ Why do you think Jews do not try to convert other people to their religion?

▶ How does belief in free choice imply that people are responsible for their actions?

▶ Look back to the Aleinu prayer. Why do you think Jews say this?

▶ Imagine that you are helping a convicted criminal to go straight. He blames his upbringing and his friends for his life of crime, and he cannot believe that he will ever be different. You are trying to get him to see that he is responsible for what he does with his life. How might the conversation go?

FOR DISCUSSION

▶ To what extent is it possible for people of different faiths to live and work together in a multi-ethnic society? (Bear in mind (a) that members of one religious group might disapprove strongly of some things that another religion may teach and (b) that some people might want to convert others to their belief.)

THE CHOICE OF ISRAEL

(another name for the Jewish people)

> *'For you are a holy people to the Lord your God, and the Lord has chosen you out of all the peoples that are on the face of the earth.'*

(Deuteronomy 14:2)

Jews are sometimes called the Chosen People. This term is often misunderstood since it suggests that God has favourites. However, Jews only ever think of themselves as chosen for responsibility, not for privilege. In Jewish thinking, all human beings have a responsibility to serve God by keeping the Noachide Laws (p. 20). But for Jews, their relationship with God depends on them keeping the 613 commandments (see below).

THE COVENANT

> *'You are standing this day all of you before the Lord your God that you may enter into the Covenant of the Lord your God . . . that He may set you this day for Himself as people, and that He may be to you a God . . .'*

(Deuteronomy 29:9–12)

Jews understand their relationship with God as a covenant. That is an arrangement whereby two or more parties agree to look after each other's interests so that they all benefit. Treaties or trade agreements between countries are examples of covenants.

When everyone plays their part in a covenant relationship, each one's needs can be satisfied. Of course, it is difficult to think of God as having 'needs'. Judaism insists that He does, though 'desires' is a more accurate term. 'God desired to have a dwelling place among low creatures', i.e. human beings, says an ancient Jewish teaching. Jews believe that when they keep God's commandments, they bring holiness into the world and prepare it for the time when all human beings will know Him (*Jeremiah 31:31–4*).

Jews believe that God has His part to play in the covenant relationship too. Even though He can do whatever He wants (p. 18) He has bound Himself never to abandon the Jewish people entirely.

The Bible describes how God made a covenant with Abraham, the first Jew (p. 6). Later, at Mount Sinai, the Israelites entered into a covenant with God (*Exodus 19–20*), and were given the rules by which they were expected to live. By keeping these rules

(mitzvot, see below) they were to become God's servants and help to fulfil His plan. The first five books of the Bible (the Five Books of Moses) contain the basic rules that God wants the Jews to keep. These books, which Jews call the **Torah** are their most sacred possession.

THE MITZVOT (COMMANDMENTS)

> *'And now Israel, what does the Lord your God expect of you? To walk in His ways . . . to keep, for your own good, the commandments of the Lord . . .'*

(Deuteronomy 10:12–13)

Mitzvah (plural mitzvot) means 'commandment'. Jews use this term when speaking of the rules that God wants them to keep. Some people take it to mean 'good deed', though this is not quite accurate. There are 613 mitzvot; 248 are positive commandments, i.e. things Jews are commanded to do, and 365 are negative commandments, i.e. those things Jews are commanded not to do. The Bible describes how God gave these commandments to Moses, who taught them to the Israelites in the desert (p. 6). The Ten Commandments (p. 26) are part of these 613; so are the seven commandments of the Noachide Laws (p. 20).

Mitzvot as a discipline

The mitzvot cover every area of life. They include those activities people usually associate with religion, such as praying or observing festivals, as well as many more which people might not think of as religious at all – industrial relations, conducting a trial, divorce proceedings and the food Jews may or may not eat. For Jews there is a right and wrong way of doing even ordinary, everyday things. Keeping the mitzvot means leading a disciplined life.

Mitzvot and ethics

Keeping the commandments is also an important part of character building. 'The mitzvot were given for the purpose of refining people,' says the Talmud (p. 31). Each mitzvah has something to teach. For example, the laws concerning the punishment of criminals (*Deuteronomy 21:22–3*) emphasize the need to respect human dignity, those concerned with damages and compensation stress personal responsibility (*Exodus 22:28–23:5*) and the laws of borrowing and lending teach compassion for those less well-off than oneself (*Deuteronomy 15:7–11*).

One class of commandment, the **chukim** (statutes), need special mention as no reason is given for them.

They are regarded as a test of a Jew's faith, and observing them strengthens it. The commandments about eating **kosher** food (p. 68) are examples of chukim.

Mitzvot as attachment to God

At a deeper level, Jews believe that by fulfilling the commandments, they are communicating with God. They understand the mitzvot to be God's way of reaching out to people. Observing them is humanity's way of reaching back to God. Indeed, the word mitzvah is related to another Hebrew word meaning 'connection'.

BECOMING JEWISH

Jews do not try to convert other people to their religion since they believe that there are many paths to God (p. 20). Nonetheless, people sometimes do wish to become Jewish and there is a procedure for converting them.

Conversions are carried out by a **bet din** (rabbinical court, p. 97). Once the **dayanim** (judges) agree to consider someone for conversion, the person is given a course of instruction in Judaism and is expected to start living as a Jew. However the dayanim will want to be convinced of the person's sincerity before finalizing the conversion.

A person converting is required formally to accept that he or she will keep all the mitzvot. This acceptance is essential since a conversion cannot normally be annulled. Male converts must be circumcised. This will normally be carried out in hospital by a Jewish doctor qualified in circumcision (p. 72). Conversion is finalized by immersion in a **mikveh**, a special pool (p. 82). Upon emerging from the water the convert becomes fully Jewish, and will remain so for life.

THE LAND OF ISRAEL

'And the Lord appeared to Abram and said,
"To your descendants will I give this land."'

(*Genesis 12:7*)

When Jews use the word Israel they mean two things: the land which God promised to their ancestors and the modern State of Israel. Although these are more or less the same, they are not completely identical. The founding of the modern state is looked at in more detail on pp. 144–7; here we are concerned with the religious significance of the land.

For Jews, Israel is not only the land of their origins;

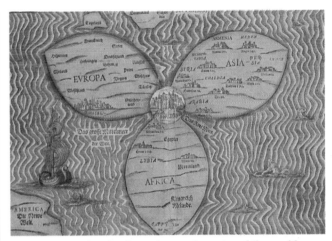

Medieval map showing Jerusalem as the centre of the world

it is the Holy Land, and Jerusalem is the Holy City. Many of the 613 commandments can only be kept in Israel, and Jerusalem is the only place in the world where a Temple (p. 7) can be built. Mediaeval maps which put Jerusalem at the centre of the world expressed the Jewish view very well. Of course, there is not really a centre point on the earth's surface, but in a spiritual sense that is exactly how Jews see it.

For Jews, Israel is God's special land. 'The eyes of the Lord your God are upon it from the beginning to the end of the year,' says the Torah (*Deuteronomy 11:12*). Jews look forward to a future time when they will all return there, the Temple will be rebuilt, and all nations will go there to worship God (*Isaiah 56:7; 66:23*). They believe this will happen in the age of the Messiah (p. 24).

FOR YOUR FOLDERS

▶ What is a covenant? How does the term describe the way Jews see their relationship with God?

▶ Explain why doing mitzvot is important for Jewish people.

▶ If you were a dayan (judge) in a rabbinical court, what questions would you want to ask someone who wants to become Jewish? Remember, you need to be convinced that the person in front of you is sincere.

▶ Explain the religious significance of Israel for Jews.

THE MESSIAH

'"Behold, days are coming," says the Lord," . . . when no person will need to teach another . . . saying, "Know the Lord", for they will all know Me . . ."'

(Jeremiah 31:31–9)

The word Messiah (**Mashiach**) means 'anointed one'. In ancient times, kings of Israel were called Messiah because they were anointed. Priests, and sometimes prophets too, were also anointed when they were called into office. Apart from these uses, the term Messiah refers specifically to a future leader of the Jewish people who will bring far-reaching changes to the world.

The prophets wrote a great deal about the age of the Messiah. From what they said we can put together a picture of a time when there will be peace all over the world, when humans and animals will not harm one another and when God's presence will be felt by everyone. This belief leads Jews to regard existing conditions as temporary. For Jews, human history is not open-ended, but moving towards a destiny when life as we know it will give way to something more spiritual.

The Messiah, who is to rebuild the Temple and usher in the new age, has always been thought of as human (not a divine being), a descendant of King David and a man of exceptional piety, learning and leadership qualities. Rabbis have always discouraged attempts to work out when he might come. Nonetheless, many people have tried to calculate the time of his coming and some have even claimed to be the Messiah. There have been at least a dozen false Messiahs throughout history. Jews still wait for the true Messiah and pray daily for his coming.

LIFE AFTER DEATH

'In this world people fulfil commandments and do not know the value of what they have brought about. In the world to come they will realize what they have achieved.'

(Midrash)

The Jewish view of life and death can only be understood in terms of people being put into the world to be workers for God (p. 22). Life can be compared to a stage. The actors enter from the wings and play their parts for a while. There are no set lines and they make up their own scripts as they go, interacting with all the other players on the stage. As each actor comes on, he or she is given a guide book. Only by referring to the guide book will they know why they are there and what tasks they are expected to perform while on stage. At times unknown to the actors, each one will be called off the stage to be assessed, after which they will be rewarded or punished according to their performance. In a similar way the period before birth, life in this world and existence after leaving it are thought of as stages in a continuum.

REWARD AND PUNISHMENT

Judaism teaches that when people leave this world, they are rewarded or punished for what they have done during their lives. Reward is understood in terms of closeness to God. 'The righteous bask in the rays of God's presence,' says the Midrash. Another ancient teaching states, 'The reward for a mitzvah is the mitzvah', i.e. the reward for carrying out a mitzvah (commandment) is the spiritual accomplishment it brings.

Punishment is thought of as a cleansing process. Jews do not believe in hell as a place of everlasting torments. They believe that there is nothing a person can do which is so evil that his or her punishment could never, ever end. The Jewish hell is a kind of laundry, a process by which souls are cleansed of their sins so that they can eventually enter the presence of God. The Talmud tells a story of Rabbi Elisha ben Abuya, a righteous man who lost his faith and began to commit sins. After he died, the heavenly court was undecided as to whether he should be rewarded for his righteousness or punished for his sins. His student, Rabbi Meir (p. 30) declared, 'It is best that he receives the judgment', i.e. it would benefit him to go through the cleansing process of hell so that he could eventually come close to God.

Jews also believe in a resurrection of the dead, when souls and bodies will be united once more. However, the Jewish sources say very little about such things. They are much more concerned with the practicalities of serving God in this world.

THE AUTHORITY OF THE RABBIS

In this and Units 9 and 10 we have looked at several Jewish beliefs. In Units 12–15, we shall examine the Jewish holy writings, the sources of those beliefs as well as of Jewish practices. We shall also see how, over the centuries, Jewish teachings have been reapplied to ever-changing conditions.

Jews have two sets of teachings. One is the written **Torah** (Unit 12), a fixed unchanging body of teaching that Jews believe to be the revealed word of

Learning the importance of the Torah begins at an early age

God. Alongside it is the oral Torah, the **halakhah** (Units 14–15), a body of laws and teachings originating with Moses, handed down and reapplied through the ages as learned men interpreted and continually reapplied its principles. The people responsible for guiding Jews in their day-to-day service of God were originally priests and judges.

In Jewish tradition, 'priests' (Cohanim) are descendants of Aaron, Moses' brother, of the tribe of Levi. In ancient times, they served in the Temple (p. 7). Judges were learned people who were not necessarily priests. Together they were the interpreters of the Torah, the Jewish Bible.

The priests' and judges' authority to interpret the Torah is laid down in the written Torah itself.

'If there is a problem that is too difficult for you . . . you shall go to the priest, the Levite, or to the judge who will be in those days; you shall enquire and he will give you the ruling. You must do according to the ruling he instructs you . . . according to the law which he teaches you and the judgment he tells you you must do; you shall not deviate from it . . . .'

(Deuteronomy 17:8–11)

Later, the priests tended to concern themselves more and more with Temple matters and the judges became the main interpreters of the Torah. During the period before the destruction of the Second Temple (p. 8), the term **rabbi** came into use.

CLASS DEBATE

▶ 'This house believes that there is no life after death.'

Two people should argue in favour of the motion and two against it. Remember to present your arguments clearly.

◇

THINGS TO DO

▶ Do you think that the Jewish belief about life after death has any practical value? Explain your answer.

▶ What does the term Messiah mean? What sort of a person is the Messiah expected to be? What do Jews believe will happen in the time of the Messiah?

▶ Who are the rabbis?

▶ On what is their authority based?

▶ What do Jews mean by the terms 'heaven' and 'hell'?

'Moses received the Torah from Sinai, he gave it to Joshua, Joshua gave it to the Elders, the Elders to the Prophets, and the Prophets to the men of the Great Assembly.'

(Ethics of the Fathers)

Torah means 'instruction'. Jews use this word in a number of ways. Sometimes they mean the first five books of the Bible; sometimes the whole of the Bible. The Bible is known as the written Torah. The word Torah can also mean the whole body of traditional teachings which explain the Bible and guide Jews in their day-to-day living. These teachings used to be passed on by word of mouth. They are known as the oral Torah.

THE WRITTEN TORAH

Jews divide the written Torah into three sections:

- **Torah** (the Five Books of Moses)
- **Nevi'im** (the books of the Prophets)
- **Ketuvim** (holy writings).

The initial letters of the section headings, T, N, K, form the word **Tenakh**. This is the name Jews give to the Bible. The Tenakh is written mainly in Hebrew. Small portions of it are in Aramaic, a language closely related to Hebrew.

THE TEN COMMANDMENTS

Seven weeks after the Israelites left Egypt, they came to Mount Sinai (p. 6). There, amid thunder and lightning and a terrifying display of God's power, Moses ascended the mountain and disappeared in the thick cloud that covered the peak. Forty days later he returned. He was carrying two blocks of stone with writing cut in to them. These were the Ten Commandments.

During the time he was on the mountain, Moses was learning all the other commandments that God wanted him to teach the Israelites, together with their meanings. When he came back he began teaching them to the people. There are 613 commandments in all, including those cut into the two blocks of stone.

Jews regard the Ten Commandments as special for two reasons. First, they are universal commandments – i.e. they must be kept by every Jew, man and woman, young and old, everywhere and at all times.

Second, Jews think of them as subject headings, rather than individual commandments, since many

The Ten Commandments

- Know that I am the Lord your God, who brought you out of slavery in Egypt.
- You must have no other god besides Me.
- You must not use the name of the Lord your God without reason.
- Remember to keep the Sabbath day holy; on it you must not do any work.
- Respect your father and your mother.
- You must not murder.
- You must not commit adultery.
- You must not steal.
- You must not give false evidence against your neighbour.
- You must not desire your neighbour's house, his wife nor anything that belongs to him.

(Exodus 20:1–14)

of the other commandments can be listed under them. For example, the command to keep the Sabbath suggests the idea of a holy day. All the festivals derive from that idea. Similarly, the command not to steal means that taking away someone else's property is wrong. All the laws about injury and compensation, loans and inheritance come from that basic idea.

TORAH

Moses wrote down everything God had taught him in five books. These, the Five Books of Moses, form the first part of the Tenakh. They contain the commandments and the ethical ideals of the Jewish people, set in a historical framework. Here are the Five Books of Moses and some of the things they contain:

1 *Genesis* (**Bereshit**)
How God creates the world; people become wicked and God wipes them out with a flood, Noah and his family are spared to start the human race anew; the life stories of the ancestors of the Jews, Abraham, Isaac and Jacob; Jacob's sons settle in Egypt (p. 6).

2 *Exodus* (**Shemot**)
The Egyptians enslave Jacob's descendants; Moses leads the Israelites to freedom, they

cross the Reed Sea, (not Red Sea) and sin by worshipping a golden calf; God forgives them, they receive the Torah at Mount Sinai (p. 52), they build a Sanctuary, a portable temple (p. 7).

3 *Leviticus* (**Vayikra**)
How sacrifices were offered in the sanctuary; the foods Jews may or may not eat (p. 68); the times of the major festivals and the special mitzvot which must be observed during them.

4 *Numbers* (**Bemidbar**)
Moses counts the Israelites, there is a rebellion against Moses; various hostile nations try to defeat the Israelites; the Israelites' conquests east of the River Jordan; an outline of the route they had taken from Egypt to the Promised Land.

5 *Deuteronomy* (**Devarim**)
Also called **Mishnah Torah**, the repetition of the Torah; this book takes the form of speeches said by Moses on the borders of the Promised Land; it contains a great many laws as well as ethical teachings, and ends with Moses' death.

Torah scrolls set in cases (Sephardi style)

Jews regard these five books as the holiest part of the Tenakh. The Torah's stories – the patriarchs and matriarchs, the Egyptian slavery and the long trek to the Promised Land – tell Jews who they are; its laws and moral teachings tell Jews how to live and fulfil God's will.

For centuries, Jews have copied the Torah's words lovingly on to parchment scrolls, (p. 85). They have read the Torah, studied it and meditated upon it, and scholars have written commentaries to explain it in a variety of different ways. It has been the Jews' source of strength and inspiration. They have lived by the Torah's laws and, in times of persecution, have died for them.

Throughout their long history, the Torah has been the Jews' most precious possession. They have carried it with them to all their lands of dispersion. For centuries, as soon as Jewish children were old enough to read, they were introduced to the Torah. Every Jewish parent's deepest wish was that their children would grow up to live by the Torah's teachings.

Today, Torah scrolls are usually only found in synagogues, where they are kept in an honoured place. In their homes, Jews have the Torah in a printed book form called a **chumash** (plural **chumashim**). This is an abbreviation for **chamishah chumshei** Torah – the five parts (literally fifths) of the Torah.

THINGS TO DO

▶ What does 'Torah' mean? What is the written Torah? How is the word Tenakh formed? In what language is it written? What is a chumash?

▶ Why do Jews regard the Five Books of Moses as holy? How do they show this?

▶ Look at the Ten Commandments. Pick out those that deal with behaviour towards other people. How would you describe the others? Why do you think Jews regard each type as equally important? Explain what is meant by the Ten Commandments being subject headings?

▶ In his novel *Exodus*, Leon Uris described a Russian mob killing a Jew as he tried to rescue a **Sefer Torah** (Torah scroll) from a synagogue that they had set on fire. Uris writes, 'He had died in the noblest way a Jew could meet death – protecting the Sefer Torah.' What do you think he meant?

The Nevi'im (prophets) and Ketuvim (holy writings) make up the rest of the Tenakh, the written Torah. Jews regard these books as sacred because they were written either by prophets or people with **ruach hakodesh**, the divine spirit. However, they are not as holy as the Five Books of Moses, to whom God spoke 'face to face' (*Exodus 33:11*). This means that Moses' five books express a more direct communication from God than the writings of any other person. For this reason, Jews would not place a book of the Nevi'im or Ketuvim on top of a Chumash.

NEVI'IM (BOOKS OF THE PROPHETS)

The books of *Yehoshua* (*Joshua*), *Shofetim* (*Judges*), *Shemuel* (*Samuel*) and *Melachim* (*Kings*) describe the history of the Israelites from the death of Moses. They tell of how the Israelites conquered their new land and settled in it and of how they fought against hostile neighbours and eventually established a monarchy. They describe the building of the Temple, the division into two kingdoms (Israel and Judah), the exile of the people of Israel to Assyria and the destruction of the Temple and the exile of the Jews to Babylon.

Although these books are written as history, their main purpose is to teach religion. They show the covenant relationship described in the second paragraph of the Shema (p. 18) working itself out through the history of the Jewish people.

The prophetic writings also contain the three long books of *Isaiah, Jeremiah* and *Ezekiel*, as well as the twelve much shorter books of other prophets, known simply as *trei asar* (the twelve). Isaiah lived at the time of the Assyrian invasion and the exile of the Northern Kingdom (p. 7). Jeremiah and Ezekiel lived at the same time, and both foretold the destruction of Jerusalem. Jeremiah lived to see it; Ezekiel was exiled to Babylon before the destruction and told his prophesy to the Jews there. These books contain very little history; their purpose is to teach faith, justice and compassion.

KETUVIM (HOLY WRITINGS)

The books in this section are rather varied. *Esther, Daniel, Ezra* and *Nehemiah* describe what happened to the Jews in the Persian period (p. 8). *Chronicles* reviews the history of Israel. Like the historical books of the Nevi'im, the purpose of the books of the Ketuvim is to set down on record how the way that Jews behaved towards God has affected their own history. The book of *Chronicles* (*divrei hayamim*) is also historical, summarizing the events from Adam, the first man, until the return from Babylonian exile (p. 8).

The book of *Psalms* (*Tehillim*) is a collection of 150 praises to God. Most were written by David; the Talmud mentions ten other authors. *Proverbs* gives advice for upright living. It is set out as a series of short sayings.

Job (*Iyov*) is the story of a righteous man whom God tested by bringing appalling suffering upon him. Job's friends tell him that he must have sinned to have deserved such affliction, but he insists that he has not. Job accepts his ordeal without complaint and, eventually, God speaks to him and explains that humans cannot fathom His motives. One of the main teachings of the book is that suffering is not necessarily due to sin (p. 102).

Ecclesiastes (*Kohelet*) considers the meaning of life. It contrasts the majestic power of God with the limitations of humanity. After looking at various earthly desires and showing that they are all futile, the book concludes, 'The end of the matter is, now that everything has been heard, fear God and keep His commandments, for this is the whole of man.'

The book of *Ruth* tells a story of a Moabite woman who lived in the period of the Judges (p. 7). She loved God and endured poverty and hardship to join the Jewish people. Her great grandson was King David. Jews expect the Messiah (p. 24) to be Ruth's descendant.

Lamentations (*Eichah*) is the saddest of all the books of the Tenakh. In it, Jeremiah describes the destruction of Jerusalem and the First Temple which he himself had warned people about for many years previously. It portrays the tragedy in graphic and poetic terms, and expresses all the anguish of the people and Jeremiah himself.

The *Song of Songs* (*Shir Hashirim*) seems, at first glance, to be a love poem in which a shepherdess seeks her shepherd lover. However, Jews have long taken it to be an allegory referring to the love of God and the Jewish people for one another. Rabbi Akiva (p. 30) said, 'If all the Books of the Tenakh are holy, Shir Hashirim is the holy of holies.'

USES OF THE NEVI'IM AND KETUVIM

Like the Five Books of Moses, Jews have always read the Nevi'im and Ketuvim, meditated on them and made them their guide to life. However, some parts of these books have specific use in worship. Extracts from the book of *Tehillim* (*Psalms*) are incorporated into the daily and weekly prayers. Some are

Reading the Megillah (scroll of Esther) on Purim

especially appropriate for certain occasions. For example, Psalms 121 and 130 are often said before praying for a sick person. Psalm 91 is sometimes said before starting out on a journey. Extracts from the Nevi'im are read in the synagogue at the end of the Torah readings. These readings are known as **haftarot** (singular **haftarah**) meaning 'partings'.

The books of *Shir Hashirim*, *Ruth*, *Kohelet*, *Esther* and *Eichah* are known as the **Chamesh Megillot** (The Five Scrolls). These are read in the synagogue on **Pesach** (p. 48), **Shavuot** (p. 52), **Sukkot** (p. 54), **Purim** (p. 58) and **Tisha b'Av** (p. 60) respectively. In some communities, *Shir Hashirim* is read on Friday afternoons before the beginning of the Sabbath. The book of *Jonah* is read on the afternoon of **Yom Kippur** (Day of Atonement) (p. 46), the day when Jews pray for forgiveness for their sins. It tells of a prophet called Jonah who was sent to Nineveh, an Assyrian city. The inhabitants were very wicked. However, as soon as Jonah tells them that God will destroy them they are shocked into sudden awareness of how far they have fallen. They repent sincerely and God forgives them.

FOR YOUR FOLDERS

▶ Why do Jews regard the Five Books of Moses as the holiest part of the Tenakh? How do they express this belief?

THINGS TO DO

▶ What is the meaning of (a) Nevi'im, (b) Ketuvim? Name the five books in each section.

▶ Why are the books of *Job*, *Kohelet* and *Shir Hashirim* important for the Jews?

▶ Jonah is famous as the man who was swallowed by a big fish. What is the main message of his book? Why do you think Jews read it on Yom Kippur (Day of Atonement), the day when they pray to be forgiven for their sins?

▶ What are the psalms? How are they used in prayer?

HALAKHAH – JEWISH LAW

The 613 mitzvot (p. 22) are stated very briefly in the written Torah. For example, the command to 'bind a sign on your arms' (*Deuteronomy 6:8*) or not to work on the Sabbath day (*Exodus 20:10*), do not explain what the sign is or what is meant by work. Another body of teachings provided this information. According to Jewish tradition, when God gave Moses the Torah, He also taught him the halakhot – how the commandments were to be kept. Halakhah (plural **halakhot**) really means 'a going', since Jews think of observing the commandments as 'going with God'. The halakhot make up the oral Torah.

In the centuries that followed, these halakhot were passed on by word of mouth. Sometimes, questions arose as people wanted clarification of halakhot. For example, the Torah specified that a Moabite could not join the Jewish people (*Deuteronomy 23:4*), but did it also exclude a Moabitess? Other questions arose out of new situations. For example, when King David conquered neighbouring countries (p. 7) people needed to know whether the new territories became part of Israel and whether crops grown there should be tithed (i.e. a portion given to the priests and Levites). The destruction of the first Temple and the exile to Babylon (p. 7) raised all sorts of questions about how Jews should pray once they could no longer offer sacrifices. These questions would be addressed by priests and judges (*Deuteronomy 17:8–11*) and, later, by rabbis (p. 25). Their decisions became part of the halakhah. Authoritative rulings would be handed down by the Bet Din Hagadol (the supreme court of Judges, later called the Sanhedrin). These rulings would also be passed on orally and other priests and judges would refer to them when faced with further questions. In this way the oral Torah made it possible for Jews to live by the teachings of the written Torah as new conditions continually arose.

In addition, judges (and, later, rabbis) made rules to prevent people from violating the Torah. For example, the Torah forbids lighting a fire on Shabbat. The rabbis forbade handling flint stones or other fire-making equipment so that a person should not create fire unintentionally. This is known as 'putting a fence round the Torah'. They also instituted **takanot**, rules for the benefit of the community.

By the end of the first century BCE, there were a vast number of halakhot (rulings) and rabbis wanted to ensure that there was a system for making them. One of the foremost was Hillel the Elder who set down seven principles for formulating halakhic rulings. This gave rabbis clear guidelines for arriving at halakhic decisions.

About a century later, Rabbi Akiva (d. 135) began classifying halakhot under specific headings. He also set out to show how the halakhot were related to the written Torah. He taught that since the written Torah is the revealed word of God, even seemingly unnecessary words or words spelt in unusual ways are significant and that halakhot can be derived from them. Rabbi Akiva's work was built on by his pupil Rabbi Meir who made his own collection of authoritative halakhic decisions. Until this time, the halakhah was still taught orally, although teachers did make notes for their own private use.

THE MISHNAH

Towards the end of the second century CE, Roman oppression had become so severe that Jews started leaving the Holy Land. The foremost Jewish leader of the day, Rabbi Judah the Prince, saw that if they migrated to regions remote from one another they would lose contact. He was afraid that different versions of the halakhah would grow up in different areas and that the Jewish people would lose its unity. He decided that the time had come to write down the oral Torah, so that wherever Jews went, they would have a book of the most important halakhic decisions to refer to. The result was the **Mishnah**, set down in about the year 200 CE. Based heavily on Rabbi Meir's work, the Mishnah ran into 63 volumes (known as tractates) which Rabbi Judah divided into six divisions. These are the topics covered:

1 **Zeraim** ('seeds') Prayer, crops which were to be left for the poor, giving tithes, **Shemitta** (the sabbatical year when no farm work was to be done).

2 **Moed** ('festivals') How Sabbaths and festivals are to be observed, sacrifices offered in the Temple on these days, the forbidden types of work, fasts and other special days, mourning.

3 **Nashim** ('women') Betrothal and marriage, marriage documents, people who are forbidden to marry, divorce and settlements, vows.

4 **Nezikin** ('damages') Injury and compensation, ownership, inheritance, the

work of a court, examining witnesses, the punishments a court could inflict. One tractate, *Pikei Avot*, 'Chapters of the Fathers' (usually known as *Ethics* or *Sayings of the Fathers*), deals with moral guidance (p. 33).

5   **Kedoshim** ('holy matters') How the different types of sacrifices were offered in the Temple, sacrifices which became unfit for offering, the layout of the Temple.

6   **Taharot** ('purities') How people and articles could become pure or impure (p. 82), the mikveh (immersion pool), purity of foods.

Material not included in Rabbi Judah's Mishnah was later collected into a work known as the **Tosefta** (addition).

A page of Talmud. The text of the Talmud is in the middle. On the right side is Rashi's commentary; the Tosafot are on the left

THE TALMUD

From the end of the second century CE, the Mishnah was studied in the academies of Israel and Babylon. Rabbis and students wanted to know how its halakhot had arisen and what they meant for the practice of Judaism. Their discussions were carefully written down and filed away in archives. In about 500 CE, two Babylonian rabbis, Rabbi Ina and Rabbi Ashi, put these archives in order. They wrote down each paragraph of the Mishnah with the discussions that had taken place around it – some of which drew on discussions and rulings that went back many centuries and had been handed down orally. The result was a massive work which became known as the the Talmud Bavli, the Babylonian Talmud. About a century earlier, a similar scholarly effort in Israel had resulted in the Talmud Yerushalmi, the Jerusalem Talmud. Of the two, the Bavli has always been studied more extensively and is known simply as the **Talmud**. Jews also call it **gemara**, an Aramaic word meaning 'learning'. To this day, Talmud is the main subject studied in **yeshivot**, Jewish academies (p. 89).

COMMENTARIES

Some rabbis wrote commentaries to guide people through the Talmud. By far the most important is that of Rashi (Rabbi Shlomo ben Yitzhak, 1040–1105, p. 9). It takes the student through the Talmud phrase by phrase, explaining the discussions. Rashi's commentary has never been bettered and is still the standard explanation of the Talmud.

After Rashi, a number of rabbis wrote **Tosafot**, additions. These analyse particular points in a discussion or compare them with points raised elsewhere. Today, the standard printed Talmud has Rashi's commentary on one side of the text and the Tosafot on the other side (see photograph).

THINGS TO DO

▶   What is the halakhah? When and why was the Mishnah written? What is the Talmud? What is the Tosefta? What does 'putting a fence around the Torah' mean?

▶   What did Rashi achieve? How did the commentaries of the Tosafists differ from Rashi's?

▶   What is the connection between the written Torah and the oral Torah?

The Talmud is not a literary work but a record of discussions. Its topics are not neatly arranged under headings, but appear as and when people talked about them. In a discussion about Passover, for example, someone might refer to the Sabbath for comparison; a discussion of mourning will include comments about mourning on the Sabbath. This means that the principles of Sabbath observance are widely scattered throughout the Talmud. The same is true of other topics. Rabbis had to be very familiar with the entire Talmud to know where to locate the material they needed for deciding questions of Jewish law. This was difficult for the Talmud is very large (studying at the rate of one page a day, it takes 14 years to complete). Also, rabbis needed to be continually updated with halakhic decisions reached by other rabbis. Two methods arose for dealing with this problem: responsa and codes.

RESPONSA

From about the seventh century onwards, rabbis began sending their most difficult questions to a handful of particularly learned rabbis. The most famous were the heads of the Babylonian academies, the **gaonim** (p. 8). These learned men would send replies (responsa) to rabbis in many lands. Later, these responsa were collected and published so that they could be made available to rabbis everywhere. Rabbis would use them for working out solutions to further problems. Their rulings were incorporated into the codes.

CODES

Other rabbis complied codes, digests of halakhah where authoritative rulings could be set down in order. Two of the most important were that of Rabbi Moses ben Maimon (Maimonides, 1135–1204) who set down halakhot under separate headings and that of Rabbi Yosef Caro (1488–1575) whose work, the Shulchan Aruch (table prepared), omitted the laws connected with the Temple and anything else that no longer applied, but included the rulings given in the responsa up until his day. Rabbi Caro set out the halakhot in clear, short paragraphs. The Shulchan Aruch became the model for all later codes.

HALAKHAH AS AN ONGOING PROCESS

Over the centuries new discoveries, new methods of manufacture, new social conditions have changed people's ways of living and thinking about the

Keeping Judaism in an age of advancing technology

world. For Jews, this has always created the need to reapply the halakhah to ever-changing conditions, for living by the halakhah is essential for Jews to fulfil their part of their covenant relationship with God (p. 22).

During this century advances in technology have led Jews to raise questions which could not have been thought of in earlier times – questions about the use of automated electrical machinery on Sabbaths, whether computer hacking is theft, whether surrogate motherhood is permissible, whether a person on a life-support machine is alive or dead.

To enable rabbis to answer these questions, up-to-date commentaries have been added to the Shulchan Aruch, and whole books concerned with specific topics of halakhah are now being published. Some rabbis specialize in particular areas of halakhah (p. 93). Sometimes religious scientists help them. The continued reapplication of halakhah is an ongoing process.

◇

AGADAH (TEACHING WHAT THE TENAKH MEANS)

Agadah ('telling') is the traditional method of explaining the verses of the Bible. Each word is examined in its own context, and is also compared with similar words in other verses. Like the halakhah, the agadah was passed on orally. From the first century people began writing down the agadah. These works became known as **midrashim**. The writers of the midrashim often used parables or examples taken from real life to illustrate what they said. Much agadah was included in the Talmud.

KABBALAH (MYSTICISM)

Kabbalah means 'that which is received'. It is a study of the secrets of the Torah. Kabbalistic writings explain the ways in which God reveals Himself, how He created the universe out of nothing, how God, who has no limitations (p. 18), can have a relationship with finite beings, the nature of the human soul and how evil can exist in a world created by a good God.

Jews never delved into these topics just to gain knowledge. Those who studied kabbalah did so because they wanted to have a better understanding of themselves and their relationship with God. This understanding helped them to serve God with great devotion.

The kabbalistic tradition has been studied since the earliest times. However, the full explanation was written down gradually over many centuries. The most important kabbalistic book, the **Zohar** (*Book of Splendour*), was published in the fourteenth century. It contains teachings going back many hundreds of years.

Until the early eighteenth century kabbalah was only taught to learned and pious people who were considered worthy of such knowledge. At this time Rabbi Israel Baal Shem Tov made its teachings more widely available by explaining it in a simplified way. Kabbalah became the basis of Hasidic philosophy (p. 130).

ETHICAL WRITINGS

Judaism has always sought to improve people's characters and behaviour. These are among the main concerns of the Bible, Talmud and Midrashim. Jews always regarded Torah study as important because it could lead to good deeds. A first-century rabbi expressed the relationship between study and behaviour: 'Anyone whose good deeds are more than his wisdom, his wisdom will endure. Anyone whose wisdom is more than his good deeds, his wisdom will not endure.'

Through the ages there was always a special type of Jewish literature devoted to character training and guidance for correct behaviour. The oldest of these is the book of *Proverbs* in the Bible (p. 28). In the Mishnah, one tractate, *Ethics of the Fathers*, deals solely with ethical guidance (p. 31). From about the thirteenth century many ethical works were written. During the nineteenth century these writings became the main tool in the educational programme of the Musar movement (p. 128).

THINGS TO DO

▶ Why do you think studying Torah is important for Jews?

▶ Explain the term 'halakhah'. How has modern technology raised new questions in halakhah (give some examples)? How is halakhah related to the covenant?

▶ What sort of topics would you expect to find in a book of kabbalah? What is the value of studying these topics?

FOR YOUR FOLDERS

▶ What is meant by oral Torah and how is it related to the written Torah?

▶ Why were codes and responsa necessary? What did they achieve?

▶ What is meant by 'the continued reapplication of halakhah is an ongoing process'?

▶ What would you say to a person who felt that Jews are too concerned about keeping rules?

'These are the festivals of the Lord, holy assemblies which you shall proclaim at their appointed times.'

(Leviticus 23:4)

Jews have many festivals and special days during the course of the year. Some of these are major celebrations when ordinary day-to-day affairs, such as working, going to school or shopping must cease, and Jews will spend a great deal of time at prayer or celebrating with their families. Others are less important occasions and daily life continues much as usual. Still others are simply days when special prayers are recited in the synagogue.

The Jewish festivals are of two main types. Some, such as Pesach (p. 48) and **Hanukkah** (p. 56) commemorate historical events. They focus on miracles through which God helped the Jewish people. They represent God intervening in human affairs and changing them according to His plan. On these festivals Jews praise God as the controller of human history. *When Jews observe these festivals they attempt, through special mitzvot, to recreate or re-enact the original event.* This is important and you should be on the lookout for these mitzvot in the following units.

Other holy days, e.g. **Shabbat** (Sabbath p. 36) and the New Year for Trees (p. 62), focus on God as the creator and controller of nature. Pesach, Shavuot and Sukkot are linked to both themes. Although they commemorate historical events, Pesach coincides with the barley harvest in Israel and Shavuot with the wheat harvest. Sukkot occurs at the beginning of the rainy season in the Holy Land.

Two exceptions are Yom Kippur, the Day of Atonement (p. 46) and **Simchat Torah**, which are linked neither to history nor to nature. The theme of Yom Kippur, and the month of Ellul which leads up to it, is re-establishing one's relationship with God and with other human beings. Simchat Torah is the day when Jews conclude the weekly Torah readings in the synagogue (p. 55), and begin the cycle all over again. It marks the Jewish people's special relationship with God.

The chart on this page shows how the festivals may be classified under these headings.

Jews use the Biblical method of reckoning time. Each new day starts at sunset, instead of at midnight (*Genesis 1:5*). For example, when the sun goes down on Thursday evening it will be Friday for Jews, and when the sun goes down on Friday it will be Saturday. This explains why the Jewish Sabbath, which occurs each Saturday, actually begins on Friday evening. For the same reason, all Jewish festivals start at sunset.

In Britain there are very large seasonal differences in the times of sunset. At the height of summer the sun does not set until after 9 pm (or even later in Scotland); in midwinter it can set as early as 3.30 pm. This means that in winter, Jewish children who observe Sabbath will leave school early on Friday afternoon. The nearer one gets to the tropics, the less variation there is between the times of sunset at different seasons.

Jews have to learn to think of those hours after sunset as being a new day as regards Jewish matters, but still the same day for secular affairs. Most Jews manage this 'double thinking' without any difficulty.

The chart opposite shows how the Jewish year (Tishrei to Ellul) corresponds to the year January to December. This correspondence is only approximate since the Jewish calendar is a combination of the solar and lunar years (p. 42). This means that the exact time when the festivals occur will vary slightly from year to year.

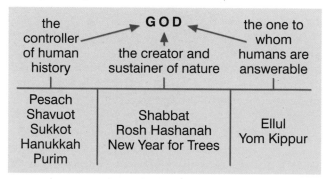

The festivals mark different aspects of a Jew's relationship with God

THINGS TO DO

▶ Imagine you are the parent of a Jewish child. Write a short letter to the head teacher asking permission for your son or daughter to leave school early on Fridays during the winter. Remember to explain fully why you are requesting this.

▶ Jews think of their festivals as regulated according to 'nature's clock'. Read *Genesis 1:14* and explain what you think this means.

▶ Which two themes are expressed in the Jewish festivals?

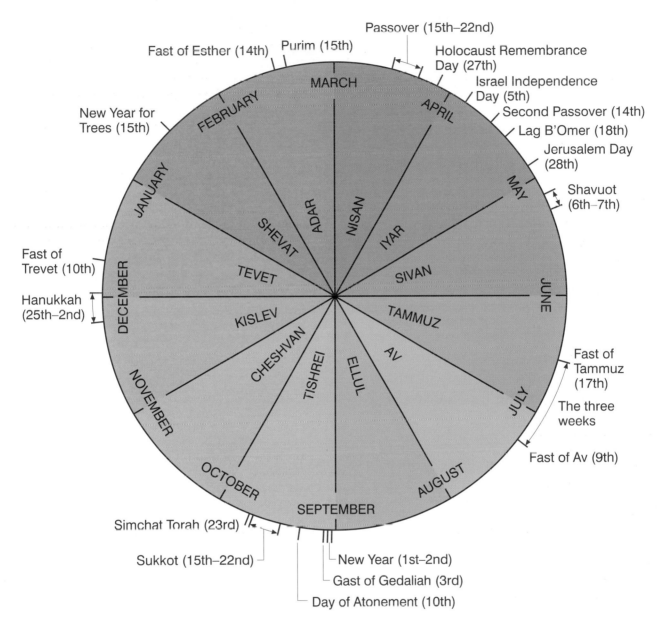

The Jewish year

'God said to Moses, "I have a precious gift in My treasure house, 'Sabbath' is its name. Go and tell the people of Israel that I wish to give it to them."'

(Talmud)

Each week Jews have a day of rest known as the Sabbath. Jews usually call it Shabbat or Shabbos. Shabbat begins at sunset on Friday and lasts until Saturday night when the stars appear.

WHY JEWS REST ON SHABBAT

Shabbat is a day when Jews are forbidden to do any work. But it is much more than just a 'day off'; it is a holy day. Jews are not meant to do any work so that they can devote themselves to prayer and Torah study. Rabbi Saadia Gaon, who lived in the tenth century, described Shabbat as an opportunity

> *'. . . to achieve rest from the abundance of one's toil so that one might acquire a little knowledge and pray a little more, and so that people might meet one another and discuss matters of Torah . . .'*

By resting on Shabbat, Jews proclaim their belief that God created the world, and that after completing His work He stopped and created nothing new (*Genesis 2:1–3*). Like God, Jews too have a day when they stop work. When they rest on Shabbat they see themselves, in a sense, as imitating God. He finished creating the world; Jews cease from exercising control over it.

Shabbat is also a time for relaxing with the family. Nowadays, many people live highly stressful lives. They are continually hurrying to get things done and families seldom have time just to be together. For Jews, Shabbat is a time when the family can spend time together in an unhurried, relaxed atmosphere.

PREPARING FOR SHABBAT

Jews try to see to it that on Shabbat the atmosphere in the home is different from the rest of the week. All the preparations must be done beforehand, as no work may be done on Shabbat itself. Some of the shopping or cooking might be done earlier in the week, but the bulk is often left until Friday. To see what happens, we are going to follow the Greens, a North London family, from early Friday afternoon until Saturday night.

Friday afternoon is a busy time for the Green family. They think of Shabbat as an honoured guest who comes to visit each week, so there is a lot to do

Friday afternoon: the Green children get ready for Shabbat

to get ready. In winter when it gets dark early, Mrs Green leaves work at lunchtime and Mr Green returns from the office in time to prepare for Shabbat. By the time Mr Green arrives home, Naomi (aged 20) and Aaron (aged 16) will already be helping to clean and tidy the house. Miriam, aged 8, helps too. This is an important part of a Jewish child's upbringing; Judaism is learnt by 'doing'.

Naomi and Aaron have lots of friends, and on Friday afternoon the phone hardly stops ringing, often up until minutes before Shabbat begins. On Shabbat the Greens do not use the phone (except for a life-threatening emergency). They do not turn on the television either. It is the peace and restfulness of Shabbat that make it a special day.

The Greens keep their best cutlery and crockery for Shabbat. The candlesticks sparkle on the table, next to the wine and **challot** (Shabbat loaves, p. 40). Challot are sold in Jewish shops. Occasionally, Mrs Green bakes her own.

Cooking is forbidden on Shabbat, so Mrs Green has prepared all the Shabbat food beforehand. Late on Friday afternoon she puts the cooked food on the stove to keep it hot. She does not place it directly on the flame as it would boil away or char to a cinder. She stands the saucepans on a sheet of metal known as a **blech**. This has been placed over the cooker rings, and she can now move the saucepans to cooler or hotter parts of the blech as required. In this way food can be kept hot for tomorrow's dinner.

When the dirtier jobs in the house have been done, every member of the family has a bath and they get dressed in their Shabbat clothes. Jews may neither turn lights on or off on Shabbat, so just before Shabbat, the Greens turn on all the lights they expect to use. They will stay on until Saturday night.

WELCOMING SHABBAT

Just before sunset, Mrs Green lights her candles. This marks the moment that Shabbat begins in the Green's house. It is always the woman's privilege to usher in the holy day. As she lights the candles, she beckons with her arms as though to welcome Shabbat into her home, and covers her eyes to recite the blessing. Like thousands of other Jewish women, Mrs Green uses this moment to say a short prayer for her family. This is a very holy moment in the Green household. Shabbat has arrived.

Mrs Green lights her candles

REFLECTIONS

'Lighting Shabbat candles connects me to an endless stream of Jewish mothers through all of time.'

(*Mrs R, North London*)

'When I light the Shabbat candles I feel like God is blessing me.'

(*Mrs M, Glasgow*)

Mr Green takes Aaron to the synagogue for afternoon prayers. Sometimes Mrs Green and the girls go too. Shabbat prayers actually begin with the evening service, when the Shabbat is greeted as a bride coming to meet her husband, the Jewish people. At the end of the service the rabbi takes a cup of wine and recites **kiddush** (sanctification). This is a blessing thanking God for having given Shabbat to the Jewish people.

As they leave the synagogue, the Greens shake hands with their friends, and they all wish each other 'Good Shabbos' or '**Shabbat Shalom**' (a Shabbat of peace).

THE FRIDAY NIGHT MEAL

Back at home, Mr Green blesses his children. This blessing, usually in Hebrew, is a prayerful wish that the children should grow up to follow the examples of the righteous men and women of Jewish history.

After this Mr Green recites kiddush. Every member of the family will listen to the blessings in silence and answer 'amen' at the end of each one. No one will have tasted any food from the moment Shabbat began until hearing kiddush, except Miriam, who is still quite young.

After kiddush they all go to wash their hands. This is not a physical cleansing, for the hands must be clean before washing. It is an act of purification (p. 65). They take their places at the table and Mr Green recites the blessing over the challot. This is a 'thank you' blessing to God for 'bringing bread out of the ground'. Jews are expected to thank God before eating any food. After cutting the bread, Mr Green dips the pieces lightly in salt (p. 61) and passes them round. The meal now begins.

For the Green family, the Shabbat meal is different from any other meal of the week. They eat special foods, sing songs between courses and Mr and Mrs Green often tell stories to their children. These might be stories from the Bible, or about the great Jewish men and women of the past. Naomi and Aaron often have a story to tell, and sometimes Miriam does too. It is a relaxed, unhurried meal, as no one is going anywhere. Like other Jewish families who observe Shabbat, the Greens look forward to this weekly opportunity just to be together and enjoy each other's company. They often have guests for the Shabbat meal.

THINGS TO DO

▶ Why do Jews not work on Shabbat?
▶ Look at the picture of Mrs Green. Explain fully what she is doing.
▶ What is kiddush?
▶ Why is Friday afternoon a busy time in Jewish homes?
▶ What do you think is meant by the phrase 'Judaism is learnt by doing'?

SHABBAT MORNING

The Shabbat morning service in the synagogue usually begins a bit later than during the week. It is also longer. During the service the rabbi will read part of the Torah. He reads it aloud in Hebrew from a handwritten, parchment scroll called a **Sefer Torah** (book of the Torah, p. 85). A certain portion, called a **sidra**, is read each Shabbat so that the entire scroll is completed during the course of the year. These scrolls are the holiest objects in the synagogue.

When the Ark (cupboard containing the Torah scrolls, p. 84) is opened, everyone stands up as a mark of respect. A Sefer Torah is taken out and carried to the **bimah** (platform, p. 84). Seven men will be called to recite blessings at certain points during the reading of the sidra. At the end, before the Torah scroll is returned to its place in the Ark, an eighth man is called to read the haftarah, a portion from one of the books of the prophets (p. 29). Sometimes Mr Green is called up to say a blessing. When Aaron reached the age of thirteen (p. 74) he, too, was called.

After the Torah scroll has been put back in the Ark, the rabbi gives a sermon. Sometimes there is a visiting speaker. The sermon might be on something in the sidra or about an item in the news. The rabbi takes this as an opportunity to encourage his congregation to keep Judaism or to teach them something new. After this there is an additional service, known as **musaf** (p. 86).

As people leave the synagogue, they again wish each other 'Good Shabbos' or 'Shabbat Shalom'.

Back home, the Green's midday meal is very much like the one the night before. Mr Green does not bless his children again, but he does recite kiddush and say a blessing over the challot. He usually has another story ready, and Miriam sits glued to every word. Even his older children, Naomi and Aaron still enjoy their father's stories.

After dinner Mr Green usually sits down with Aaron and Miriam to go over their Jewish studies. Naomi runs a Shabbat playgroup for younger children and she has to go out. Sometimes Miriam visits friends who live nearby (the Greens do not use their car on Shabbat) or she might have some friends round to play. On the long summer afternoons Mr and Mrs Green might have a short nap or take a stroll in the park.

Later on in the afternoon, Mr Green and Aaron go to the synagogue again. Afternoon prayers are fairly short. The Sefer Torah is taken out and the first part of the following week's sidra is read. Mr Green

Mr Green performs havdalah. Miriam holds the candle

and Aaron study the Torah with the other men until nightfall. Mrs Green and the girls usually go to a women's study group in a neighbour's house. The neighbours take turns to host it, and sometimes it will be in the Green's house.

SHABBAT GOES OUT

When the stars appear on Saturday night, Shabbat is over and the congregation prays the weekday evening service. This includes a prayer asking for God's blessing for the coming week. At the end of the service the rabbi performs **havdalah** (separation), a ceremony to mark the end of the holy day. He says a blessing over a cup of wine, followed by another over spices. A third blessing is said over the light of a candle, showing that Jews are allowed to light fire once more. He says one last blessing over the wine, and the separation of the holy day from the ordinary is completed.

As soon as Mr Green gets home, he too performs havdalah. The Greens now start their tidying up. They could not do any of this on Shabbat. They have all the dishes to wash up, dry and put away.

FIND OUT

▶ A Sefer Torah is written in Hebrew. Try to find out in which direction Hebrew is read, how many letters there are in the alphabet and the names of some Hebrew letters, in particular the first two.

▶ On Friday afternoon Shabbat begins when the sun sets, but on Saturday it does not end until the stars appear. Find out how long it is from the time the sun goes down over the horizon until the time when you can see the first stars. Sometimes a bright object appears in the sky shortly after sunset. You might mistake it for a star. Try to find out what it is.

◇

THINGS TO DO

▶ Which of these statements is true?

1 Resting on Shabbat is the Jews' way of showing that they believe God created the world.

2 Jews may not cook on Shabbat so they only eat cold food.

3 Jewish women light their candles a few minutes after sunset.

4 Shabbat is welcomed as a bride coming to meet her bridegroom.

5 On Friday night Jewish children and parents bless each other.

6 After cutting the bread, father pours salt on each slice.

7 Children listen to Jewish stories at the Shabbat meal.

8 Many Jews think of Shabbat as a time for being with the family.

▶ Write a letter to a friend describing a Shabbat morning service you went to. If you want to include some details about the synagogue, look at pages 84–5.

▶ A rabbi has asked you to help him prepare a sermon. Choose one or more items of recent news and suggest how they could be used as examples of good behaviour which are worth copying, or of bad behaviour which should be avoided.

▶ Why do you think havdalah is an important ceremony?

▶ Shabbat is very much a family event. How might it be celebrated by:

a people living on their own

b residents of an old age home

c a patient in hospital?

THE SYMBOLISMS OF SHABBAT

So far we have followed the Green family through Shabbat, without explaining what they were doing or why. We must now go back over some of the things the Greens did and see what they mean. Shabbat is very rich in symbols (make sure you know what a symbol is).

The challot (Sabbath loaves)

The two challot represent the manna, the miracle food which the ancient Israelites ate during their journey through the desert (*Exodus 16:14–18*). The manna appeared outside the doors of their tents each day, except Shabbat. Instead, God gave them a double portion on Friday. This is represented by the double loaves at the Shabbat meal.

In the desert the manna was enveloped between two layers of dew, one above and one below. This is represented by a plate or board underneath the challot, and a cloth on top. The challot are usually plaited loaves. They have twelve plaits to represent the twelve loaves of bread which were laid out in the Temple (p. 7) on the eve of each Shabbat.

Mr Green says a blessing before cutting the challot

The candles (p. 37)

Before the days of electric lights, Jews would light large numbers of candles on Friday evening. This gave the house a festive atmosphere, for during the week candles would only be lit where and when they were needed. Today two symbolic candles are lit. These represent the Biblical commands, 'Remember the Sabbath day' (*Exodus 20:8*) and 'Observe the Sabbath day' (*Deuteronomy 5:12*). In many families an extra candle is lit for each child.

Havdalah spices

Shabbat is a holy day. Many Jews feel more spiritual on Shabbat than on other days. The ancient rabbis described this as having an 'extra soul'. With the close of Shabbat the extra soul leaves. Spices are smelled to refresh the soul after the departure of its 'companion'.

Havdalah candles

On Shabbat, Jews are not permitted to create fire (*Exodus 35:3*). At the havdalah ceremony, they use a plaited candle so that the flames of several wicks mingle. This shows that they can now create fire in any form.

WORK FORBIDDEN ON SHABBAT

People often find it difficult to understand exactly what Jews mean by 'work' on Shabbat. They see the rabbi leading the service in the synagogue and think that he must be 'working', as that is the way he earns his living. On the other hand, they see that observant Jews do not turn on light switches on Shabbat nor carry a handkerchief in their pockets when they walk in the street, and they wonder how doing these things could possibly be regarded as work.

The difficulty arises because when Jews speak of 'work' on Shabbat, they mean something quite different from the general accepted idea of work. Work usually means following a profession or using up energy. As far as Shabbat is concerned, work means doing a **melachah**. A melachah (plural **melachot**) is simply a type of job. On Shabbat there are 39 melachot which are forbidden. These are the 39 types of job which were necessary for building the Sanctuary, the portable Temple that the Israelites built in the desert (p. 7). These tasks include not only building and shaping operations, but also agricultural and cooking activities which were necessary for producing dyes from plants. It would be less confusing if instead of using the word 'work' when talking about Shabbat we used the Hebrew term 'melachah'.

The 39 forbidden melachot are:

1 ploughing	23 sewing
2 sowing	24 tearing
3 reaping	25 trapping or hunting
4 sheaf-making	26 slaughtering
5 threshing	27 skinning
6 winnowing	28 tanning
7 selecting	29 scraping pelts
8 sifting	30 marking out
9 grinding	31 cutting to shape
10 kneading	32 writing
11 baking	33 erasing
12 sheep-shearing	34 building
13 bleaching	35 demolishing
14 combing raw materials	36 lighting a fire
15 dyeing	37 putting out a fire
16 spinning	38 the final hammer
17–19 various	blow (putting the
weaving operations	finishing touch to a
20 separating into	newly made article)
threads	39 carrying from a
21 tying a knot	private to a public
22 untying a knot	area (and vice versa).

These tasks are ways of controlling our environment (p. 36) and are forbidden on Shabbat no matter how they are done. For example, we could light a fire by rubbing two sticks together. We could also press a switch and produce fire in an electric light bulb. The first method is very hard work in the generally accepted sense; the second method involves no work at all. However, both of them result in fire being produced, so each is a melachah and is therefore forbidden. The same is true for all 39 melachot.

Jews are forbidden to drive on Shabbat, to use the telephone (except in emergencies), watch television, play computer games, take photographs or go fishing. They may go for a walk in the park, but are forbidden to take a ball with them; they may stroll past shops and look in windows, but may not buy anything. In Israel the buses do not run. Each of these involves doing a melachah.

It sometimes seems to non-Jews that all this turns Shabbat into a dreary, unpleasant day. Nothing could be further from the truth. To Jews it is a day of joy; it is simply a day when they enjoy themselves in different ways from the rest of the week. Jews who observe Shabbat look forward to its coming. Each week, when they celebrate Shabbat, they feel that the rabbis of old were right when they said, 'all the days of the week are blessed by the Shabbat'.

THINGS TO DO

▶ The 39 forbidden melachot are not single tasks, but broad categories. For example, ploughing means preparing ground for planting and includes digging, fertilizing soil and removing stones. Similarly, sowing means helping plants to grow and includes pruning bushes and watering the lawn. Sewing is joining two materials permanently by means of a third substance. It includes stapling bits of paper together.

Try to work out which categories the following come under (Jews are forbidden to do any of them on Shabbat):

a making a bouquet of flowers

b filing metals

c shaving

d ironing

e putting on make-up

f knitting

g sealing envelopes

h squashing a spider

i polishing shoes

j smoking.

▶ Imagine you are helping Naomi Green run her Shabbat afternoon playgroup. Plan some games so that the children can enjoy Shabbat without violating it.

▶ Shabbat is a day for making spiritual progress. How might avoiding the 39 melachot help accomplish this?

▶ Why are Jews not permitted to make toast on Shabbat?

▶ It is a sunny Saturday afternoon and you are going cycling with a few friends. They want to call on another friend who is Jewish to go as well. How would you explain to them that it would not be appropriate to call?

▶ Do you think observing Shabbat has any value today? Explain your answer.

'O our God and God of our ancestors, renew this month for us for good and for blessing . . .'

(Prayer book)

As well as the calendar which everyone uses (January–December), Jews have a calendar of their own (p. 34). Their months are lunar months; that means that they follow the phases of the moon. In some months **Rosh Chodesh** (new moon) stretches over two days. This depends on when the actual change in the moon's phase occurs.

THE JEWISH MONTHS

It takes about $29\frac{1}{2}$ days for the moon to orbit the earth. During this time the moon appears to grow in size and then shrink away to nothing. Its reappearance is called the new moon. For Jews this is the start of a new month. Jewish months have either 29 or 30 days. There are 12 months in the Jewish year, except in leap years (see below) when there is an extra month. All the Jewish festivals occur at set dates in this calendar.

The Jewish months do not coincide with those of the January–December calendar, although they do not vary from it a great deal. For example, the Jewish New Year is on the first two days of the month of Tishrei. Tishrei is always in autumn. However, it can fall anytime between early September and early October (see the chart on p. 35). Jews have to learn to regulate their religious life according to the Jewish calendar, and their business or other secular activities according to the general calendar.

ROSH CHODESH IN ANCIENT TIMES

Even in ancient times, astronomers were able to calculate where and when the new moon would appear. Nevertheless, Torah law required that people who had seen it should come to the **Bet Din Hagadol** (p. 30), the supreme rabbinical court, and state that the new moon had appeared. As soon as the rabbis had questioned the witnesses and were satisfied that the new moon had been seen, they would stand up and proclaim, 'It [i.e. the new month] is sanctified, it is sanctified.' They would then dispatch messengers to Jewish communities everywhere to inform people that they should start reckoning a new month.

The rabbis also had to make sure that the festivals occurred in their right seasons. The lunar year, which governs the Jewish months, is about ten days shorter than the solar year, which governs the seasons. As each lunar year went by, the festivals would have shifted further and further back in the seasons. Within ten years, Passover, which is meant to be a spring festival, would have occurred in midwinter. To overcome this difficulty the rabbis inserted an extra month from time to time. This kept the lunar and solar years in line with one another. Years of thirteen months are leap years. They occur seven times in every cycle of nineteen years.

After the destruction of the second Temple (p. 8) it became difficult to continue with the system of examining witness. A permanent calendar was then worked out. This could be used indefinitely since it recurred every nineteen years. This is the calendar that Jews use today.

The chart on p. 35 gives the Jewish months and their approximate equivalents.

In ancient Israel, Rosh Chodesh was a day of rest, almost like Shabbat. During the Middle Ages various communities adopted different customs about what kind of work could be carried out, though in most places it was a day when women rested. Nowadays, all Jews work on Rosh Chodesh, though in some communities women still refrain from certain tasks.

THE SABBATH OF BLESSING

The Shabbat before Rosh Chodesh is called **Shabbat Mevarchim** (Sabbath of Blessing). After the Torah has been read, everybody in the synagogue stands up to hear announcement of the time of the forthcoming new moon. This is like the ancient rabbinical court which stood to proclaim the new month. Following this, the congregation prays to God asking Him to bless the coming month as a month of 'life and peace, gladness and joy, deliverance and consolation'.

PRAYERS

On the day of Rosh Chodesh itself, special prayers are recited in the synagogue. These include part of **Hallel** (a reading of Psalms 113–118). These are special hymns of praise and are read on most festivals. A passage from the Torah scroll is also read, describing the sacrifices for Rosh Chodesh in the ancient Temple. Unlike Shabbat, when seven men are called to the Torah reading, on Rosh Chodesh only four are called.

WOMEN'S ROSH CHODESH GROUPS

In recent years, some women have begun getting together on Rosh Chodesh to strengthen their Jewish commitment. In these groups, they have revived some ancient Rosh Chodesh customs that

Women at a North London Rosh Chodesh group listen to a visiting speaker

had fallen into disuse – for example, lighting a candle floating in water to represent the moon floating in space. Each group decides what it will do. There is no set pattern. Some read extracts from the Tenakh or more recent Jewish writings, some have formal study sessions associated with the events of the coming month, others discuss selected topics and how they relate to Jewish women. Many have a light celebration meal. Almost all have a charity collection. However, all the women who take part in these groups share the common ideal of wanting to deepen their spiritual awareness.

BLESSING OVER THE MOON

During the first half of the month, when the moon appears to be growing in size, **Kiddush Levanah** is recited. This is a blessing thanking God for having renewed the moon. It is an acknowledgement that God maintains order and harmony in the cosmos. Kiddush Levanah is usually said on Saturday night, immediately after Shabbat.

There is also a blessing that Jews recite over the sun. This is the most infrequent of Jewish observances; Jews say it only once every 28 years. It is said when the earth and sun are in the same

relative positions as they were at their creation. Jews recite this blessing to acknowledge that God created the universe and continues to take care of it.

THINGS TO DO

▶ Try to find out the date of your birthday in the Jewish calendar. Use the chart on p. 35 to see whether it is near to a festival. Use this information to write a card to a Jewish friend inviting him or her to your birthday party. Does 1 January always occur on the same date in the Jewish calendar? Explain your answer.

▶ What do you think Jews mean when they praise God for maintaining order and harmony in the cosmos?

▶ On Rosh Chodesh Jews read Psalm 104. Read this psalm and jot down ten things it mentions. Why do you think it is included in the Rosh Chodesh prayers?

'"Seek the Lord while He may be found" (Isaiah 5:6). This refers to the ten days between Rosh Hashanah and Yom Kippur, when God is closest to those who sincerely want to return to Him.'

(Talmud)

Rosh Hashanah (New Year) and ten days later Yom Kippur (Day of Atonement) are known as the Days of Awe. Some Jews also refer to them as the High Holydays. Jews think of Rosh Hashanah and Yom Kippur as two stages in the process of judgement and atonement.

THE SIGNIFICANCE OF THE DAYS OF AWE

In Jewish tradition, Rosh Hashanah is the birthday of the human race. It is the anniversary of the day when God created the first human beings (p. 20). Jews believe that on this day God judges all people for their deeds of the previous year, and decides what their circumstances shall be during the following year. For this reason Rosh Hashanah is also called **Yom Hadin**, the *Day of Judgement*. This passage from the Rosh Hashanah service, shows the kind of decisions Jews believe that God makes on this day.

'. . . how many shall pass away and how many shall be born, who shall live and who shall die . . . who shall be at peace and who shall be harassed, who shall be poor and who shall be rich, who shall be humbled and who shall be promoted . . . .'

Jews think of Rosh Hashanah as the day when these decisions are written down, and Yom Kippur as the day when they are sealed (finalized).

THE MONTH OF ELLUL

'The gates of repentance are always open,' says the Midrash. People can ask God to forgive them at any time. However, the month of **Ellul** has always been a special time when Jews prepare themselves for the coming judgement. Traditionally, 1 Ellul is the date that Moses went up Mount Sinai (p. 26) the second time, to receive the tablets of stone with the Ten Commandments engraved in them. He had smashed the first tablets when the Israelites sinned by worshipping the golden calf (p. 27). Forty days later on 10 Tishrei (the day now celebrated as Yom Kippur), Moses came back. The new tablets in his hands showed that God had forgiven the Israelites

A rabbi shows a class how to blow the shofar

for their sin. This span of time, therefore, is strongly associated with repentance and forgiveness. Jews have always regarded Ellul as a time for putting right the mistakes and misdeeds of the previous year and preparing themselves to renew their pledges to God.

The Greens take Ellul very seriously. For the whole month, Mr Green listens to the **shofar** (ram's horn) blown each morning in the synagogue. He usually takes Aaron with him. The shofar is one of the oldest musical instruments known. In ancient times it signalled the advance or retreat of armies on the battlefield, or was sounded to announce the approach of the king. Each morning it reminds Mr Green that Rosh Hashanah is getting nearer. On Rosh Hashanah it will be blown again as Jews renew their promises to their King (God).

Oriental Jews (**Sephardim**) rise early during the month of Ellul to recite selichot, special prayers for forgiveness. Western Jews (**Ashkenazim**) start saying **selichot** only during the last part of the month.

In the past, whenever Jews wrote letters at this time of year, they would end with a wish for a Happy New Year. Today the Green family sends New Year greetings cards to their friends bearing these wishes.

THE EVE OF ROSH HASHANAH

On the last day of the old year, special selichot are said. Mr Green and Aaron arrive in the synagogue much earlier than usual. On this day the shofar is not sounded. This is to draw a distinction between the month of Ellul, when the shofar is blown to herald the coming day of judgement, and Rosh Hashanah, when it will be blown in fulfilment of one of the 613 commandments (p. 22).

The Green family prepare for Rosh Hashanah in much the same way as for Shabbat (p. 36). They buy a new fruit, one they have not eaten during the past season, such as a pomegranate. This symbolizes renewal, and a special blessing will be recited before eating it on the second night of Rosh Hashanah. Just before sunset, Mrs Green ushers in the holy day by lighting candles (p. 40).

ROSH HASHANAH

As with all Jewish festivals, prayers start with the evening service (p. 34). On this night God is addressed as a king sitting in judgement over His world. The main theme of the prayers during the entire two days of Rosh Hashanah is asking God to accept once again the kingship of the world.

As they leave the synagogue, the Greens greet their friends. They bless one another with the words, 'May you be written down for a good year.' At home Mr Green makes kiddush (p. 37), and they eat slices of apple dipped in honey. This symbolizes a 'sweet new year'. They eat other symbolic foods, such as a fish head.

The high point of the Rosh Hashanah morning service is the blowing of the shofar. Unlike in the month of Ellul, when a few notes were blown each morning, on Rosh Hashanah itself 100 notes are blown. They are made up of three sounds: **tekiah**, a single long note, **shevarim**, three shorter notes, and **teruah**, nine or more very short notes blown in staccato. They all represent different types of crying, for the shofar expresses the crying of the soul yearning to be reunited with God.

Later in the day there is an afternoon service. After afternoon prayers on the first day of Rosh Hashanah, the Greens go to **tashlich** (casting away). Tashlich is a prayer asking God to remove the sins of His people. They say this prayer by the banks of a river or pond symbolizing the verse '. . . and You will cast all their sins into the depths of the sea . . .' (*Micah 7:19*). If the first day of Rosh Hashanah is Shabbat, they go to tashlich the following day.

THE TEN DAYS OF RETURNING

The period from 1 Tishrei (Rosh Hashanah) until 10 Tishrei (Yom Kippur) is known as the ten days of returning. It is a time of stock-taking, when Jews consider their deeds of the past year and resolve to do better during the year that has just begun. In many communities selichot are said before morning prayers each day. Judaism teaches that God does not forgive a wrong done to another person unless one has first asked that person for forgiveness. During this time Jews try to contact anyone they might have wronged, to ask them for forgiveness.

The Shabbat which occurs during this week is called **Shabbat Shuvah** (Sabbath of Returning). The scriptural reading for this Sabbath (*Hosea 14*) urges Jews to turn to God and to make themselves dependent on Him alone.

A fish head on the table: a symbol of good deeds multiplying like fish

FOR YOUR FOLDERS

▶ During Ellul (and for most of Tishrei) Jews read Psalm 27 twice a day. Read it and jot down six ideas it contains. What might this psalm have to do with returning to God?

▶ Why is Rosh Hashanah called the Day of Judgement?

▶ Jews believe that God decides many things on Rosh Hashanah but not *who will be righteous and who will be wicked*. Why not?

THE EVE OF YOM KIPPUR

The day before Yom Kippur – 9 Tishrei – is a time of preparation. There is a very old custom of distributing chickens to the poor for their pre-Yom Kippur meal. These represent the sacrifices of the ancient Temple. Early in the morning, before the chickens are killed, **kaparot**, a special prayer for forgiveness, is said. Like many people today, the Greens give money to the poor instead.

Sometime during the afternoon Mr Green and Aaron go to the mikveh, an immersion pool (p. 82). Immersion is an act of spiritual cleansing. Throughout the year only married women have an obligation to visit the mikveh (p. 83). The eve of Yom Kippur is the only time in the year when men have an obligation to go (there is a separate mikveh for men).

Yom Kippur is a 25-hour-long fast. Miriam, who is eight, is not permitted to fast. On the Yom Kippur before her **Bat Mitzvah** (p. 74) Miriam will be encouraged to fast if she feels able. People often think that Yom Kippur must be a sad day, since Jews fast, reflect upon their sins and pray for forgiveness. This is not so. The Greens approach it joyfully, happy because they are given this opportunity each year to atone for their misdeeds. The last meal before the fast begins is a festive meal.

After the meal everybody gets ready for the evening prayers. The Greens do not wear leather shoes, as these are a symbol of luxury. Mr Green wears a white smock-like garment called a **kittel**, over his clothes. This symbolizes the verse, 'Even if your sins will be as red as scarlet they will become as white as snow' (*Isaiah 1:18*). Mrs Green, Naomi and Miriam wear white dresses (or, at least, dresses with white in them). They do not wear gold jewellery, just like the high priest in the ancient Temple, who did not wear his golden garments for the holiest parts of the Yom Kippur service. Gold would have called to mind the sin of the golden calf (p. 27). Just before sunset Mrs Green lights candles and the holy day begins.

YOM KIPPUR (DAY OF ATONEMENT)

Yom Kippur is the holiest day of the Jewish year, and the synagogues are usually packed. Thousands of Jews who might be absent the rest of the year feel compelled to attend on this special day. Mr Green wears his **tallit** (p. 86). It is the only time the tallit is worn at night time.

Before the evening service begins, the **Kol Nidrei** declaration (annulment of vows) is chanted. It was written during the Spanish Inquisition, when Jews

Mr Green puts on his kittel

were forced to accept Christianity or be killed. Many Jews in Spain lived outwardly as Christians and swore vows of allegiance to the Church (p. 15). Secretly, however, they lived as Jews, gathering in cellars to pray, and observing Shabbat behind closed doors. Each year, before the Yom Kippur service, they declared null and void any vows that they might be called upon to make to the Church during the coming year. Today Jews chant this before Yom Kippur prayers begin. It calls to mind a time when their ancestors took great risks to live as Jews.

During the prayers of Yom Kippur each member of the Green family confesses their sins and asks for forgiveness. Confession may only be made to God, never to a person, and it is always said quietly so that no one should hear. It is regarded as disrespectful to God to let other people hear that one has sinned against Him. The prayer books have printed lists phrased in very general terms, like this:

'And so, may it be Your will, Lord our God and God of our fathers, to have mercy on us and forgive us all our sins, grant us atonement for all our iniquities, and forgive and pardon us for all our transgressions:

- *for the sin which we have committed before You under duress or willingly*
- *and for the sin which we have committed before You by hard-heartedness*
- *for the sin which we have committed before You inadvertently*
- *and for the sin which we have committed before You with an utterance of our lips*
- *for the sin which we have committed before You with immorality*
- *and for the sin which we have committed before You openly or secretly*
- *for the sin which we have committed before You with knowledge and with deceit*
- *and for the sin which we have committed before You through speech . . .'*

People who know that they have been guilty of a particular sin are expected to make a special confession of it. The Green family will pray five times on Yom Kippur, starting with the evening service at the beginning of the fast. The day starts with the morning service. This is followed by a reading of the Torah, when they will hear about the Yom Kippur service in the ancient Temple (*Leviticus 16*). After this is the additional service, which includes a step-by-step follow-through of the Temple procedure. At this point most synagogues have a short break. A little after midday Mrs Green takes Miriam home to give her lunch. During the afternoon service the Torah is read again. The reading is from *Leviticus 16*, which warns the people of Israel not to be influenced by the ways of the heathen nations. After this, the book of *Jonah* is read (this is a fairly short book and you might like to read it). Its theme is the great power of repentance.

The day's prayers conclude with **Neilah**, 'the closing of the gates', the final service before the decrees made by God on Rosh Hashanah are sealed. Throughout this service, the doors of the Ark (p. 84), symbolizing the gates of heaven, remain open. At the end of Neilah, the Green family make the three declarations of faith:

'Hear O Israel, the Lord is our God, the Lord is One.'
This is the daily declaration of God's oneness, (p. 47). They say this once.

'Blessed is the name of His glorious kingdom forever and ever.'
This is said three times.

'The Lord is God.'
They say this seven times. It is the declaration which the Israelites made in the time of Elijah, when they rejected idolatry and turned wholeheartedly to God (*I Kings 18:39*).

After nightfall, a single blast of the shofar announces that the fast is over. The Greens pray the evening service (it is now the following day, p. 34). At home Mr Green makes havdalah (p. 39) and they all 'break' their fasts. After eating, Mr Green and the children start building the **sukkah** (p. 54) to prepare for the next festival.

REFLECTION

'Fasting is something I definitely do not enjoy. But Yom Kippur is different. I always feel so cleansed at the end of the day.'

(Mrs C, Manchester)

THINGS TO DO

▶ Test yourself with this quiz. See if you can write down the meaning of the following in less than 5 minutes:

Ellul shofar Shabbat tashlich kittel Shuvah selichot Kol Nidrei kaparot Yom Kippur

Now check back and see how many you got right.

9–10	Excellent
6–8	Good
4–5	Fair
3 or less	Read these pages again!

▶ Look up 'atonement' in a dictionary. How do Jews pray for atonement? Does atonement have any relevance today?

▶ What do you think is achieved by confessing one's sins?

▶ What does Judaism encourage people to do if they know they have wronged someone? What does this tell you about the Jewish attitude to other people?

'Three times during the year all your males shall appear before the Lord your God, . . . on the feast of Unleavened Bread, the feast of Weeks and the feast of Tabernacles . . .'

(Deuteronomy 16:16)

The festivals of Pesach, Passover (in spring), Shavuot, Weeks (early summer) and Sukkot, Tabernacles (early autumn), are known as the pilgrim festivals. In ancient times men used to make a pilgrimage to Jerusalem on these occasions to offer sacrifices in the Temple (p. 7). They usually took their families with them, (e.g. *I Samuel 1:3–4*). Today there are no pilgrimages in Judaism (but see p. 151), and people celebrate these festivals at home and in the synagogue. Some people like to celebrate one or more of them in Israel, especially in Jerusalem where they can pray by the Western Wall, the last remaining wall of the Temple, (p. 151).

Pesach marks the departure of the Israelites from Egyptian slavery (p. 6). Shavuot commemorates the giving of the Torah at Mount Sinai, seven weeks later (p. 52). Sukkot marks the Israelites' journey through the desert on their way to the Promised Land. Everywhere in the world these festivals are observed for one day longer than in Israel. This practice began in ancient times when the Jews living in the diaspora could not know when the rabbis had proclaimed a new month (p. 42) until the messengers arrived to tell them. They therefore observed an extra day of each festival in case the new month had started a day later than expected, as sometimes happened. Today, continuing the practice gives Jews a way of expressing the special sanctity of the Holy Land. The spiritual attainments of Passover, for example, which may be achieved in Israel in seven days, take eight days everywhere else in the world.

HOW PESACH BEGAN

About 3500 years ago Jacob and his family settled in Egypt (p. 6), and soon grew into a sizeable nation. By that time, however, Egypt had lost much of its wealth, its empire was falling apart and there was widespread unemployment. A new king came to the throne. He blamed all of Egypt's problems on the Israelites. He announced that they were a threat to national security and decreed that they should become slaves. All able-bodied Israelite men were put to work on the king's building projects or in the mines.

Many years earlier, God had told Abraham that this was going to happen (*Genesis 15:13–14*). He also promised him that one day He would set the Israelites free. When the time came for God to fulfil His promise, He chose Moses, who had fled from Egypt years earlier, to go to Pharaoh and ask him to free the slaves. Pharaoh refused, and God tormented the Egyptians with ten plagues.

The last plague was terrible. God warned Moses that on a certain night He would kill all the firstborn sons of the Egyptians. The Israelites were to sacrifice sheep and goats and smear the blood on the doorposts of their houses. In this way those who wanted to identify themselves as Israelites would be known and their children would be spared. That night there was crying all over Egypt. Pharaoh, whose firstborn son had also died, begged Moses to leave. The Israelites set out on their journey across the desert.

During the days that followed, Pharaoh and his advisers changed their minds. They missed having slaves to do their work. Finally, Pharaoh decided to bring back the Israelites. He took a huge army headed by 600 chariots and raced across the desert in pursuit. By this time the Israelites were approaching the shores of the Reed Sea (not the Red Sea). God parted the sea with a strong wind and the Israelites passed across between two walls of water. As the last of the Israelites reached the shore, the Egyptians rushed into the path. God lowered the wind and the waves came crashing down. Hundreds of Egyptians were drowned, and the Israelites knew that from then on they were really free.

PREPARING FOR PESACH

God commanded the Israelites to mark their freedom with an annual festival. During this festival, to be called Pesach, they were neither to eat nor to possess any **chametz**. Chametz means leaven, i.e. grain products which become swollen during baking. Bread and cake are chametz (think of how disappointed people are when their cakes do not rise), so are cereals and anything else that contains grain. During Pesach, Jews eat only chametz-free foods.

Jews regard chametz as a symbol of pride, since it swells as it bakes. In the English language too, we speak of a person being 'puffed up' with pride. Pride can lead people to rely on themselves for everything and exclude God from their lives, whereas a humble person is prepared to admit that he or she depends on God. Pesach commemorates the Israelites' total reliance on God's help, for no human power could have taken them out of slavery. Jews express this by having no contact with chametz during the week of Pesach.

Let's see how the Goodman family prepare for Pesach. The Goodmans live in Glasgow. Removing all chametz from their home means a total spring clean. Michael (aged 6) usually find crumbs in her pockets. Michael and Daniel (aged 10) help their mother clean out drawers and cupboards. Michael likes searching out the recesses of armchairs with the nozzle end of the vacuum cleaner.

Mrs Goodman cleans all the kitchen appliances which have been used for preparing food throughout the year. She spends a long time cleaning the cooker and oven with steel wool. The Goodman family change their cooker tops and cover their work surfaces, since the Pesach food must not be allowed to come into contact with any of these. Preparing the sink is a hard job, and this is left to Mr Goodman. After cleaning it and leaving it unused for 24 hours, he scalds it with boiling water and then covers it with a layer of foil. Some Jews do their washing-up in bowls.

Jews must not have any chametz in their possession during Pesach, and Mr Goodman sells his to a non-Jew before the festival. He signs a form empowering his rabbi to sell the chametz for him. The Goodmans change all their crockery, cutlery and saucepans for Pesach. Mrs Goodman and Daniel lock away the things they use throughout the year.

Daniel searches for chametz with a candle and feather

Mr Goodman brings out the Pesach sets.

Before the festival the Goodmans have been stocking up with Pesach food. This must all be chametz-free. They have been buying specially supervised products, which bear a 'Kosher for Passover' label called a **hechsher** (p. 70).

THE SEARCH FOR CHAMETZ

As soon as night falls on 14 **Nisan** (see chart on p. 35), Mr Goodman and the boys carry out **bedikat chametz**, the search for chametz. This makes sure that no chametz was overlooked while the house was being cleaned.

Before the search, Mrs Goodman hides ten pieces of bread around the house. Her husband and the boys do not know where they are. This is a good guide to how well they have searched. If they find only nine pieces, they have not searched thoroughly enough! The search is made with a candle and feather (the ancient equivalents of torch and brush!). If they find any chametz, they collect it in a paper bag. After the search, Mr Goodman makes a declaration giving up ownership of any chametz that he might have missed. On the following morning they all have their last meal of chametz. Then Mr Goodman makes a bonfire in the garden and burns the bag, with its ten pieces of bread.

During the afternoon Mrs Goodman and the boys prepare the food for the **seder**, the Pesach meal, and set the table.

Prep.

THINGS TO DO

▶ Look up 'pilgrimage' in a dictionary. Why are Pesach, Shavuot and Sukkot known as 'pilgrim festivals'? Why are there no pilgrimages in Judaism today in quite the same way?

▶ What would you say to someone who thought that on Pesach Jews just stop eating bread for a week?

▶ What is chametz? How do Jews make sure their Pesach food is chametz-free?

▶ Suppose you are going to make a home video of some members of your family doing bedikat chametz. What would you particularly want to record?

THE SEDER

About an hour before nightfall, Mrs Goodman lights her candles and welcomes the festival into her home (p. 37). Mr Goodman and the boys go to the synagogue where they thank God for freeing their ancestors from Egyptian slavery. On their return, the seder meal begins. On the table will be wine, three matzot (plural of matzah, unleavened bread) placed in a special cloth cover, and a plate set out like the one in the photo. Mr Goodman makes kiddush (p. 37) and the meal begins. Seder (rhymes with 'raider') means 'order'. The meal follows a set order during which Jews recall the slavery and the departure from Egypt. This is set down in the **hagadah** (telling), the book Jews read at the seder. Michael, who is the youngest at the table, asks four questions:

'Why is this night different from all other nights?

1 *On all other nights we may eat chametz or matzah. Tonight, why do we eat only matzah?*
2 *On all other nights we may eat any kind of herbs. Tonight, why do we eat bitter herbs?*
3 *On all other nights we do not dip our food at all. Tonight, why do we dip twice? [see below]*
4 *On all other nights we eat sitting or leaning. Tonight, why do we all lean?*

During the rest of the seder these questions are answered as the Goodmans read through the hagadah. The story is not only told through words. Each item of food on the seder plate is a symbol calling to mind a different aspect of the story. On Pesach Jews celebrate the passage from slavery to freedom. Most of the symbolic foods have associations with both slavery and freedom.

Matzah   This is the bread the Israelites ate during their long slavery in Egypt. It takes very little time to bake, and it keeps a person going for a long time. By feeding the slaves matzah, the Egyptians got the maximum working time from them. But matzah is also the bread of freedom. When the Israelites went out of Egypt they did not have time to bake proper bread, and could only bake matzah.

When Jewish people eat matzah, the same food their ancestors ate as slaves, they feel they are

reaching out across time to those Israelites of long ago. It links them with all the Jews who have observed Pesach in the past, as well as those who will celebrate it in the future. This reinforces the Jew's sense of belonging to a world-wide family (p. 5).

Wine During the seder everyone drinks four cups of wine. These stand for the four ways that God spoke about setting the Israelites free: 'I will bring you out', 'I will deliver you', 'I will redeem you', 'I will take you to Me' (*Exodus 6:6–7*). Red wine is used as that is the colour of blood. It recalls the blood of the slaves who were beaten without mercy. But it is also the blood of freedom. The Israelites smeared blood on the doorposts of their houses (p. 48) on the night the firstborn sons of Egypt died. Soon after that, they left Egypt.

Salt water Some of the food is dipped in salt water. Salt water represents the tears of the slaves. But it also symbolizes freedom. After the Israelites had crossed the Reed Sea (p. 48), their pursuers were drowned, and they were really free. The salt water represents the sea.

Haroset This is a paste that has the appearance and texture of river mud. It represents the mud bricks which the Israelite slaves had to make. Ashkenazim make it with crushed almonds and apples, sprinkled with cinnamon and wine. Some Sephardim use dates boiled many times to make a pulp. Others make it from the 'seven special fruits of the Holy Land', – wheat, barley, grapes, figs, pomegranates, dates and olive oil.

Bitter herbs Though Jews use various vegetables for bitter herbs, the ideal one is long lettuce. The leaves of a lettuce are crisp and pleasant, but they grow from a green-white stalk which is very bitter. The bitter stalk represents slavery, and the crisp leaves stand for freedom.

Carpas This is a vegetable, usually potato. The word 'carpas' is made up of the letters of the Hebrew word *perech*, meaning hard labour. It is, therefore, a symbol of slavery. It is dipped in salt water to commemorate the bunch of hyssop which the Israelites dipped in the blood of the Pesach sacrifice, to smear on their doorposts. In this way, carpas is also a symbol of freedom.

Bone and egg There is also a burnt egg and burnt bone (the neck or shank bone of a chicken) on the seder plate. These are not connected with slavery and freedom. They represent the sacrifices which the Israelites used to offer in the ancient Temple.

Not all the seder foods are symbolic. About halfway through the seder, the Goodmans eat a proper dinner. They sing songs about the departure from Egypt, and about how God helped the Jewish people. At the end of the meal they eat a piece of matzah known as the **afikomen** (dessert). Mr Goodman set this aside at the beginning of the seder. It represents the Pesach sacrifice, the last food eaten after the service in the ancient Temple.

The Goodmans have a second seder the following night. Their cousins in Israel have only one (p. 48).

THE REST OF PESACH

During the rest of Pesach the Goodman family eats only chametz-free foods. The first two and last two days are holy days when Mr Goodman does not go to work. The middle four days are known as **chol hamoed**, the 'ordinary days of the festival'. They are 'ordinary' in the sense that Jews may do some kinds of work.

On each day of Pesach, the Goodmans go to the synagogue. They say Hallel (p. 42), as this expresses joy. On Pesach, however, there is a reason for not rejoicing too much. When the Israelites crossed the Reed Sea, the Egyptians foolishly chased after them, and were drowned (p. 48). The Israelites gained their freedom, but other human beings had to be destroyed to achieve it. To this day, Jews recall that sad event by leaving out part of the joyous Hallel prayer.

After nightfall on the eighth day of Pesach, Mr Goodman recites havdalah (p. 39). Everybody then gets busy washing and packing the Pesach utensils and putting them away until the following year.

Mr Goodman and the children bring out the other utensils and crockery and put them back in their cupboards. Mrs Goodman usually bakes a cake to have ready when they have finished. They can now eat chametz again.

THINGS TO DO

▶ Michael (aged 6) is the youngest member of the Goodman family. What part does he play in the seder?

▶ Look up 'symbol' in a dictionary. In what way are matzah, bitter herbs and burnt bone symbols?

▶ What is Hallel? Why is the full Hallel not said for the whole of Pesach? What does this tell you about the Jews' attitude to their enemies? Do you think this attitude is relevant today? Explain your answer.

Shavuot commemorates the giving of the Torah on Mount Sinai, seven weeks after the departure from Egypt. Jews regard this as the most important event in the history of the human race. It was an unearthly experience, totally unlike anything else. The Bible describes how the Israelites gathered around the mountain, how thunder and lightning shook the sky and how the voice of God called to Moses from the thick cloud which surrounded the peak. You can read about it in *Exodus 19–20*. There, God spoke the Ten Commandments. Moses then spent 40 days and nights learning the rest of the Torah, which he was to teach the Israelites. On his return he carried with him two stone cubes containing the Ten Commandments.

COUNTING THE OMER

Pesach coincides with the time of the barley harvest in the Holy Land. From the second day of Pesach until Shavuot, by which time the wheat harvest will have started, Jews count 49 days. This is known as the Counting of the Omer, since during this period an **omer** (roughly 2.25 litres) of barley was offered in the Temple.

Counting 49 days determined when Shavuot should occur. Of all the festivals listed in the Bible, Shavuot is the only one which had no fixed date. In ancient times, when the start of each new month depended on witnesses appearing before the rabbinical court (p. 42), each month might have been 29 or 30 days long. Shavuot could have fallen on 5, 6 or 7 of **Sivan**, whichever was the fiftieth day after Pesach. Today, with a fixed calendar, Shavuot always occurs on 6 Sivan, (and also 7 Sivan outside Israel, p. 48).

The counting of the days between Pesach and Shavuot also represents the Israelites' eagerness to receive the Torah, just as someone waiting for an important event would count each day leading up to it.

Like other festivals, Shavuot starts in the evening. However, whereas some synagogues start Shabbat and other festivals prayer before nightfall, on Shavuot everyone waits till after dark. This is because the Torah commands Jews to count seven *complete* weeks of the Omer. This means complete not only in days but also in hours.

CELEBRATING SHAVUOT

Shavuot differs from every other Jewish festival that marks an historical event. There is no special mitzvah through which the original event is recreated (p. 34). This is because the Torah which the Israelites received became their link with God (p. 23). The giving of the Torah was so overwhelmingly important that there is no action which could recapture it.

In the Shavuot prayers Jews thank God for having given them the Torah. During the morning service, Hallel is said. The Torah reading describes the scene at Mount Sinai when God gave the Israelites the Torah and lists the Ten Commandments (p. 26). In Israel, Shavuot is only one day. Everywhere else it lasts for two (p. 48).

SOME SHAVUOT CUSTOMS

Shavuot is a joyous occasion and many synagogues are decked with flowers for the event. This calls to mind the flowers that bloomed all over Mount Sinai.

Although there is no special mitzvah associated with this festival, in some communities people stay up the whole of Shavuot night to study the Torah. Some communities recite **tikun**, a collection of excerpts from Tenakh, Mishnah, Zohar and other holy writings. There are various reasons for this. When the Israelites were due to receive the Torah, instead of spending the night preparing for the great event, as they should have done, they slept. Early the next morning, Moses had to wake them up to receive the Torah. Some people believe the Israelites did wrong, and by staying awake to study the Torah or read tikun through the night they are putting right their ancestors' mistake. Studying the Torah through the night is also a way of Jews expressing their commitment to fulfilling God's plan by forcibly overcoming their tiredness and studying the holy books. The Talmud also says, 'A house in which the words of the Torah are heard at night will never be destroyed'. Studying through the night is a preparation for the rebuilding of the Temple which, Jews believe, will never be destroyed again.

Dairy foods, especially cheesecake, are eaten on Shavuot. According to Jewish tradition, the Israelites ate dairy foods because they were not sure about the many laws connected with preparing meat (p. 69). They avoided meat until they had learnt them.

On Shavuot the synagogue is decorated with flowers

THINGS TO DO

▶ The Midrash tells the following story:

'The Jewish people had gathered round Mount Sinai, waiting for God to give them the Torah. Suddenly they heard His voice, "What guarantee can you give Me that you will keep My Torah?" God asked. They replied, "Let our holy ancestors, Abraham, Isaac and Jacob be our guarantee. We will keep Your Torah for their sakes." "No," came God's voice, "I do not accept such a guarantee." The people thought again. "Let our holy prophets be our guarantee." "No," came God's voice again.

They thought some more. Finally they said, "Our children will be our guarantee. We will undertake to teach it to them and they to their children and so on." "I accept this guarantee," said God. "Now I will give you My Torah."

a What do you think this story means?

b How might studying the Torah or reciting tikun through the night be appropriate ways of celebrating Shavuot?

c Why does Shavuot not have a special mitzvah like other festivals?

Sukkot is celebrated from 15 to 22 Tishrei (p. 35). As on Pesach, the first two and last two days are holy, the middle four days are called chol hamoed, the ordinary days of the festival. Jews are permitted to do some work during chol hamoed.

A sukkah (plural sukkot) is a dwelling with a roof made of leaves. When the Israelites left Egypt, they needed some form of shelter in the desert. Some had tents, but many did not. Each time they encamped at an oasis they built small huts and covered them with leaves from the palm trees. The sukkah was a perfect shelter for these conditions; the leafy roof kept out the heat and dust of the desert, but allowed air to circulate.

Today, Jews commemorate their ancestors' trek through the desert by building sukkot and living in them for an entire week. The sukkah itself is a symbol of harmony, since it encloses those inside it as one unit. It is also a visible link with the events their ancestors lived through. Living in the sukkah reinforces a Jew's sense of belonging to an ancient people (p. 5), like eating matzah on Pesach.

◇

BUILDING THE SUKKAH

Like many other Jewish families, the Levys of Manchester start to build their sukkah straight after Yom Kippur (p. 47). It is quite simple to make. Mr Levy builds it against the house, because this gives him two of the sukkah walls. Some families use their garden sheds, which they have fitted with lifting roofs.

A sukkah must have at least three walls. Any materials may be used to make them. It should not be too small for a person to sit inside, though there is no limit to how large the floor area may be. A sukkah built in a synagogue yard might be large enough to seat an entire congregation.

The most important part of the sukkah is the covering of leaves. Any non-edible vegetation may be used, provided that it has been cut from the ground or a tree. The leafy covering should be thick enough to provide more shade than it lets in sunlight, without being so dense as to make it impossible to see the sky. For this reason, a sukkah must not be placed under anything that obscures the sky, such as a building or a tree.

Mr Levy always uses evergreen, as other leaves shrivel up before the end of the festival.

Debbie and David decorate their sukkah

LIVING IN THE SUKKAH

The Levys live in their sukkah for the whole week of the festival. They eat their meals and entertain their visitors there. When it is warm enough Mr and Mrs Levy sleep in the sukkah. In this way, they try to recreate their ancestors' living conditions (p. 34).

Debbie (aged 10) and David (aged 8) like to decorate the sukkah. They make paper chains and buy coloured lights with their pocket money. Sometimes they draw pictures of Jewish themes and hang them up. Their father prefers the traditional decorations of fruits hanging from the leaves, but he does not stop the children putting up their own.

REFLECTION

'I like Sukkot. It's a bit like a camping holiday when we all go and eat outside the house. I like the leaves over my head and being together with everyone else in the sukkah.'

(Justin T, Northeast London)

TORAH

THE FOUR SPECIES

Before Sukkot, Mr Levy buys his **arba'at haminim**, 'four species': a citron (**etrog**), a palm branch (**lulav**), two sprigs of willow (**aravot**) and three branches of myrtle (**hadassim**). On each day of Sukkot, except Shabbat, he holds them during part of the synagogue service. He takes the etrog in his left hand, and the others, which will be bound together, in his right.

Sukkot occurs during the autumn, just before the start of the rainy season in the Holy Land. The four species are all plants that need an abundance of water, and at the end of Sukkot, prayers for rain will be said. As a preparation for praying for rain, Mr Levy holds these plants together and moves them to and from all six directions towards his heart. This symbolizes God's presence everywhere and the blessings which He showers upon His creatures from all sides.

HOSHANAH RABBAH

Sukkot occurs at the beginning of the rainy season in Israel, and on each day of the festival (except Shabbat), Jews pray for rain. As they pray, they circle the bimah (p. 84) holding their four species, just like the service in the ancient Temple (p. 7), when the worshippers used to circle the altar. On the last day of chol hamoed, called **Hoshanah Rabbah**, the worshippers make seven circuits. It is the last occasion on which prayers for rain are said.

SIMCHAT TORAH (REJOICING OF THE TORAH)

The day following Sukkot is Simchat Torah (Rejoicing of the Torah). It is the day when Torah readings in the synagogue (p. 86) end and begin again.

The meaning of Simchat Torah

This festival has two names, **Shemini Atzeret** (Assembly of the Eighth Day, i.e. the eighth day after the start of Sukkot) and Simchat Torah. Outside of the Holy Land, where Sukkot lasts for eight days (p. 48), the eighth day is known as Shemini Atzeret, and the ninth is Simchat Torah.

Simchat Torah is not a part of Sukkot but a distinct festival that marks the end of the annual cycle of Torah readings (p. 86). Almost immediately after concluding *Deuteronomy* therefore, the first chapter of *Genesis* is read and the cycle of readings begins again.

Simchat Torah is one of the most joyous occasions in the Jewish year. Whereas at other times one or two Torah scrolls might be taken out of the Ark (p. 84) and only for reading, on Simchat Torah all the synagogue's scrolls will be taken out. Some people dance round the synagogue with them while other members of the congregation follow them, singing songs and clapping their hands as they go. Children carry flags. They make seven circuits (called **hakafot**). The whole scene is one of great merriment. In many synagogues packets of sweets and chocolates are handed out to the children.

CHATAN TORAH AND BERESHIT

Before Simchat Torah, a **Chatan Torah** (bridegroom of the Torah) and **Chatan Bereshit** (bridegroom of Genesis) will be selected. The Chatan Torah will conclude the annual cycle by being called to the reading of the final portion of *Devarim* (*Deuteronomy*). The Chatan Bereshit will be called to begin the new cycle of readings.

The term *chatan* (bridegroom) is taken from ancient Jewish imagery, where the giving of the Torah on Mount Sinai (p. 52) is referred to as the wedding of the Jewish people to God. There, God is the bridegroom and the Jewish people are the bride. It is a great honour to be selected as Chatan Torah or Chatan Bereshit. Those chosen usually treat the congregation to a celebratory meal after morning prayers.

THINGS TO DO

▶ What does Sukkot commemorate?

▶ Why was the leafy covering ideal for desert conditions?

▶ What do Jews do with the four plants?

▶ Which Torah readings may be heard in the synagogue on Simchat Torah?

▶ How do Jews celebrate Simchat Torah?

▶ Why do Jews regard Simchat Torah as important?

▶ About 320 years ago, an English writer called Samuel Pepys visited a synagogue. His visit happened to be on Simchat Torah and he later wrote about how Jews dance and shout in their synagogues instead of praying properly. Imagine you could go back in time and speak to Mr Pepys. How would you prepare him for his visit?

Hanukkah and Purim (p. 35) are not mentioned in the Torah. Jews celebrate them because of important events which the rabbis of long ago decided to commemorate. For this reason they are known as celebrations 'of the rabbis'.

HANUKKAH

> *'We kindle these lights on account of the miracles, the deliverances and the wonders, which You performed for our ancestors . . .'*
>
> *(Prayer book)*

Hanukkah (dedication) is an eight-day celebration which occurs in midwinter. It marks the victory of a small army of Jews over the overwhelming forces of the Syrian Greeks nearly 22 centuries ago. The enemy the Jews fought was a king who wanted to force them to change their religion.

HOW HANUKKAH BEGAN

In 323 BCE Alexander the Great died, having conquered the massive Persian Empire (p. 8). His generals divided up the empire among themselves. One of them, Seleucus, took control of a large area stretching from the Mediterranean Sea to the borders of India. This became known as the Seleucid Empire. The empire was populated by so many different nations that Seleucus and his successors found it difficult to rule them all. They tried to solve this problem by encouraging their subjects to Hellenize, i.e. adopt the Greek way of life. They were quite successful. Within a few generations many orientals began to dress like Greeks, speak Greek and worship the Greek gods.

Many Jews changed their way of life too, and as a result Jewish society became divided. On one side were the Hellenists, who believed that by giving up Judaism in favour of Greek ways they were entering the wide world of universal brotherhood. Opposed to them were the traditionalists, who refused to give up the ways of their ancestors. In 175 BCE, Antiochus IV came to the throne. Unlike the earlier kings, Antiochus decided to use force to make the Jews hellenize. He passed laws forbidding the Jews to keep the Sabbath or circumcise their sons (p. 72). He also set up an idol in the Temple and ordered the Jews to sacrifice to it. Those who refused were tortured and killed. Many Jews showed amazing heroism and kept their Judaism in spite of the enormous risks they were taking.

The turning point came when Antiochus began sending soldiers to the outlying towns and villages to force Jews everywhere to worship his idols. At one of these assemblies an aged Jew, Mattathias, rose and killed a Greek officer. He and his sons then fled to the hills. Mattathias became a national hero and young men flocked to the hills to fight with him. Mattathias put his son Judah in command and began waging a guerrilla war against Antiochus's troops. This is known as the Maccabean Revolt (p. 8). The name comes from the nickname, Maccabi – 'hammer' – given to Judah. To the Jews of his day Judah was the 'Hammer of the Greeks'.

Victory followed victory, and eventually Judah felt strong enough to fight on the open battlefield. After three years the enemy was driven out.

Judah and his men turned their attention to restoring the Temple. It was a shocking sight. There was rubbish everywhere and weeds were growing through the flagstones. They broke up the idols and set about cleaning the holy house. While cleaning up they found a small bottle of oil with the seal of the High Priest still intact. They filled the oil lamp even though they only had enough oil to burn for one day. Each day, as they returned to carry on with their work, they found the oil lamp still burning. Only after they had prepared fresh oil, eight days later, did the lights go out. The Jews knew that they had witnessed a miracle. It made them realize that the battles they had fought and won had been miracles too. With God's help the few had overcome the many. To commemorate this the rabbis decided to hold an annual festival, when oil lamps would be lit and praises sung to God.

HOW JEWS CELEBRATE HANUKKAH

Throughout the eight days of Hanukkah there are special prayers and Torah readings in the synagogue, and Hallel is read (p. 42). Jews try to recapture something of the original event (p. 34) by lighting special lamps.

From the outset, Jews wanted to commemorate the fact that as each day passed, the miracle seemed to get bigger. Oil which should have burned for only one day burned for two, three and eventually for eight days. Jews expressed this by lighting one oil lamp on the first night, two on the second and so on, up to eight on the last night. These lamps were placed side by side in a straight line, outside the front door or near a window overlooking the street. This reminded anyone who passed by about the miracle. Eventually, someone thought of making a single oil lamp with holes for eight wicks in a row, and the Hanukkah lamp (also called a **Hanukiah**) came into being.

Lighting an oil Hanukkah lamp

spinning top with some letters of the Hebrew alphabet on it. Children spin the top and make up words with the letter that falls uppermost when the dreidle stops spinning. The origins of this game are thought to go back to the time when the Greeks tried to stop the Jews studying the Torah. The children hurriedly hid their books and pretended to be playing with their spinning tops whenever soldiers came by.

Hanukkah is also a time for giving presents. Children look forward to receiving their Hanukkah gelt – spending money.

WHY HANUKKAH IS IMPORTANT FOR JEWS

Although Hanukkah was instituted by the rabbis more than 2,000 years ago, it still inspires Jews today. First, Hanukkah is a time of remembering the heroic self-sacrifice of those who faced torture and death to keep God's commandments. Second, the story shows God playing His part in the Covenant (p. 22) and not abandoning His people, even though many of them had turned their backs on Judaism.

Jews always tried to burn olive oil in their Hanukkah lamps, as this was the oil used in the Temple. Today, although many people still burn oil lamps, many more use candles.

The Hanukkah lights are lit from a 'servant' candle. This candle is also used for taking a light if anyone needs to, as the Hanukkah lights themselves are holy and may not be used.

While the Hanukkah lamps are burning, women sit back and do not do any work. This is a way of honouring the Jewish women who displayed outstanding heroism during the persecutions of Antiochus. When the king tried to abolish circumcision, many men were too frightened to disobey him. The women defied the king and circumcised the babies themselves. Each time one was caught, the baby was strangled and hung around its mother's neck while she was paraded through the streets as a warning to others. In spite of this, the women refused to give in and continued to circumcise their sons.

Among the traditional foods eaten during Hanukkah are doughnuts and latkes, a kind of shredded potato-cake fried in oil. These are all ways of commemorating the miracle of the oil.

During Hanukkah Jewish children play a traditional game called **dreidle**. A dreidle is a

FIND OUT

▶ Try to find out what you can about Hellenism. Why do you think some Jews found it attractive? Why did others regard it as a threat to their traditional way of life?

FOR YOUR FOLDERS

▶ Bearing in mind what the Seleucid kings wanted to do to the nations they ruled, why do you think Antiochus tried to ban circumcision?

▶ A visitor to a Jewish house wants to light a cigarette. They have no matches so they move towards the Hanukkah lamp. What would you say to them?

▶ What special heroism did Jewish women display at the time of Antiochus? How is this remembered today?

'And these days should be remembered and observed throughout every generation . . . so that the days of Purim should not pass away from among the Jews . . .'

(Esther 9:28)

Purim, celebrated in late winter, is one of the most joyous days of the Jewish year. It marks the Jews' deliverance from a threat of annihilation, about 25 centuries ago. The main details are in the Biblical book of *Esther*.

HOW PURIM BEGAN

In 586 BCE the first Temple was destroyed and the Jews living in the Holy Land were deported to Babylon (now Iraq, p. 6). About 50 years later the Persians conquered Babylon. They gave the Jews permission to return and rebuild their Temple and homeland. Although several groups of Jews did return, hostile neighbours did everything in their power to prevent them from resettling. They even persuaded the Persian authorities to stop the Jews rebuilding the Temple. Among the Jews' enemies was a group called the Troublers of Judah and Benjamin. They made repeated accusations about the Jews to the Persian Emperor.

In 481 BCE, Xerxes I (called Ahasuerus in the Bible) came to the throne of Persia. The book of *Esther* describes two events which were to have far-reaching effects for the Jews living in his empire. First, as a result of a domestic quarrel, Xerxes had his queen executed. A Jewish girl named Esther was chosen to replace her. Esther had an uncle called Mordecai, who visited the palace each day to find out how she was. On one of these visits Mordecai uncovered a plot to assassinate the king. Second, after the assassination attempt, some of the Persian nobles fell from favour. Xerxes now appointed Haman, a foreigner, as his prime minister. Haman, was one of the 'Troublers of Judah and Benjamin', and he realized that he could use his new position to destroy the Jews. He found the excuse he wanted when Mordecai, whom he met in the palace yard, refused to bow to him.

Haman accused the Jews of disobeying the laws of Persia and obtained the king's consent to kill them. Haman was a superstitious man and he cast lots (*purim* in the Assyrian language) to choose the right day for the slaughter. He sent letters to the provincial governors all over the empire ordering them to stand back while the Jews' enemies killed and plundered them. The Jews were not to be allowed to defend themselves.

Mordecai informed Esther about the plot and she told Xerxes. Although he was unable to change the decree, he had Haman executed and issued a second order allowing the Jews to defend themselves.

On the appointed day, fighting broke out in many places as the Jews' enemies rose against them and they in turn rose to defend themselves. By the end of the second day the Jews had overpowered their enemies and were safe. They celebrated their deliverance with prayers of thanksgiving and banquets.

One year later, Mordecai and Esther wrote to all the Jewish communities of the empire instructing them to commemorate what had happened. The rabbis agreed to this and the festival of Purim came into being.

HOW JEWS CELEBRATE PURIM

The Fast of Esther

Jews see Purim as a turnabout 'from anguish to joy, from mourning to festivity' (*Esther 9:22*). They recapture this change of mood by the events of the day preceding Purim and Purim itself.

The day before Purim is a fast, called the Fast of Esther. It commemorates the three days of fasting and prayer which Queen Esther ordered the Jews to undertake before she went to plead with the king. It also marks the days of fasting and praying during those uncertain weeks when the Jews did not know what their fate would be.

During the fast there are special prayers and Torah readings in the synagogue. Before the afternoon service the **machazit hashekel** (the value of half a shekel) is given. This is a special charity collection. It is not connected with Purim, but commemorates the tax which all Jews used to pay towards the upkeep of the Temple. It used to be collected at this time of the year. Today the machazit hashekel goes towards the running costs of the synagogue.

Reading the Megillah

At nightfall Purim begins. People came to the synagogue dressed in their Shabbat clothes. Although they are still fasting, the joyous day has begun. They recite the evening prayers and the book of *Esther* is read. Jews call this book the **Megillah** (scroll), for it is read from a scroll of parchment. Before the reading it is unrolled and folded over on itself several times so that it resembles a wad of pages. This is the way royal proclamations were read in the Persian Empire.

While the Megillah is being read, the congregation, especially the children, stamp their feet and make a noise each time Haman's name is mentioned. This is an ancient custom. It symbolizes blotting out the names of the Jews' enemies. In some synagogues this is done only at certain points during the reading.

After hearing the Megillah, people go home to break their fasts and the evening festivities begin. Purim is a special time for giving charity and in Jewish areas children dress up and visit houses to collect for various worthy causes.

On the following morning, after prayers, the Megillah is read a second time.

Gifts to the poor

Charity is an important Jewish virtue (p. 116). It is considered especially important on joyous occasions to make sure that the poor can also rejoice. Jews usually try to give charity in such a way that the giver does not know who receives the gift and the recipient does not know where it came from. Jews give their donations to the charity organizers who distribute the funds to the needy of the community.

Sending food to friends

Even with the best methods of distributing charity, there are always poor people who are too embarrassed to accept. To make sure that these people have enough food to celebrate the Purim feast, everybody sends gifts of food to friends and acquaintances. Both rich and poor give and receive and in this way everyone can accept without embarrassment.

Children taking Purim gifts to friends

The Purim meal

Purim afternoon prayers are recited earlier than the usual time so that people can get home and celebrate with a feast. Children put on fancy dress, and there are usually guests at the table. It is a joyous, festive occasion.

Shushan Purim

The day following Purim is called **Shushan Purim**. There are no special prayers for this day, though people still wear their Shabbat clothes. It commemorates the struggle of the Jews in Shushan, the capital of the Persian Empire, who did not overcome their enemies until the following day. In certain very ancient cities, such as Jerusalem, the Megillah is read on this day.

WHY PURIM IS IMPORTANT FOR JEWS

The importance of Purim for Jews far outweighs the significance of the event in Jewish history. The Talmud goes so far as to say, 'If all the festivals would pass away, Purim would still be observed'.

The story of Purim focuses upon the affairs of the Persian court and the social problems of the empire. God seems to be entirely absent. In fact, His name is not mentioned at all in the book of Esther. Yet, for Jews, this teaches a very important lesson. Jews take Purim as the prime example of God being there behind the scenes and guiding events, even though His presence is not obvious.

THINGS TO DO

▶ List the ways in which Jews try to recreate the original events of Purim.

▶ How are children involved in celebrating Purim?

▶ The book of *Esther* tells us that Xerxes ruled 'from India to Ethiopia' (*Esther 1:1*). Find these countries in an atlas, and try to work out the size of his empire.

▶ 'When the Jews rose to defend themselves against their enemies many thousands of people lost their lives. This is not something to celebrate – it's about time Purim was abolished.' How might a Jewish person respond to this view?

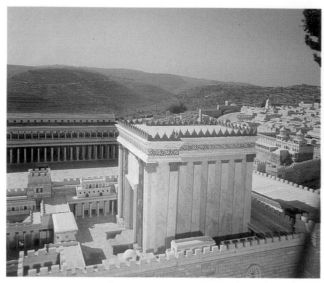

A scale model of the second Temple

> *'If I forget you Jerusalem, may my right hand forget its skills.'*

(Psalm 137:5)

Jews have had two Temples. The first was built by King Solomon in Jerusalem about 29 centuries ago. It was destroyed by the Babylonians in 586 BCE (p. 7). The second Temple, built on the same site, was destroyed by the Romans in 70 CE. For the last 19 centuries Jews have prayed daily for its restoration.

WHY THE TEMPLE IS IMPORTANT

Read this section together with unit 39.

For Jews the Temple was the holiest place in the world. It was always crowded with worshippers, especially on festivals when pilgrims came from many countries. Of the 613 commandments (p. 22), 244 of them were connected with the Temple.

Jews have always regarded the Temple as the place where God's presence could be felt. The Mishnah tells us about ten miracles that occurred there each day:

> *'. . . the rain did not put out the fire on the altar, the wind did not move the vertical column of smoke . . . when the people stood they were crowded together but when they bowed they had ample room . . . .'*

The loss of the Temple was so severe that Jews have mourned it for nearly 2000 years.

THE THREE WEEKS

On 17 **Tammuz** (p. 35) in the year 70 CE the Roman armies broke through the walls of Jerusalem. Three weeks of fierce hand-to-hand fighting followed, as the Jews were driven back towards the Temple. On 9 **Av** the Temple was set on fire. Both of these days are fasts, and the period between them is known simply as the three weeks. It is the saddest time of the Jewish year.

From 17 Tammuz onwards, Jews observe mourning customs. They do not cut their hair or listen to music (p. 81) and no marriages take place. As soon as the month of Av begins they stop eating meat and drinking wine, except on Shabbat when no mourning is permitted. This lasts until 9 Av, a period called 'the nine days'.

TISHA B'AV (9TH OF AV)

The 9th of Av is a day of mourning. Both Temples were destroyed on this date. It has also been a day of many tragedies throughout Jewish history. Tisha b'Av is a fast, the second most important after Yom Kippur (p. 46). From sunset on 8 Av until nightfall on 9 Av, Jews neither eat or drink nor wear leather shoes (p. 80). Sexual relations between husband and wife are forbidden. Jews are allowed to wash if they get dirty, but not simply to freshen up.

Late on 8 Av, just before the fast begins, Jews eat their last meal. They sit on low chairs or on the ground (p. 80). The traditional mourners' meal of hard-boiled egg is eaten and the bread is dipped in ash to symbolize the burning of the Temple.

In the synagogue, the lights are low and the curtain is removed from the front of the Ark (p. 84). People do not greet one another. Evening prayers are recited quietly and the book of *Lamentations* (p. 28) is read in a mournful chant. This describes the destruction of Jerusalem and the massacre of its population.

On the following day, morning prayers are said quietly. Men do not put on the **tallit** and **tefillin** (p. 86) until the afternoon. The service is followed by reading **kinot** (dirges). This is a collection of poems written over a period of many centuries, describing some of the persecutions which Jews have suffered. Some of them were written in remembrance of entire communities massacred in the Middle Ages; others refer to the more recent Holocaust (p. 16). Tisha b'Av is considered an appropriate day for remembering these tragedies.

Midday marks a turning point, since by that time the fire of the Temple had died down. People get up from their low mourners' seats and set about their daily tasks again. After nightfall they break their fasts. Some mourning customs are observed until the following day, since the ashes of the Temple were smouldering until then.

Although Tisha b'Av is a sad day, its prayers express a strong element of hope. Jews look forward to a glorious Messianic Age (p. 24) when, according to the ancient Jewish traditions, the Temple will be rebuilt and 9 Av will become a day of rejoicing.

THE FASTS OF TEVET AND GEDALIAH

There are two other fasts which commemorate the destruction of the first Temple.

Asarah b'Tevet, 10 **Tevet**, marks the day when the Babylonians began the siege of Jerusalem in 587 BCE. From that day on, no one could get in or out of the city and the Jews were starved into surrender.

The fast of Gedaliah takes place on 3 Tishrei, the day after Rosh Hashanah. After the destruction of the first Temple thousands of Jews were deported to Babylon (p. 7). The Babylonian authorities appointed Gedaliah ben Achikam, a former cabinet minister in the government of Judah, over the Jews who remained. Gedaliah was a man of peace. For two years he encouraged the Jews to take up farming and trade and to give up all ideas of further rebellion. He persuaded the soldiers who were still roaming the countryside to hand in their weapons and settle down and he even gained the confidence of the Babylonian officials.

On the second Rosh Hashanah after the destruction, Gedaliah was assassinated by a Jewish prince who was jealous of his success. The Jews who had lived under his rule fled to Egypt and all hopes of rebuilding the Temple and restoring the old order were lost. On the fast of Gedaliah, Jews mourn for the loss of an entire age.

KEEPING THE TEMPLE ALIVE

Since the Temple was destroyed, Jews have kept its memory alive in many ways. Some of these are:

- In synagogues the daily prayers are read at the times when the sacrifices in the Temple were offered (p. 86), and the Temple is mentioned in all of these prayers.
- The Torah readings on all festivals describe the Temple sacrifices for those occasions.

- Whenever bread is eaten, the first piece is dipped lightly in salt (p. 37). This is to recall the sacrifices, which were sprinkled with salt before being placed on the altar.
- Before grace after meals on each weekday, Psalm 137 is read. This psalm expresses the bitterness of the Jews who were exiled to Babylon after the destruction of the first Temple.
- At the end of wedding ceremonies a glass is broken. This symbolizes destruction and reminds Jews that their joy is never complete without the Temple (p. 7).

When Jews observe these customs they do not see themselves as gloomily dwelling on past misfortunes. They are keeping alive their hope for a future restoration.

THINGS TO DO

▶ Draw a time chart covering the period 17 Tammuz to 9 Av. Show what happened at each stage of this period, and what mourning customs Jews observe. From your chart explain how the mourning increases. If you have already studied pp. 80–1, compare your chart with the one you drew there. How are these mourning customs similar to those and how are they different?

▶ You are spending a few days with a Jewish friend and it is now the night following 8 Av (in Jewish thinking this would be 9 Av). Write a letter home describing the events of the day.

▶ Read Psalm 137. How do you think the Jewish exiles felt about the loss of the Temple and their deportation to Babylon?

▶ How might a Jew respond to the suggestion that mourning for the Temple is no longer relevant?

THE NEW YEAR FOR TREES (15 SHEVAT)

The Bible commands farmers to tithe their crops, i.e. to set aside a certain percentage as gifts for the priests and the poor.

The New Year for Trees falls on 15 **Shevat**. It is the cut-off date for all tithes of fruit. Fruit harvested before 15 Shevat belongs to the previous year's crop and must be tithed separately from fruit harvested after that date.

The Talmud describes the New Year for Trees as marking the time when the rainy season (in Israel) is over and the trees are beginning to produce their new crop of fruits. Since Jews regard the cyclic changes of nature as evidence that God constantly cares for His world (p. 43), the New Year for Trees is always observed as a semi-joyous occasion.

Today, many Jews mark the New Year for Trees by eating many different kinds of fruit. In Israel, the day is celebrated by planting trees.

LAG B'OMER (18 IYAR)

Starting on the second day of Pesach (Passover) Jews count 49 days until Shavuot (Feast of Weeks). This is called the Counting of the Omer (p. 52). The first 32 days are observed as a period of semi-mourning when many Jews do not cut their hair (p. 80) and no marriages take place. The thirty-third day is known as **Lag b'Omer** and is celebrated as a joyous occasion.

The origin of Lag b'Omer goes back to the period between the fall of Jerusalem in the year 70 CE and the Bar Kokhba revolt in 132 CE (p. 8). The Roman rulers of Judea (Israel) were very harsh. The Jews were driven to the point of revolt many times, and only the wise council of the rabbis held them back. During the 120s, however, Roman oppression became so severe that it was only a matter of time before the Jews rebelled. During that time an epidemic broke out, and in 32 days thousands of Jews died. Among them were many rabbinical students. It looked as though there would be no leaders to guide the Jews through the difficult times ahead. On the thirty-third day of the Omer the plague stopped. Ever since then Jews have celebrated Lag b'Omer as a symbol of survival and hope. It reminds them of their belief that God would never totally abandon His people (p. 22).

On Lag b'Omer Jews cut their hair and marriages take place. It is also a time when Jewish families and sometimes schools, arrange outings, usually with a picnic lunch. Cities with large Jewish communities sometimes have parades with floats and bands (see photograph p. 130). In Israel bonfires are lit.

YOM HASHOAH (HOLOCAUST REMEMBRANCE DAY, 27 NISAN)

In 1933 the National Socialist (Nazi) Party came to power in Germany. Almost immediately it began persecuting the Jews. It published anti-Jewish propaganda and passed laws which gradually stripped the Jews of Germany of all their citizens' rights. During the Second World War the German armies occupied most of eastern and central Europe, as well as France, the Netherlands, Denmark and Norway. Jews living in the countries which the Germans occupied were rounded up and sent to concentration camps. There they were to be killed. About 6 million Jews perished in what has come to be known as the Holocaust (p. 16).

Yom Hashoah – 27 Nisan – is observed as a day of remembrance for those Jews who perished. Some synagogues hold special memorial services. In Israel it is a sad day when many Israelis cease their regular social activities. The armed services have their own memorial services.

Yad Vashem is the Holocaust memorial in Jerusalem. It has the names of all the concentration camps engraved in Hebrew and English, with candles burning around them. Visitors can see photographs of the camps and the Jews who were imprisoned there. Their clothing and other possessions are on display, as well as horrific photos of camp life, including executions and mass graves.

On Holocaust Remembrance Day many people visit Yad Vashem to light candles and recite psalms on behalf of the martyrs. Some people go there at other times of the year. They regard this as a personal pilgrimage (p. 151).

Holocaust Remembrance Day is not observed by all Jews, as many rabbis did not wish to add another day of mourning to the calendar. They preferred to remember the Holocaust martyrs on Tisha b'Av (p. 60), when many of the sad events of Jewish history are called to mind. Some even composed special memorial prayers for the Holocaust victims to be recited on Tisha b'Av.

Memorial sculpture at Yad Vashem

Independence Day celebrations in Israel

YOM HA'ATZMAUT (ISRAEL INDEPENDENCE DAY, 5 IYAR)

During the latter years of the nineteenth century a large number of Jewish settlements had been established in the Holy Land (p. 144). By the end of the Second World War, the need to resettle Holocaust survivors made it urgent for the Jews to form their own state.

In November 1947 the United Nations General Assembly voted on partition, i.e. the division of Palestine into separate Jewish and Arab states. The Arabs opposed the idea of a Jewish state. As the British troops were leaving, the provisional Jewish government declared the creation of a Jewish state with the name Israel (p. 13). The new state was immediately attacked by the armies of Egypt, Iraq, Lebanon, Syria and Transjordan. They wanted to destroy the new Jewish state as soon as it was born. Fierce fighting broke out, particularly in Jerusalem, and the Arab armies were defeated. This became known as the War of Independence. It was the first major conflict between the Jews and the Arabs. The anniversary of the Declaration of Independence, **5 Iyar**, has been celebrated every year since then as **Yom Ha'atzmaut**, Israel Independence Day.

In Israel, Independence Day is a national holiday. Schools, banks and businesses are closed and many people go out on picnics. However, Jews are divided in their attitude towards Israel Independence Day (p. 148). In some synagogues, both in Israel and the diaspora, there are thanksgiving services and Hallel (p. 42) is recited. In others, no special service is held.

YOM YERUSHALAYIM (JERUSALEM DAY, 28 IYAR)

In 1948, at the end of the War of Independence, the United Nations Armistice Commission divided the city of Jerusalem. Jews lived in the west; Arabs in the east, (the Old City). A barbed-wire fence cut Jerusalem in two. The Jews' most holy place, the Western Wall (the last remaining wall of the ancient Temple), was in the Arab sector. No Jew could visit it (p. 151).

In 1967 the Jews and Arabs fought their third major conflict. The war lasted for six days (it is known as the Six Day War) and on 27 Iyar the Israeli army entered the Old City. The shofar (p. 45) was blown at the Temple Wall and Jerusalem became one city again. Since then the Wall has been the scene of daily services and both Jews and Arabs have free access to all parts of the city.

In Israel, 27 Iyar is celebrated as **Yom Yerushalayim**, Jerusalem Day. About 100,000 people gather at the Western Wall to pray and some synagogues hold special services. Many Israeli schoolchildren do projects on Jerusalem. In Britain some synagogues mark the day with special thanksgiving services.

You will have a better understanding of Israel's Independence Day and Jerusalem Day after you have read pages 144–7.

THINGS TO DO

▶ The Nazi Party came to power in Germany in 1933. From that time on it passed a number of laws restricting the rights of Jews. Find out what some of these laws were.

▶ Look back to the chart on p. 35.

   a Explain why the New Year for Trees is included in nature festivals.

   b What does Lag b'Omer commemorate?

   c How is it related to the covenant between God and the Jewish people?

   d Why did some rabbis want to remember the Holocaust on Tisha b'Av?

   e Would you describe Israel Independence Day as a mainly religious or mainly political occasion? Explain your answer.

   f Why is Jerusalem important for Jews?

   g Look at the picture of the Holocaust memorial. Try to describe it to a friend. What do you think the sculptor was trying to convey?

The family is one of the two pivots around which Jewish life revolves (the other is the community). For Jews, the home is where children receive their earliest education; it is where parents show them, by personal example, how to live as Jews and where the regular daily practices, weekly Sabbaths and cycle of festivals help children develop their Jewish identities. In the home, children are taught what it means to bring holiness into everyday affairs. Ordinary actions, such as getting dressed, eating a meal or going to bed, are all transformed into ways of serving God. In a Jewish home, children are brought up to fulfil the Biblical directive, 'Know Him in all your ways' (*Proverbs 3:6*).

THE DAY BEGINS

Sarah starts the day by thanking God for her waking up. This 'thank you', known as **modeh ani** is the first sentence on her lips in the morning.

After this, before getting out of bed, she washes her hands using the jug of water and a bowl she placed by the side of her bed the night before. This is not part of her morning wash, for straight after this she goes to the bathroom. Sarah washes her hands as an act of purification. This is like the priests of old who used to wash their hands and feet before entering the Temple (p. 7). Since each day is full of opportunities for serving God, beginning the day is thought of as entering a 'Temple'. Like the ancient priests, Sarah pours water three times on each hand.

When Sarah was very young she had this done for her. Generations of Jewish parents have washed tiny hands each morning. In this way children grow up never having known a time when they did not purify themselves at the start of each day.

Sarah gets up and washes her hands

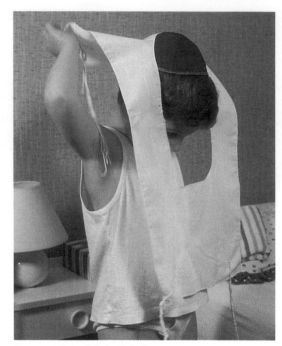
Simon puts on his tallit katan

GETTING DRESSED

Judaism teaches people to dress modestly, and not to be showy or provocative.

Boys are expected to wear a **tallit katan** (small robe, p. 86). In the photo you can see Sarah's brother Simon putting his on. A tallit katan is a four-cornered garment, often made of wool, with a hole for the head. It fits over the shoulders so that it drapes over the front and back of the body. On each corner are eight-fringed tassels called **tzizit** (fringes). Jewish men and boys wear it to fulfil the commandment '. . . They shall make for themselves fringes on the corners of their garments . . . and you shall see them and remember all the commandments of the Lord . . .' (*Numbers 15:38-39*). Ideally, the tallit katan should be worn in such a way that the fringes may be seen, though some Jews tuck them inside their shirts. Simon was given his first tallit katan when he was three years old.

Simon also covers his head as a mark of respect for God. He wears a small cap, known as a **kippah** (also called a **kupple** or **yarmulke**). It reminds him that there is another intelligence in the world far greater than that of human beings. Married women are also expected to cover their heads, though this is because of modesty. Jews are also forbidden to wear any garment which contains **shatnez**, mixtures of wool and linen (*Deuteronomy 22:11*). The Torah gives no reason for this rule; it is one of the chukim (p. 22). Observing it is simply an act of faith and obedience.

BLESSINGS

Jews pray three times each day (p. 86). Men usually go to the synagogue for they have an obligation to pray with a **minyan** (a group of ten men, this being regarded as the smallest communal unit). Simon started going with his father as soon as he was old enough to read some of the prayers. Women are not under an obligation to pray together as a community (p. 91), although some choose to do so. Sarah usually prays at home during the week. On Sabbaths and festivals everybody attends the synagogue if they can. The prayers will be explained in more detail on pp. 86–7.

As well as praying, Sarah and Simon bless God before and after food, and at various other times during the day. Each type of food has its own special blessing. For example, before eating an apple Jews say (in Hebrew), 'Blessed are You Lord our God, King of the universe, who creates the fruit of the tree,' and before bread, 'Blessed are You Lord our God, King of the universe, who brings bread out of the ground.' Bread is considered to have a special importance, and Jews wash their hands before eating it (p. 37). They also say the full grace afterwards, whereas all other foods only require a short 'thank you' blessing after eating them. Sarah and Simon began learning these blessings as soon as they were talking properly.

As well as the blessings before and after food, Jews are expected to acknowledge God's overlordship on many other occasions. Sarah has had to learn the blessings to be said on seeing lightning, hearing thunder, on smelling fragrant flowers or herbs and on seeing such wonders of nature as the sea, shooting stars and mountains. Jews even bless God when they hear of someone's death: 'Blessed are You Lord our God, King of the universe, the true judge.' In homes where children are taught these blessings and encouraged to say them, it becomes natural for them to see ordinary things as opportunities for serving God.

◇

PERSONAL STUDY

Every Jew has an obligation to know as much about Jewish beliefs and practices as possible. Setting aside time for Torah study is one of the 613 commandments. Most synagogues offer a variety of study groups for both sexes, though men sometimes prefer to study with a companion (**chavruta** system, p. 89). As soon as children begin to read Hebrew, parents will review their Jewish studies with them.

GOING TO BED

The day ends as it began, in praising God. Before going to bed Sarah says the Shema (p. 18), and finishes, '. . . may it be Your will . . . that You should lay me down in peace and raise me up to good life and peace . . . Blessed are You God, who lights up the whole world with His glory.' When she was younger her parents said this with her as they tucked her in.

FOR YOUR FOLDERS

▶ Look at the photo of Sarah washing her hands. What time of day is it? Explain what she is doing.

▶ Look at Simon. Explain what he is putting on. Why is he wearing this?

▶ Imagine that you are organizing a summer camp for Jewish children. How would you plan this timetable to combine outings and sports events with the children's Jewish obligations?

▶ What advice might Jewish parents give to their fashion-conscious daughter who is about to go out to buy some new clothes?

▶ Mitzvot that involve the individual with other people include charity, hospitality, visiting the sick and comforting mourners. How might these be carried out today?

'And these words which I command you this day shall be upon your heart . . . and you shall write upon the doorposts of your houses and upon your gates.'

(Deuteronomy 6:9)

Look closely at the photo below. There is a rectangular object fixed to the right-hand doorpost. This is a **mezuzah**; it is the sign of a Jewish house.

A mezuzah (plural **mezuzot**) is a scroll with two passages from the Torah (*Deuteronomy 6:4–9* and *11:13–21*) written on it in Hebrew. These are the first two paragraphs of the Shema (p. 18). They declare the oneness of God and the covenant relationship between God and the Jewish people (p. 22). A mezuzah must be handwritten by a trained **sofer**, scribe (p. 94), on parchment. Parchment is the inner membrane of an animal skin, treated to make it smooth. It is one of the oldest writing surfaces known. Only the skin of a kosher animal (see p. 68) may be used. Parchment from the skin of kosher birds is unusable because it is full of holes from where the feathers grew.

Rolling a mezuzah to put it in its case

When you look at the door of a Jewish house you will probably not see the parchment scroll at all. It is usually inside a protective case. This has led to some confusion as to what the mezuzah actually is. Some people make the mistake of thinking that the scroll and the case together make up the mezuzah. Others think that the case itself is the mezuzah. People have even bought empty cases thinking that they were buying mezuzot! The mezuzah *is* the parchment scroll. The case is just there to protect the mezuzah from damp and dust. Some Jews do not have cases at all on their indoor mezuzot. They wrap them in clear plastic so that they can see the mezuzot rather than the cases.

WRITING A MEZUZAH

Before starting to write the mezuzah, the sofer cuts the parchment into squares varying in size from about 5 cm × 5 cm for a small mezuzah, up to about 15 cm × 15 cm for a fairly large one. He will then score lines lightly across to make sure that the writing will be straight. The letters are written *below* each line, as though they are hanging from it.

A mezuzah on the right-hand doorpost – sign of a Jewish house

A mezuzah must be written in order. This means that if a sofer writes a word wrongly and only discovers it after having written further, he may not simply go back and correct that word. If he did so, that word would have been written *after* the words that are meant to follow it. Instead, he must erase everything from where he made the mistake and then write it all over again. If one of those words should be the name of God, then it is impossible to correct the mezuzah for the name of God may not be erased. Mezuzot with mistakes that cannot be corrected are **pasul**, unfit for use, and must be buried. Such mezuzot and tefillin (p. 87), as well as old and worn-out sacred books, will be buried in a Jewish cemetery.

After completing a mezuzah, the sofer will give it to another qualified sofer to check. Some soferim (plural of **sofer**) check their own mezuzot. Ensuring that people have perfect mezuzot is a great responsibility, and having another sofer check it serves as an extra precaution.

Sadly, in recent years some unscrupulous (and totally irreligious) people have started selling fake mezuzot. These are either printed on parchment or on paper treated to look like parchment. This is a despicable practice because Jews are tricked into buying these worthless objects, thinking that they are performing a mitzvah. However, any rabbi or trained sofer can spot such fakes quite easily.

FIXING A MEZUZAH

The mezuzah is fixed to the doorposts of every room in a Jewish house and place of work, except the bathroom and lavatory. These are not considered suitable places for a holy object.

Its correct position is on the post to the right-hand side as one enters the room. It should be in the upper third of the doorpost, but not higher than 10 cm from the top. Ideally, it should be inclined slightly inwards towards the room. Where the doorpost is too narrow for this, the mezuzah is placed vertically. It would not be fixed to the doors of cupboards, except very large walk-in cupboards which are, in effect, small rooms.

CARE OF THE MEZUZAH

Mezuzot are holy objects and Jews have to look after them. In particular, it is important that the writing remains legible. Every three years Jews take down their mezuzot so that they can be checked by a rabbi or a scribe. Sometimes, partially faded mezuzot can be written over with fresh ink. If the ink has cracked or faded too much it must be replaced.

People sometimes make the mistake of not taking the mezuzot off their doors before decorating. If paint seeps into a mezuzah it can ruin it.

THE SIGNIFICANCE OF THE MEZUZAH

The mezuzah, placed on each door of the house, is a constant reminder that the affairs of the house and everything that takes place within its walls are to be used in the service of God. It also symbolizes the dedication of God and the Jewish people to one another, since it contains a summary of the covenant (p. 22). As Jews walk around their houses they are continually reminded of their covenant obligations. At the same time the mezuzah, placed on every door of the house, calls to mind the verse, 'You are blessed when you come in, you are blessed when you go out' (*Deuteronomy 28:6*). This represents God fulfilling His side of the covenant.

THINGS TO DO

▶ Which of the following are true?
a A mezuzah is a plastic case with a scroll inside it.
b Inside the mezuzah are the Ten Commandments.
c Mezuzot are written by scribes.
d Mezuzot may be printed as long as parchment is used.
e Bathrooms and lavatories do not have mezuzot on their doorposts.
f Mezuzot must be checked every three years.
g A mezuzah should be fixed to the left-hand doorpost.
h If paint seeps into the mezuzah, it will ruin it.

▶ Read the paragraphs from the Torah that are written in the mezuzah. Make a summary of the contents. How does the second paragraph express the covenant (p. 22) between God and the Jewish people?

▶ Some Jews touch the mezuzah as they enter or leave the house. Why do you think they do this?

'These are the animals which you may eat . . . anything which has a completely split hoof and chews the cud, this you may eat . . .'

(*Leviticus 11:2–3*)

The food Jewish people are permitted to eat is known as **kosher**. Kosher means 'fitting', or 'correct'. From this we get the word **kashrut**, the state of being kosher. The opposite of kosher is **treifah**. All plants are kosher, but not all animals, birds or fish are. Animals must also be killed in a special way, and all their blood must be removed before the meat may be eaten by Jews. Some people think that kosher food is food which a rabbi has blessed. This is not so.

KOSHER ANIMALS

Kosher animals can be easily recognized by two features. First, their hooves are completely parted at the bottom to form two horny pads; second, they chew cud. Cud is the name given to the little balls of grass that certain animals (known as ruminants) form in their stomachs after swallowing it. Later, they bring the grass up into their mouths and chew it a second time before digesting it. Cows, sheep, goats and deer have these two features and are therefore, kosher. Pigs have split hooves, but do not chew the cud; camels chew the cud, but have only partially split hooves. These are not kosher animals.

Which of these are kosher?

KOSHER POULTRY

There are no special ways of recognizing kosher birds. The Torah gives a long list of birds which are not kosher (*Leviticus 11:13–19*). This list includes many birds of prey. In theory, Jews may eat any bird not on the list, though in practice they only eat chicken, turkey and duck. Even animals and birds of the right type might become treifah if they are found to have defective internal organs. Sometimes people find things wrong with chickens, and take them to a rabbi for him to decide whether they are kosher (p. 92).

KILLING ANIMALS AND BIRDS (SHECHITAH)

Read this section together with p. 125.

Jews may only eat animals and birds which have been killed by **shechitah**. Shechitah is a cut across the throat made with a razor-sharp knife. Causing pain to any living creature is strictly forbidden in Jewish law. Shechitah has been shown to be a humane way of killing animals.

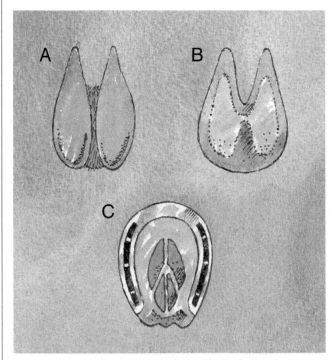

*Hoof prints of **a** cow, **b** camel, **c** horse. Only the first is completely parted underneath.*

The key to shechitah's painlessness lies in the sharpness of the blade and the smoothness of the stroke. Think of the last time you cut your finger. It probably hurt quite a bit if you cut it on something blunt. If you cut your finger with a very sharp knife, you often do not become aware of it until a few moments later. Sometimes you only realize when you notice the blood; you have not felt anything at all. The shechitah knife is kept razor sharp so that the animal will not feel the cut. On either side of the animal's neck are arteries that take blood to the brain (the carotid arteries). When these arteries are cut through, blood pressure in the brain falls immediately to zero and the animal loses consciousness. By the time it becomes possible to feel anything, it is already dead.

REMOVING THE BLOOD

The Torah commands Jews not to eat the blood of animals and birds. If a blood spot is found in an egg, the egg is treifah (not kosher) and is thrown away. Jews use salt and water to remove the blood from their meat before they cook it. This is how they do it:

1   The meat is soaked in water for 30 minutes. This removes any congealed blood on the surface and softens the meat, so that the salt can act.

2   The meat is laid out on thin boards. These are placed a few centimetres apart to allow the blood to drain away.

3   Every part of the meat is covered with salt. Coarse salt has to be used, as table salt would just dissolve. It is left like this for 60 minutes, and the blood drips out between the boards.

4   The meat is rinsed thoroughly several times to remove the salt. It is now ready for cooking.

In the past this was carried out at home. Today, it is usually done by the butcher before the meat is sold. Nonetheless, some people still prefer to do their own salting so that their children will see it and learn how it is done.

Jews treat liver differently since it is difficult to remove the blood completely by salting. After sprinkling the liver with salt they roast it over an open flame. Roasting does not remove the blood but changes its physical nature.

THINGS TO DO

▶ What would you say to someone who thought that kosher food was food that a rabbi had blessed?

▶ Take a piece of raw meat and try soaking it and salting it in the way described. Watch how the blood drips out of it.

▶ You have read an article in a newspaper claiming that the Jewish method of animal slaughter is cruel. (Such claims appear from time to time.) Compose a reply to the editor of the newspaper.

KOSHER FISH

There are two features which help Jews recognize kosher fish. Fish that have fins and scales are kosher. All other seafood is forbidden. This gives Jews a wide range of fish which they may eat: plaice, cod, herring, haddock, mackerel, salmon, tuna and pike are all kosher. Eels are not kosher as they have no scales. Shell fish, such as crabs, lobsters, prawns, mussels and shrimps, are not permitted to Jews, nor is octopus or squid.

LOOKING FOR INSECTS

Jews are also forbidden to eat insects or other 'creepy crawlies'. This might sound strange, for most people would not want to eat them anyway. For Jewish people, however, eating an insect is not only repulsive; it is a sin. Before eating vegetables and fruit Jews have to make sure they are free from insects.

Most people wash leafy vegetables such as cabbage and lettuce before eating them. However, this does not always remove all the insects. You can see this for yourself. Wash a lettuce leaf until you are certain that it is clean. Then hold it up to the light and look closely under each fold. You will sometimes be amazed at what you find. Jews always have to check their vegetables like this.

Worms and maggots sometimes burrow into fruit and Jews are required to remove these too. In Jewish households children are often encouraged to help examine the vegetables. Some kinds of fish may also be infested with worms, especially at certain seasons. Jews are expected to remove them before cooking. Cod is particularly prone to infestation.

BUYING KOSHER FOOD

Jews can buy fruit, vegetables, eggs and most drinks anywhere without any problem. They can also buy fish from any fishmonger, but have to ensure that the fish have fins and scales. Meat and poultry are usually bought from a licensed kosher butcher, though some supermarkets now sell kosher meat in sealed packs.

Products such as packet soups, confectionery and other items contain colouring, flavouring, preservatives, emulsifiers or stabilizers, and some of these come from non-kosher sources. To overcome the problem of knowing which food products are kosher, rabbis sometimes supervise the manufacture. These rabbis will certify that the product is kosher by a label printed on the packet or carton. This label is called a **hechsher**.

Today there is a wide range of products bearing a hechsher. These include sweets, chocolates, soups, margarine, oil, biscuits, butter and cheese. Most of these are manufactured in Israel or the USA, and increasing numbers are being produced in Britain. Keeping a kosher home is probably easier today than at any time in the past.

Kosher butchers' shops always display a licence from a rabbinic board. The board takes responsibility for making sure that the butcher does everything properly. They frequently send inspectors to check the shop. If a butcher is found to be selling non-kosher meat, he loses his licence immediately.

Kosher restaurants also have to have a licence from a rabbinical authority. These restaurants normally serve either meat or non-meat meals, e.g. fish or dairy foods, but not both.

Some medicines may also be non-kosher. They might contain non-kosher ingredients or come in capsule form (the capsules are often made of gelatin, a compound produced from animals' bones). In most cases, Jews may use them because they are needed to make people well and many of the rules are relaxed for sick people. However, if a kosher medicine is available as an alternative, Jews would prefer to use it. For this reason many Jews feel the need for a Jewish doctor or pharmacist.

Some items of kosher food

Washing up – notice the bowl in the sink

IN A KOSHER KITCHEN

Based on the Biblical verse, 'You must not cook a young goat in its mother's milk' (*Exodus 23:19* and elsewhere), Jews who keep kosher homes do not eat meat and dairy foods together. A kosher kitchen would be laid out in two parts, a meat section and a dairy section. Work surfaces will be used for either meat or milk foods, and crockery, cutlery and utensils will be stored in drawers and cupboards on the appropriate side.

Cooking needs a certain amount of care and good management. Jews find electric cookers easier to manage than gas, since the rings may be brought to red heat and any spillage can be burned away. Those who can afford it will have two cookers or hobs. They might also have two sinks. Where there is only one sink it will certainly be treif (not kosher), since everything will be poured down it. Families with one sink do their washing up in bowls. There is never a need for two refrigerators or freezers, since cold foods are not affected in the same way.

Foods which contain neither meat nor dairy produce, (i.e. vegetables, eggs) and have not been prepared in meat or dairy utensils are known as **parev** or **parve** (rhymes with 'carver'). Parev foods may be eaten with either meat or milk.

Sometimes, even with the most careful kitchen management, meat and milk foods get mixed or spilled on to one another. When this happens a Jewish person consults a rabbi, who decides whether the food and utensils are still kosher.

THINGS TO DO

▶ You have been invited to eat with a Jewish family. You want to buy them a box of chocolates. What would you look for?

▶ 'The dietary laws were important in the past; they kept Jewish people healthy. But today with meat inspection and food hygiene laws we no longer need them.' How might a Jewish person respond to this view?

▶ A Jewish couple move into a new flat. How might they arrange the drawers, cupboards and working surfaces in the kitchen to enable them to use it for kosher food?

▶ On p. 92 there is a photo of a rabbi examining a chicken. Look at the photo and write a few sentences explaining what might have happened to make the woman bring the chicken to him.

▶ A Jewish family takes a holiday at a seaside resort where no kosher food is available. Is there anything they could buy there? How do you think they would manage?

CIRCUMCISION

'Then God said to Abraham, "You must keep my covenant, you and your children after you throughout their generations. This is My covenant which you shall keep . . . you shall circumcise every male."'

(Genesis 17:9–1)

Circumcision is the first Jewish rite of passage, i.e. rites (rituals or ceremonies) that mark the passage from one stage of life to the next. It marks the entry of Jewish males into the covenant between God and the Jewish people (p. 22). It is also an important event in the life of a family. It gives them the feeling of being linked in a long chain reaching all the way back to Abraham, who was the first Jew to perform this ceremony.

Circumcision is the removal of the foreskin, the skin that overhangs the tip of the penis. Not only Jews carry out circumcision. It has been practised by many peoples, past and present. There are carvings of ancient Egyptian priests being circumcised and in Roman times singers underwent the operation because they thought it improved the voice. Today, many non-Jewish men are circumcised as the foreskin can easily become a reservoir of infection if it is not kept clean. Nonetheless, Jewish circumcision differs from surgical circumcision. The reason for doing it is religious rather than medical and it involves procedures not found in other forms of circumcision.

Jewish males are normally circumcised at the age of eight days. It is a quick operation and the child heals within a few days. If the child is ill or too weak, the circumcision is postponed until the baby is fit and strong enough. If a Jew was not circumcised in infancy, he has an obligation to have himself circumcised when he reaches adulthood. Non-Jewish males who wish to convert to Judaism must be circumcised too (p. 23).

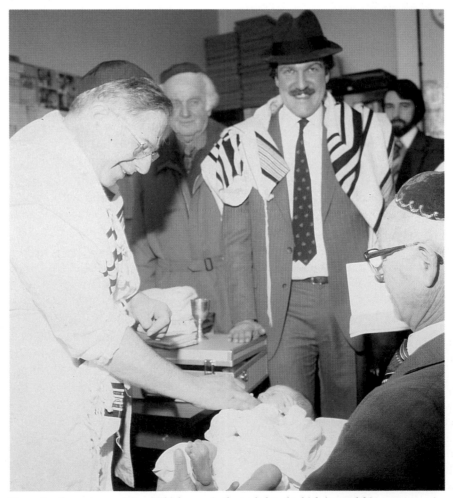

Preparing for a circumcision. Which man is the mohel and which is sandek?

The circumcision of an adult is more complicated than that of a child. It is carried out in hospital by a Jewish doctor who is qualified in Jewish circumcision. The operation can be performed under local anaesthetic.

Circumcision is carried out by a trained person called a **mohel**. Sometimes the mohel will be a doctor, although this is not necessary. It is essential however, that the mohel is a deeply religious person. He has to know all the laws of circumcision and must be trained in the necessary surgical technique.

A circumcision is a joyous event. Many circumcisions are carried out in the maternity hospital before the mother and baby leave (like the one in the photograph). Sometimes they are performed at home or in the synagogue and friends and relatives will come together to celebrate. A synagogue circumcision usually takes place immediately after morning prayers.

Prior to the circumcision, the parents will have selected a man and a woman, usually a married couple, to act as **kvatters**, bearers, i.e. those who carry the child to his circumcision. When the mohel is ready, the woman takes the child from his mother and carries him, on a cushion, to the room where the men are gathered. There she hands the infant over to her husband who carries him to the mohel. The child's father will be standing nearby. Before performing the circumcision, the mohel will place the child, still on his cushion, on an empty chair known as the Chair of Elijah. There is an ancient belief that the spirit of Elijah the prophet visits every circumcision.

The child is then placed on the lap of the man chosen to be **sandek**, where the circumcision will actually take place. It is considered a very great honour to be selected as sandek. Parents will often choose the child's grandfather or some highly respected member of the congregation.

As soon as the child has been circumcised, the father recites a blessing acknowledging that God has commanded this operation so that the child can enter the covenant. The mohel will then hold the child, bless and name him. The name will have been chosen beforehand by the parents. The child, still on his cushion, is then handed to the kvatter who brought him in, who passes him to his wife. She then carries him back to his mother for feeding.

After the ceremony there is a festive meal to celebrate the entry of a new Jewish soul into the 'Covenant of father Abraham'. The mohel will usually check the baby again before he leaves, just to make sure that the dressing is firmly in place and everything is in order. Within a few days everything will be healed.

NAMING GIRLS

Jewish girls are given their names in the synagogue. This takes place on the Sabbath following the birth. There will usually be a celebration, either in the synagogue or at home. Some Sephardim name their daughters at a ceremony called **zeved habat** (the gift of a daughter). This takes place when the baby is seven (in some communities 30) days old. The rabbi blesses the child and there is a celebration meal.

REDEMPTION OF THE FIRST BORN

Originally, first-born sons were intended to be priests. When the Israelites worshipped the golden calf (p. 27) the priesthood was transferred to the tribe of Levi, who did not take part. This means that first-born sons are now born into a priestly role which they cannot fulfil. They must be 'redeemed', i.e. taken out of their priestly status.

The ceremony takes places when a child is 30 days old. The father hands five silver coins (or an object of the same value), to a priest and 'buys' his son out of the priesthood. Relatives and friends gather for a celebration meal, for the child has now been transferred to a role he can fulfil, i.e. an ordinary Jew. A first-born son who reaches adulthood without being redeemed has an obligation to redeem himself.

THINGS TO DO

▶ Read *Genesis 17*. Explain why Jews regard circumcision as a sign of the covenant.

▶ Apart from baby boys who else may be circumcised?

▶ Why do you think a circumcision is a joyous family event?

▶ Write a short paragraph entitled 'Jewish naming ceremonies'.

▶ What does the sandek do?

▶ Why do you think being a sandek is considered a great honour?

'Five is the age for starting to study scripture, ten for Mishnah, thirteen is the age for observing the commandments.'

(Ethics of the Fathers 5:21)

Bar mitzvah (son of the commandments) and **bat mitzvah** (daughter of the commandments) are names given to boys and girls when they become adults. Jews also use the terms to mean the ceremony that marks the passage from childhood to adulthood.

JEWISH ADULTHOOD

Individuals mature at different ages. There are also different kinds of maturity; a person may be mature physically but not emotionally, or vice versa. Jews define adulthood as being able to take responsibility for one's actions. In Jewish law that age is twelve for a girl and thirteen for a boy. This is when a young person enters the covenant relationship with God (p. 22), both as an individual and as part of the community.

BAR MITZVAH

A boy's thirteenth birthday is an occasion for a family gathering and meal. On the following Shabbat most boys are called up to recite a blessing on the Torah. Some will have learnt to read part or even the whole of the sidra (section, p. 38) for that Shabbat. This requires a lot of practice and boys spend many weeks learning the parts they will read.

In some synagogues a boy will only be allowed to read from the Torah if he has passed a test of competence beforehand. The idea of being tested usually gives boys an additional incentive and makes them work especially hard to reach the required standard. Most rabbis will also see to it that a boy approaching bar mitzvah has a pair of tefillin (p. 87) and that he knows how to use them.

REFLECTION

'I was very nervous when I went up to read my part. My legs felt all wobbly. But it was all right once I'd got started. At the end I felt a bit sorry it was over.'

(David P, Brighton)

On the Shabbat when a boy is to be called up, friends and relatives will come to the synagogue to hear him. Many of them will be honoured by being called to recite a blessing on some part of the reading.

After the boy has finished reading his portion, his father recites **baruch shepatarani**. This is a brief statement in which he thanks God for having brought the boy to maturity and declares that the boy is now responsible for his own actions. In his sermon, the rabbi will usually congratulate the boy and give him some words of encouragement. In some synagogues the boy himself declares his intention to accept his obligations as a Jewish man. After the service there will often be a small celebration in the synagogue hall.

In recent years some people have started to lay on lavish banquets and balls as bar mitzvah celebrations. Much of this is contradictory to Jewish teaching, which treats the occasion as a serious religious affair, not an opportunity for extravagance and ostentation. The celebration is really of secondary importance – boys become bar mitzvah whether they have a celebration or not. In traditional communities there will be a celebration dinner with family and friends. The boy will deliver a speech on some Torah theme. Rabbis and other communal leaders offer the boy and his family encouragement to continue learning and practising Judaism. The most important presents he receives will be Jewish books (p. 89).

BAT MITZVAH

Bat mitzvah is a girl's entry into womanhood. As in the case of boys, any celebration is secondary to the meaning of bat mitzvah itself; the girl becomes a woman and is herself responsible for observing the commandments.

Until recent years Jewish families did not celebrate their daughters' bat mitzvah. Nowadays many do and customs vary widely. Sharon marked her bat mitzvah with a festive meal to which her friends were invited. She held this on a Shabbat afternoon during the summer months. Her friend Naomi had hers in the winter when nightfall is earlier (p. 34), so her parents made it after Shabbat. Sharon made a speech on a Torah theme. In some Sephardi communities this celebration meal is the occasion when the girl's father recites baruch shepatarani, thanking God for having raised his daughter to womanhood and formally declaring her responsible for her own actions. Sharon's father does not have this custom. Like her brothers, Sharon received gifts

Sharon delivers a speech at her bat chayil ceremony

from friends and members of her family. These included a number of Jewish books (p. 89).

BAT CHAYIL

Most synagogues have **bat chayil** (daughter of excellence) ceremonies for girls when they reach the age of twelve. Sharon prepared by studying the laws of Shabbat, festivals and kashrut (p. 68), as well as Jewish history, prayers and blessings. Her class was taken on a visit to a mikveh (p. 82). They were tested on all this before the ceremony. They also did projects on some aspect of Jewish womanhood.

Bat chayil ceremonies are usually held on a Sunday. For Sharon's ceremony the synagogue was decked with flowers and her family and friends joined in the celebration. The **chazan** (cantor, p. 93) sang, accompanied by the choir. Sharon made a short speech and read a passage of her choice in Hebrew. She was then presented with a **siddur** (prayer book, p. 86).

THINGS TO DO

▶ Explain the terms bar mitzvah and bat mitzvah.

▶ Your Jewish friend recently celebrated his bar mitzvah and you attended the synagogue. Write a letter to your grandmother telling her what happened.

▶ How do Jewish girls celebrate their coming of age?

▶ Your neighbour's son is going to be bar mitzvah soon. He tells you that he has hired a large hall and is planning a dinner with a cabaret and a ball. He asks you what you think. What would you tell him?

▶ To what extent is a person 'mature' at twelve or thirteen? Explain your answer.

▶ You are a rabbi preparing to speak at a bar or bat mitzvah celebration. Write out the part of your speech in which you address the young adult.

'All the blessings that a man receives come to him only in the merit of his wife.'

(Talmud)

In Hebrew, marriage is referred to as **kiddushin** (sanctification) or **nisuin** (elevation).

Jews see marriage as necessary and not only to bring children into the world. In Jewish thinking unless people become part of a couple (what scientists currently call a 'bonded pair') their personalities will not develop fully. 'A man without a wife is incomplete,' said the Talmud. 'An unmarried woman is an unfinished vessel,' echoes the Zohar. Marriage is the most intimate of relationships, quite different from any other relationship in creation.

'The mating of animals is a temporary and purely physical act. Through the sanctification of marriage however, a husband and wife become the closest of relatives.'

(Maimonides)

PARTNER SELECTION

Marrying a Jewish partner is important mainly for the sake of the children. Whether a child is Jewish or not is determined solely by its mother; if she is Jewish, so is the child. The child of a non-Jewish mother is not Jewish, even if the father is (but see p. 141). Marriages between Jews and non-Jews sometimes run into difficulties when conflicts arise over how the children should be brought up.

Certain partner combinations are forbidden in Jewish law. Apart from the prohibitions of incest, a cohen (priest, p. 25) may neither marry a divorced woman, a convert, nor a woman whose father was not Jewish.

Today, many Jews select their marriage partners by dating members of the opposite sex, just like most other people in the western world. In the more traditional Jewish communities people try to learn as much as they can about a proposed partner's character, background, interests and ambitions before meeting the other person. If two people are obviously unsuited to one another, they do not meet and there is no heartache. If they seem reasonably well suited, the couple meet. It is then up to them to decide whether they want to meet again and develop a relationship. With this method of partner selection, marriages are usually successful and the divorce rate is low.

PREPARING FOR THE WEDDING

The wedding might be set for any day of the week (except Shabbat or festivals). The bride will try to plan it for a time of the month when she expects not to be menstruating, as sexual relations may not take place at that time. A few days before the wedding, the bride will visit the mikveh – an immersion pool (p. 82). Her mother or close female friend will go with her. If she is menstruating, then the visit to the mikvah will be postponed until after the wedding. Sexual relations before marriage are strictly forbidden.

On the Shabbat before the wedding, the groom is called to the reading of the Torah (p. 38). People throw nuts and raisins or sweets on him as a symbol of a sweet life. In some Sephardi communities, synagogues will be filled with the scent of fragrant spices.

THE WEDDING

Jewish weddings take place under a **huppah**, a canopy held up by four poles. The couple stand under it as though enclosed in their own little capsule, for it is a symbol of harmony. However, it is open on all sides, symbolizing that they are not separated from the community. Sometimes weddings are held outside under the sky. The ceremony is conducted by a rabbi.

Although it is a day of great joy for the couple, it is also a day of stock-taking and asking for forgiveness before setting out upon a new stage of life. Both the bride and groom fast until after the ceremony. In their afternoon prayers they make a confession of sin as in the Yom Kippur service (p. 47).

An outdoor wedding: bride and groom leaving the huppah

The marriage ceremony

The order of the ceremony is:

1 Birchat eirusin (initial blessings)
The rabbi recites two blessings over a cup of wine. The first is the blessing always recited before drinking wine (which the bride and groom will shortly do). The second praises God for sanctifying the People of Israel by His commandments about marriage. The wine is then passed to the groom and bride in turn, who both drink from the same cup.

2 The ring
The groom then places a ring on the bride's finger and says (in Hebrew), 'With this ring you are sanctified to me according to the Law of Moses and Israel.'

3 Reading of the ketubah (marriage contract)
The **ketubah** is simply a statement of the husband's intention to feed, clothe and care for his wife. It is usually written in Aramaic, a language similar to Hebrew (p. 152). Sometimes a brief English translation is read. In Sephardi communities the ketubah is read to the groom before the ceremony begins.

4 Birchat nisuin (the final blessings)
The rabbi then recites seven blessings, praising God for creating the human race, creating joy and gladness and bringing happiness to the couple. After the ceremony the groom breaks a glass with his foot (it will be well wrapped in paper for safety). The sound of breaking glass is a symbol of destruction calling to mind the ancient Temple (p. 61). It reminds people that although they are happy, they would be even more joyful if they could fulfil those commandments which depended on the Temple.

5 Yichud (private togetherness)
Immediately after the ceremony the bride and groom will be taken to a private room. Here they can be alone together for a short while before rejoining their guests. They break their fast and spend a few moments just relaxing.

6 Shiva brachot (seven blessings)
In traditional communities the wedding celebrations continue for a whole week. There is a celebration feast each night and the bride and groom will be honoured guests in the homes of different people. At the end of each meal, shiva brachot (seven blessings) will be said. These are the same seven blessings which were said under the huppah.

TAHARAT HAMISHPACHA (FAMILY PURITY)

Read pp. 82–3 together with this section.

For much of their married life, a couple's relationship will be regulated by the laws of family purity. Judaism strictly forbids sexual relations during menstruation. Each month, from the time her period starts until she has immersed in a mikveh (p. 83), a wife is in a state of **nidah**, separateness from her husband. She remains nidah throughout the time she is menstruating plus the following seven days. It is never less than twelve days. During this time there may be no physical contact between her and her husband. Only after her return from the mikveh may they resume the physical side of their marriage.

To an outsider it might seem that this would put a great strain on a relationship. In fact, the reverse is true. Couples who observe family purity think of the monthly separation as being engaged again, when they expressed their love in non-physical ways. It helps to make a marriage more stable as it prevents a couple becoming bored with one another. When the wife comes back from the mikveh and she and her husband can both touch once again, they both feel a tremendous sense of renewal. The Talmud describes it as being under the huppah all over again.

THINGS TO DO

▶ What does kiddushin mean? What does it tell you about the Jewish view of marriage?

▶ Why do Jews, as a rule, marry Jewish partners?

▶ Would you describe a Jewish wedding as a happy or solemn occasion? Why?

▶ Your local rabbi is going to write a booklet for brides and grooms, explaining some of the laws of nidah and mikveh. Write a brief introduction to the booklet.

▶ How might a Jew respond to the view that a couple should live together for a while before deciding whether to marry?

'Whoever divorces his first wife, even the altar sheds tears on her behalf.'

(Talmud)

Judaism places great value on marriage. If a marriage seems to be faltering every effort will be made to save it. Nonetheless, Judaism recognizes that in some cases divorce is the only realistic solution. Jewish divorce involves writing and giving a **get**, a document of divorce.

GROUNDS FOR DIVORCE

In spite of the importance of marriage in Judaism, no 'grounds' are needed in order to divorce. When two people have tried to save their marriage and in the end agree to divorce, no real obstacles are put in their way. If people were aware of how simple it is to obtain a Jewish divorce, many more Jews who divorce through the civil courts would have a Jewish divorce too. Nor are any obstacles put in the way of divorced people remarrying, even remarrying each other. Only the cohen (priest, p. 25) may not marry a divorced woman.

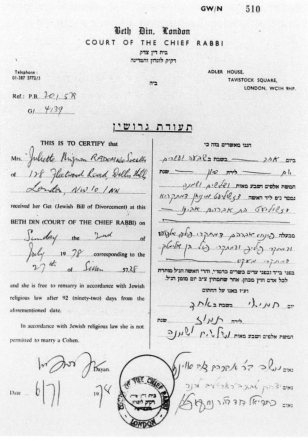

A certificate stating that a get has been received

THE GET (DOCUMENT OF DIVORCE)

A get is a document certifying that a marriage has been terminated. It must be written on parchment by a trained scribe (p. 94). A get is a very exact document. It must mention every name that the husband and wife might be known by and must state clearly where and when the divorce took place. Although the get remains the property of the woman, today it will usually be kept by the **bet din** (rabbinical court, p. 97). It will issue the wife with a certificate. She will be required to produce it if she should ever wish to remarry.

DIVORCE PROCEDURE

Once two people have agreed to terminate their marriage, the Jewish divorce procedure is very simple. They apply to a bet din and a date will be fixed for them to attend. There, a scribe will write the get in the presence of the **dayanim** (judges) and the husband will hand it to his wife in front of two witnesses. If the husband and wife do not wish to face each other in the courtroom, either partner (or both) may appoint a representative, he to give the get, she to receive it. The divorce takes effect from the moment that the wife or her representative receives the get.

If husband and wife are not living in the same town, the husband will apply to his nearest bet din. There, the dayanim will have the get written and it will be delivered to the bet din in the town or country where the wife resides. The wife will then be asked to come to the bet din to receive the get in front of witnesses.

In most countries a get is only given after the civil divorce; in Israel the Jewish divorce *is* the civil divorce. A civil divorce has no validity in Jewish law (but see p. 141). A Jewish couple who divorce in the civil courts but fail to have a Jewish divorce are still married in Jewish law. This means that if they marry new partners without a get they are committing adultery.

MAMZERUT

There can be very serious consequences if a woman remarries without having a get from her former husband. Since, in effect, no divorce has taken place, the second husband will be having a sexual relationship with a woman who is still married to someone else. A child born from such a relationship is a **mamzer** (plural **mamzerim**). 'Mamzer' is often translated 'illegitimate'. This is incorrect and misleading. 'Illegitimate' implies being born outside

Reading the get in the Bet Din (c. 1920)

may refuse to accept a get. Here, too, a bet din can do nothing. A get is only valid if it is freely given and freely accepted.

Today, some rabbis are trying to work out a formula for prenuptial agreement, i.e. a clause written into the marriage document whereby both bride and groom agree that if their marriage should fail they will neither refuse to give nor to accept a get. Achieving this formula is not as easy as it sounds. If the agreement is such that it has to be enforced in a court of law, it would mean that the get was not being given (or accepted) freely. On the other hand, if it could not be enforced in a court of law, it would be worthless.

of marriage. Judaism attaches no stigma to children born of unmarried parents. A mamzer is a child born to a married woman who has committed adultery. **Mamzerut** (the condition of being a mamzer) is one of the most tragic of situations. Through no fault of their own, mamzerim may never marry into the Jewish community.

THE AGUNAH

Another tragic situation is that of **agunah**, the 'chained wife', i.e. a woman whose husband is missing, but who has no proof that he is dead. Until such proof can be produced, she remains an agunah, tied to the missing husband and unable to marry again.

Rabbis have gone to great lengths to free agunot (plural of agunah) from their condition. They have even accepted the slightest reliable evidence – evidence that would not normally be accepted in a bet din – that the husband is dead. Straight after the Holocaust (p. 16), rabbis were particularly lenient in freeing agunot from missing husbands.

If a man refuses to give his wife a get, she too becomes, in effect, an agunah and cannot remarry. If she does, she will be an adulteress, with possible tragic consequences for her children. A bet din can neither compel a man to give a get nor annul the marriage. A get may only be given of the husband's own free will. The reverse may also happen. A wife

THINGS TO DO

▶ Why do Jews make every effort to save a faltering marriage? Whose help do you think they might seek?

▶ What is a get? What might happen if Jewish people divorce and do not have a get?

▶ How does a Jewish divorce take place if husband and wife are living in different countries?

▶ Why do you think it is important for a get to be freely given and received? Why might one Jewish partner refuse to give the other a divorce?

▶ Try to summarize the Jewish attitude to divorce. How does it square with the high regard Jews have for marriage?

FOR DISCUSSION

▶ Divorce is usually a traumatic experience, not only for the husband and wife but also for their children. Discuss ways in which religious leaders might help people over their most difficult period.

'When a man leaves the world, neither silver nor precious stones nor pearls accompany him, but only the Torah he has learnt and the good works he has carried out.'

(Ethics of the Fathers)

We all feel grief when someone we love dies. However, Judaism regards excessive or prolonged mourning as undesirable. The Jewish mourning customs help people gradually to phase out their grief.

THE DYING PERSON

Jewish families like to come together to be near a loved one who is dying. If possible, a person's last moments would be spent making a final confession and reciting the Shema (p. 18). It is considered an act of great kindness to stay with a person during the moment of death and to make sure that the eyes are closed. Those present will then bless God as 'the true judge' (p. 65) and make a short tear in their clothes as a sign of grief (*Genesis 37:34*).

A MOURNER BEFORE THE BURIAL (ONAN)

From the time of death until the body is buried, a mourner is known as an **onan** (immediate mourner). An onan's main priority is to arrange the burial – halakhah, Jewish law, forbids cremation (but see p. 138). To do this as quickly as possible, an onan is exempt from all the positive commandments of the Torah (p. 22). Jews consider it very disrespectful to delay a burial, except in exceptional circumstances (p. 106). It is also considered disrespectful to leave a dead person alone. Someone will always stay with the body from the time of death until the funeral, even if it is in a mortuary.

THE FUNERAL

As soon as a doctor has issued a death certificate, members of the **chevra kaddisha** (burial society, p. 97) will prepare the body for burial. They wash the body thoroughly and, if possible, immerse it in a mikveh (p. 82) – not the same mikveh used by living people. Men's bodies are washed by male attendants, women's by female. The body is then wrapped in a plain linen shroud. A man is usually buried wearing the tallit (p. 86) in which he prayed during his life. Once the body is ready it is placed in a simple, unpolished wooden box with no brass handles or internal padding. In death, rich and poor are treated alike.

REFLECTION

'The first time I went to prepare a body I was very worried. I thought it would be gruesome. Actually it wasn't like that at all, it was a very uplifting experience. When we had finished there was a man all ready to meet his Maker.'

(Mr S, Northeast London Chevra Kaddisha)

The funeral is a simple affair. Some psalms are read, followed by a short prayer praising God for granting life and for taking it away. A rabbi sometimes says a short speech about the dead person. No idle chatter takes place in the cemetery, as this is considered very disrespectful. Sephardim walk round the coffin seven times before the burial and recite prayers for angels of mercy to accompany the soul. The coffin is then lowered into the ground and people heap earth upon it to close up the grave. They then offer words of comfort to the mourners and everyone washes their hands before leaving the cemetery. From now on a mourner is no longer an onan, but an **avel** (plural **avelim**), a prolonged mourner. On returning home, the avelim are served a meal of hard-boiled eggs. The egg, which has no opening, symbolizes the mourners' inability to open their mouths and put their grief into words (p. 60).

THE FIRST WEEK (SHIVA)

The first week after the funeral is known as the **shiva** (seven). This is the most intense period of mourning. During this week the avelim usually gather in one of their homes and are forbidden to leave it unless absolutely necessary. Three times each day friends and fellow synagogue members will come to pray with the mourners (p. 86). At these prayers the male mourners will recite **kaddish**. Kaddish is often mistaken for a prayer for the dead. In fact, it is a declaration of God's greatness and a prayer for the coming age of universal peace (p. 24).

Throughout the shiva the mourners sit on low chairs (p. 60), except on Shabbat when no mourning is allowed. They cut neither their hair nor nails, though a sick person who feels uncomfortable is allowed to do these things. All the mirrors of the house are covered so that people are discouraged from attending to their appearance and sexual relations are forbidden. They do not listen to any music. Leather shoes are not worn. A candle is kept burning night and day. This symbolizes the verse, 'A person's soul is the candle of the Lord' (*Proverbs 20:27*). During this week, friends come to spend time with the mourners, chat to them and offer them words of comfort. Refreshments are not served to the visitors since it is considered wrong to take anything from the mourners, even food. At the end of the week they leave the house and commence their daily tasks once more.

THE FIRST MONTH (SHELOSHIM)

Sheloshim (thirty) is the name given to the first month of mourning. It includes the week of shiva.

Once the shiva has ended, the worst part of the mourning is over. From now on the mourners no longer sit on low chairs and they may cut their nails, though hair is left to grow for a while longer. Each day the male mourners go to the synagogue and recite kaddish.

A headstone may be set up over the grave at any time after the shiva. Some people try to have the headstone in place by the end of the sheloshim. Many leave this until a year has gone by. Sephardim usually have a horizontal stone slab covering the whole grave instead of a headstone.

Jews mourning parents remain avelim throughout the first year. They will neither play music or listen to it, except for professional musicians who depend on playing for their livelihoods. Male mourners continue saying kaddish for 11 months. The anniversary of the death is usually known by its **Yiddish** name **yarzheit**. For all relatives, a candle is kept burning through the night and day and kaddish is again said. For as long as the immediate relatives live, they will light a candle and say kaddish on each yarzheit.

◇

THINGS TO DO

▶ Draw a time chart to cover the period from the death of a close relative until the end of the first year. Show what customs Jews observe at each stage and as mourning decreases. If you have already studied pp 60–1, compare your chart with the one you drew there. How are these mourning customs similar to those and how are they different?

▶ Why do you think prolonged or excessive mourning is not a good thing?

▶ People often find it difficult to talk to someone who has just lost a close relative. How would you try to comfort a person whose loved one had died?

▶ Why do you think Jews consider it wrong to take food from the mourners?

▶ In Jewish writings, preparing a body for burial is called 'true kindness'. Why do you think it is called this?

▶ How do Jews show respect for a dead person? Do you think it is important to have respect for the dead? Explain your answer.

A mourner during shiva. The photograph shows several mourning customs. How many can you spot?

'The principles of purity and impurity . . . are not reckoned among those things that the human mind has determined; they are among the chukim.

(Maimonides)

Mikveh (plural **mikvaot**) means 'a place where water has gathered.' Jews use the word to refer to a special pool where people can immerse to purify themselves. A mikveh is vital for keeping the laws of family purity (p. 77). These laws are so important that a Jewish community has to build a mikveh before it builds a synagogue.

THE IMPORTANCE OF THE MIKVEH

In ancient times people brought sacrifices and other gifts to the Temple, (p. 7) and so they were often in contact with holy things. They had to be in a constant state of purity. Touching a corpse or a dead animal (except those killed for food or sacrifice) made a person impure; so did menstruation. People could only regain their purity by immersing themselves in natural water. Rivers and ponds might

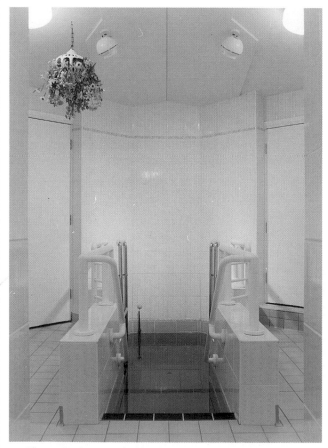

Inside a mikveh: stairs leading down to the immersion pool

have been used, but usually people would have visited the mikveh, a special pool in which rain water had collected. Now that Jews have no Temple, the mikveh is mainly used by women who immerse themselves after menstruation and childbirth. Although menstruation is a natural bodily function, each time a woman has a period she loses something which could have become a new human life.

Men are obliged to visit the mikveh on the day before Yom Kippur (p. 46). Some also go on the eve of Shabbat and festivals. Non-Jews converting to Judaism must also immerse in a mikveh as part of the conversion procedure (p. 23).

◇

PURITY AND IMPURITY

The terms 'purity' and 'impurity' are very misleading. They are poor translations of the Hebrew words **taharah** and **tumah**. These are spiritual states and are rather difficult to understand. They have nothing whatever to do with hygiene or cleanliness. Although the English language has no exact equivalent for tumah and taharah, purity and impurity (or cleanliness and uncleanliness) have long been used as translations. For that reason they are used here, though you should remember that they are not at all accurate.

◇

THE STRUCTURE OF A MIKVEH

A mikveh is a tiled pool, usually built into the ground. Mikvaot vary from about 3 to 5 metres in length and from 2 to 3 metres in width, and contain upwards of 350 litres of water. Stairs with a hand rail lead down into the water.

Ancient mikvaot would have been full of rain water. Today, the immersion pool itself will be filled with tap water, but connected by a pipe to a second pool which does contain rain water. The pipe is usually sealed with a cork stopper, which can be removed before immersing so that the two pools are joined. The immersion pool is drained and cleaned out each day. Unlike ancient mikvaot the water in modern immersion pools is heated.

Attached to mikvaot for men there are usually large changing rooms. Beyond these are showers because a person must be physically clean before immersing in the mikveh itself. The facilities surrounding women's mikvaot are more private and much more luxurious. Separate bathrooms with showers open into the mikveh area – you can see the doors leading from the shower rooms in the photograph opposite. A female attendant calls each woman to immerse in turn, as soon as she indicates that she is ready.

A week after menstruation has ceased, a woman is ready for immersion in the mikveh. Except in special circumstances, this will always take place after nightfall. Upon arrival at the mikveh, she goes straight into a bathroom and begins preparing for her immersion. If no bathroom is available she will sit in the waiting room until one is free.

Each woman is given as much time as she wants to prepare for her immersion. She will remove rings and nail polish, for, once in the mikveh, nothing must come between her body and the water.

She goes into the pool and immerses. A female attendant will be standing over her to check that she has done it properly (p. 9). She then folds her arms and, while the attendant covers her hair with a towel, she recites a blessing and then immerses a second time. As she comes out of the water she returns to her 'pure' state. She is now ready to resume sexual relations with her husband.

TRENDS IN MIKVEH ATTENDANCE

In the past, mikveh attendance was taken very seriously. Excavations at Massada, the rock fortress in the south of Israel where 1,000 Jews held out against the Romans for three years have revealed the mikveh the women used, even while under siege. Jewish women in Russia used to cut holes in the ice of the village pond to carry out the monthly immersion.

About three generations ago, mikveh attendance began to decline. This was part of the general trend among the Jewish refugees who came to the west before the First World War. Although many had kept Judaism faithfully in eastern Europe, they gradually abandoned many Jewish practices here. Their daughters and granddaughters were not taught the importance of mikveh. They came to associate it with cleanliness and saw no reason to go to the mikveh when they could wash in their own bathrooms. Nowadays, this is beginning to change. An increasing number of modern women are

discovering the significance of the monthly immersion and mikveh attendance is increasing.

IMMERSING UTENSILS

Not only people use the mikveh. New utensils, unless they have been manufactured by a Jew, must be immersed too. Only those which come into contact with food in its edible state, i.e. crockery, cutlery, glasses and saucepans, have to be immersed. Nothing must come between the utensils and the water and someone immersing utensils will remove labels or other manufacturers' marks first.

The mikvaot for immersing utensils are separate from the ones people use. They usually contain only rain water, since the utensils can be washed thoroughly afterwards. Also, it would be unsafe to immerse utensils where people immerse. Glasses or cups occasionally get dropped, and broken glass or china on the mikveh floor would be a real hazard for anyone coming to immerse.

THINGS TO DO

▶ Why is the mikveh important in Jewish life?

▶ Where did people immerse themselves in ancient times?

▶ Why is it difficult to explain what 'purity' and 'impurity' are all about?

▶ Why did many Jewish women not use the mikveh in the past?

▶ You are about to interview someone for the job of mikveh attendant. What questions would you ask her? (You might want to read p. 96 before answering this question.)

▶ You are going to conduct a class of pupils round a mikveh (not while it is in use). Write down the talk you plan to give them as you show them round.

▶ How does the immersion of utensils differ from that of people? How is it similar?

'God asks, "Did anyone ever enter a synagogue and not find My presence there?"'

(Midrash)

A Jewish house of worship is called a synagogue. As a rule Jews rarely use that name: Ashkenazim speak of the **shul** (pronounce it to rhyme with 'pool'); Sephardim (oriental Jews) usually call it **Bet ha Knesset** (house of assembly). Many synagogues are really community centres.

HOW SYNAGOGUES BEGAN

Most historians believe that synagogues originated about 25 centuries ago in Babylon, some years before the first Temple (p. 7) was destroyed. The Jews who were deported there began gathering in each other's houses to pray together and study the Torah. Later, separate buildings were set aside for prayer; these were the first synagogues.

THE LAYOUT OF THE TEMPLE

Although synagogues differ from one another, their layout is based on the Temple which, in turn, was modelled on the Sanctuary built by the Israelites in the desert (p. 7). The Sanctuary was made of posts, boards and curtains. The Israelites assembled it whenever they encamped. You can read about how it was made in the book of *Exodus 25–30*. It consisted of a rectangular enclosure. Inside was a washstand where the priests washed their hands and feet before commencing the service and an altar where animals were sacrificed. Beyond that was a tent-like structure known as the Holy Place. Only the priests were allowed to enter this. Deep inside, and hidden by a parochet, a screen, was a room known as the Holy of Holies. It contained the Ark, a wooden box overlaid with gold. In the Ark were the blocks of stone with the Ten Commandments engraved on them (p. 26).

When King Solomon built the Temple, he used the same layout as the Sanctuary, but he made everything out of stone. A rectangular stone wall marked off the courtyard and the washstand and altar were placed there. A stone building replaced the Holy Place with the Holy of Holies inside. He also built an adjoining courtyard where women could pray.

SYNAGOGUE DESIGN

Synagogues are always built facing Israel, if possible towards Jerusalem, where the Temple stood. At the

Interior of a modern synagogue

entrance is a sink where worshippers wash their hands before prayer. The synagogue is usually rectangular, with separate areas for men and women (but see p. 138). At the front of the synagogue, where the Holy Place would have stood in the Temple, there is a large cupboard (sometimes an alcove) covered by a screen called a parochet. This is called the Ark and represents the golden box in the Temple that contained the Ten Commandments. Inside it are the scrolls of the Torah, the holiest objects in the synagogue.

In the centre of the synagogue there is a raised platform called a **bimah** or **almemar**. The Torah is read from this platform and there is a table in front where the scroll is laid. This is modelled on the dais in the Temple from which the Torah was read.

Above the Ark there is the **ner tamid**, the 'continual light'. It is never put out. This represents the **menorah**, the oil lamp of the Temple. The menorah had seven wicks, one of which was kept burning continually. Near the ner tamid there is often a stone or bronze plaque with the Ten Commandments engraved on it. In Jewish tradition the tablets were perfect cubes, though they are usually shown with rounded tops.

By the side of the Ark is the rabbi's seat. There is often a similar seat on the other side of the Ark reserved for the chazan or visiting speakers. In front of the Ark, or to one side of it, there is usually a pulpit, where speakers stand to give their sermons.

These features are common to most synagogues, although the interior design can vary enormously from one to another. Some synagogues are modern structures of tubular steel, concrete and glass. Others have a classic design with wooden panelling and leather seats. Some have stained glass windows, showing scenes of the Jewish festivals; others do not.

Jewish law strictly forbids the presence of images, either sculpted or painted, so none are found in the synagogue. Some synagogues do, however, have two lions embroidered on the screen in front of the Ark. These represent the tribe of Judah from which the Messiah (p. 24) is expected to come.

THE TORAH SCROLL (SEFER TORAH)

The Torah scrolls are the holiest objects in the synagogue. These scrolls are made from animal skins stitched together to form a long, continuous writing surface. The Five Books of Moses (p. 26) are written on these skins in vertical columns. There are 250 columns in each Torah scroll. An average scroll is about 60 metres long. Each end is stitched to a wooden pole called an **etz chaim** (tree of life). The 'trees of life' are used for winding the scrolls to the part that is to be read. The writing and repair of the scrolls is the work of a trained scribe (p. 94). Writing a scroll takes about 1,000 working hours.

The scrolls are kept in the ark. In Ashkenazi synagogues, the scrolls are kept tightly wound up, tied round with silk or velvet binders and covered with velvet mantles. In Sephardi synagogues they are fixed into wooden cases (p. 27) covered with silk. They are often decorated with silver ornaments.

The presentation of a new Torah scroll to a synagogue is a joyous ceremony. The writing will be completed on the day of the presentation and various people will be honoured with writing one of the last letters. The new scroll is then carried through the street under a huppah (bridal canopy, p. 76), accompanied by people carrying candles and singing. All the other scrolls will be taken from the Ark and carried into the street, where the officials await the arrival of the new scroll. As the procession reaches the synagogue, all the scrolls will be carried together in a dance that continues round the synagogue, as on Simchat Torah (p. 55).

USES OF THE SYNAGOGUE

Synagogues have always been community centres. Ancient synagogues were often used as classrooms and the local bet din, rabbinic court (p. 97), might have sat in an adjoining building. Synagogues often had guest rooms where travelling Jews could stay, with a stable large enough for several animals. The mikveh (p. 82) was usually part of the building and so synagogues were often built near rivers.

In modern synagogues, there are usually classrooms above the synagogue or next to it,

though not rabbinic courts, for these no longer sit in each area. Very few synagogues today have a mikveh attached to them and they are not necessarily built near rivers. Most synagogues have a hall which is used by members of the community for holding weddings and bar mitzvah celebrations, as well as for meetings and lectures. Many of the surrounding rooms are used by the mother and toddler group, senior citizens' club and similar communal activities.

Youth activities are also held on synagogue premises. These might include regular youth club meetings, scout and guide groups and day camps during school holidays. Adult study groups also take place in the synagogue building, as do public lectures by visiting speakers.

FIND OUT

▶ Try to find out which is the oldest synagogue in Britain. When was it built?

THINGS TO DO

▶ When did Jews start building synagogues? Why did they do this?

▶ Make a list of the parts of the Temple. Next to it make a list of the parts of a synagogue so that your list shows how each item in the synagogue represents something in the Temple.

▶ A synagogue is trying to increase membership. Design a pamphlet to inform Jewish people of all the facilities which the synagogue offers.

▶ Why do you think the presentation of a Sefer Torah to a synagogue is a joyous event?

▶ In which direction would a synagogue face if it is built in (a) London, (b) Cape Town, (c) Tokyo, (d) Moscow? How might this help give Jews a sense of kinship with other Jews?

'When you pray, do not regard your prayer as a fixed task, but as a plea for mercy and an entreaty before God.'

(Ethics of the Fathers)

Jews believe that a person can pray to God whenever and wherever he or she wishes. Throughout the Tenakh and Talmud, we encounter people praying spontaneously, i.e. speaking their thoughts and feelings to God. There are also set daily prayers. These are based on the way Jews used to worship in the Temple.

Jews regard both as important. Spontaneous prayer might be accompanied with deep devotion, but if people only addressed God when they had a need, they would not pray very often. Set prayers create a framework of regular times for setting aside one's own affairs and turning to God.

A Jewish prayer book (containing the set prayers) is called a siddur (plural **siddurim**) meaning 'set order'. Siddurim are printed in Hebrew. Although Jews believe that they can address God in any language, they call Hebrew **leshon hakodesh**, 'the holy tongue,' and regard it as the most appropriate language for prayer. However, siddurim usually have page-by-page translations so that those who are not familiar with Hebrew can pray in a language they understand.

DAILY PRAYERS

Each day there are three services in the synagogue: **shacharit**, the morning prayer; **minchah**, the afternoon prayer; and **arvit**, the evening prayer. In Jewish tradition, praying at these times began with the Patriarchs. Abraham wanted to start his day with prayer; Isaac prayed in the afternoon, breaking off his own activities to devote time to God. Jacob prayed in the evening, to thank God for having helped him through the day.

In the synagogue, the times of these prayers coincide with the times when Jews used to offer sacrifices in the ancient Temple. They offered one regular sacrifice during the first three hours of the day and another between midday and sunset. These determine the times of shacharit and minchah today. The day's sacrifices would then be left burning on the altar until dawn the next day. This is the time when Jews may say their evening prayer, though they usually try not to leave it later than midnight.

On new moons and festivals, there is an additional service (**musaf**). This is said at the time when Jews used to offer an additional sacrifice for these occasions.

The most important Jewish prayer is the Shema (rhymes with 'bazaar'). It contains three paragraphs: *Deuteronomy 6:4–9* and *11:13–21* and *Numbers 15:37–41*. It begins with a declaration of God's oneness, after which Jews pledge themselves to accept God's kingship and keep His commandments. The Shema is recited in the morning and evening services. Jews say it again before going to sleep (p. 65).

On Shabbat and festivals the Torah is read in the synagogue (p. 38). It is also read on Monday and Thursday mornings. This began during Temple times, when it was read for the farmers who came into the towns on these days to sell their produce. Continuing the practice today ensures that people do not go more than three days without hearing the Torah read.

Many parts of these services, and all public Torah readings, require the presence of ten Jewish males over the age of thirteen. This is called a minyan (required number). Without a minyan the set prayers may be said, but certain parts are omitted.

THE TALLIT (PRAYER ROBE)

During morning prayers, Jewish males wear the tallit (plural tallitot) and tefillin (see opposite). Its full name is **tallit gadol** (large robe) to distinguish it from the tallit katan (small robe, p. 64).

The tallit is a four-cornered square (or rectangle) of white cloth. It is usually made of wool or silk, though any natural fabric will do. Attached to each of the four corners are fringes known as tzizit. These are the same as the fringes worn on the tallit katan. If you visit a synagogue you will often see men wearing very small tallitot hanging round their necks like scarves. This is one of those inexplicable practices that has grown up over the years and has given rise to the mistake of calling the tallit a 'prayer shawl'. A tallit is meant to cover the major part of a small man's body since it is also used as a shroud in which the wearer will eventually be buried (p. 97). In some congregations it is worn over the head like a cowl. A full-size tallit measures about 2 metres by 1.5 metres.

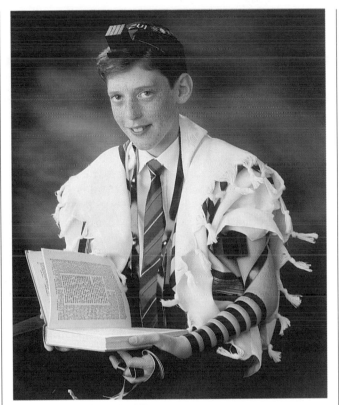

Boy wearing tallit and tefillin

If you look at a tallit, you will see blue or black stripes along the sides. This is because, in ancient times, one fringe on each corner would be dyed dark blue. The dye was obtained from a shellfish that lived in the Mediterranean Sea. Today, no one knows how to identify this creature, so all the fringes are white. The stripes are there to remind Jews of the dark blue dye.

Customs vary from one synagogue to another. There are synagogues where boys wear small tallitot; in others they wear them after bar mitzvah (p. 74). In some congregations only married men wear them.

TEFILLIN (SINGULAR TEFILLAH)

Jewish males over the age of thirteen wear tefillin (singular **tefillah**) at morning prayer each day, except on Shabbat and festivals. Boys usually start wearing them a few weeks before their Bar Mitzvah to practise putting them on properly.

The tefillin consist of two black leather boxes, one worn on the upper arm, the other on the head. Inside the boxes are small parchment scrolls containing four passages from the Bible. These are the first two paragraphs of the Shema, and also *Exodus 13:1–10* and *13:11–16*. The scrolls must be handwritten by a trained scribe (p. 94). The arm

tefillah contains all four passages written on a single scroll. The head tefillah is made up of four separate compartments pressed together, each of which contains one of the passages. The boxes are sewn up underneath with sinews. The parchment scrolls, boxes, stitching and straps may only be made from the hides of kosher animals (p. 68).

Tefillin are a good example of ideas being translated into actions. The arm tefillah is bound to the top of the biceps muscle of the left arm (or right arm for a left-handed person). When the arms are at rest it points to the heart. This reminds the wearer that he must serve God with his heart, i.e. his emotions. The head tefillah is bound to the centre of the forehead, just above where the hair begins to grow. This is to remind the wearer that he must serve God with his mind, i.e. his thoughts.

These are important symbols. It is very easy to appear righteous on the outside. What really matters is what is going on inside a person, i.e. the thoughts and feelings that other people do not see. The daily wearing of the tefillin is a personal reminder that the wearer must work hard at ridding himself of undesirable thoughts and feelings (bearing a grudge, planning revenge, etc.) and develop desirable ones (love of God, caring for other people, etc.).

Tefillin are very sacred objects for Jews. They have to be opened up and checked about every three years as the writing can fade or crack. This is done by a qualified scribe (p. 94). If you ever handle tefillin be sure to do so with great respect.

THINGS TO DO

▶ What is a siddur? What language is it in? Why are the siddurim often printed with translations? Would a siddur be of use in spontaneous prayer? Explain your answer.

▶ What is a tallit? What is its eventual purpose? How might wearing it help put Jews in the right frame of mind for prayer?

▶ The rabbi of your local synagogue has asked you to design a short instruction sheet for Jewish boys explaining what tefillin are and how to put them on. Try to design one. Make your instructions as brief and as clear as possible.

▶ What do you think is the value of symbolic actions like putting on tefillin?

'And these matters which I command you today you shall take to heart. And you shall teach them carefully to your children and you shall speak of them . . .'

(Deuteronomy 6:6–7)

Education is very important in Jewish life. It is not limited to the young, as studying the Torah is one of the 613 commandments (p. 22). Education is an ongoing process, continuing into old age.

JEWISH EDUCATION IN THE PAST

From the earliest times Jewish parents tried to see that their children grew up knowing how to live as Jews. Most education took place in the home, by personal example (p. 64). On Shabbat and Rosh Chodesh (New Moon) priests and prophets used to address audiences of both sexes (*II Kings 4:23*), and people used to gather in the Temple courts to listen to learned men.

In the first century CE, a High Priest called Joshua ben Gamla started an elementary school system. He set up schools all over the Holy Land and made communities pay teachers' salaries. During the Middle Ages, wealthy parents employed resident tutors for their sons. The education of the poor was provided by the communities. Yeshivot (singular **yeshiva**), Talmudic academies, offered higher education for boys. Old men would spend much of their day studying in synagogues, where the younger men would join them after their day's work was over. There was no similar educational provision for girls.

During the nineteenth century many changes began taking place in Jewish life (p. 11). People saw that girls also needed a sound Jewish education. Schools and seminaries for girls were opened in Germany, Poland and other places. There, girls began studying the Hebrew language, Bible, Shulchan Aruch (p. 32) and Jewish history (see Unit 44).

JEWISH EDUCATION IN BRITAIN

At the beginning of the twentieth century there was a handful of Jewish elementary schools for the children of refugees who came to Britain to escape persecution in eastern Europe (p. 12). By the First World War many of these schools were in decline and the most common form of Jewish education became the Talmud Torah. This was a system where classes were held on synagogue premises after school hours and on Sunday mornings. There,

boys and girls learned to read Hebrew and were taught basic Jewish subjects. These classes were quite widespread, but largely ineffective. During the 1920s and 1930s many Jews began drifting away from Judaism (p. 12). There was little a Talmud Torah teacher could achieve by telling children that they should not travel on Shabbat (p. 41), for example, when their parents were taking them to football matches on Saturday afternoons.

Jewish education in Britain really began to develop after the Second World War. The Holocaust (p. 16) and the establishment of the State of Israel in 1948 (p. 13) made British Jews begin to feel that their Jewishness mattered (p. 13). Also, during the late 1950s and 1960s there was more money available to support new projects. The result was a steady growth of Jewish schools. Today, there are about 40 Jewish nursery schools, 30 primary schools and 20 secondary schools in Britain. There are two special schools for Jewish children with disabilities. Of the 45,000 Jewish children of school age in this country, about 30 per cent are in Jewish schools. The rest receive their Jewish education by attending **cheder**, a system of part-time learning similar to the old Talmud Torah.

In Jewish schools time is devoted to Jewish subjects. Nursery and primary school children have Jewish songs and stories and act out Shabbat and festival observances. Classrooms are decorated with Jewish motifs. In secondary schools, Jewish texts such as Bible, Talmud and Shulchan Aruch (p. 32) are studied. Some schools prepare boys for yeshiva or girls for seminary (see Unit 44). Most Jewish schools study the life and culture of modern Israel. Jewish secondary schools provide a range of GCSE and A level choices and these usually include Biblical or Modern Hebrew (or both).

Acting out shabbat in a Jewish nursery (see photograph on p. 37)

HIGHER EDUCATION

Most Jews who leave school either start work or go to college or university. For those who want higher Jewish education, there is yeshiva for boys and seminary for girls (p. 91).

The yeshiva is the oldest of all Jewish educational institutions. There is no set course to be followed as in a university, nor a written diploma at the end. Boys are normally accepted from the age of sixteen. They mainly study certain parts of Talmud (p. 31) and are continually assessed by oral examinations. As their standard improves they move up to higher classes where they study the Talmud in greater depth.

Boys prepare for lectures and revise them in a chavruta (companionship), a system where two boys of similar ability work together. Those who have completed all the classes study in a chavruta all the time. They consult the lecturers only when they need to clarify difficult points. To anyone used to the quiet study of a university library, entering a yeshiva can be something of a shock. The learning can become very animated as boys read aloud, question, discuss and dispute. A yeshiva study hall is a lively, noisy place. Each student has to learn to block out the other voices and openly hear his **chaver** (companion).

Other subjects studied are Bible and Shulchan Aruch with their commentaries, Jewish philosophy (mainly Ethics) and Midrashim (p. 33). Yeshiva students study for long hours, sometimes starting before prayers in the morning and usually continuing until about 9 pm.

Very few boys who go to a yeshiva do so because they want to become rabbis. Most yeshiva students simply want to raise their standard of Jewish knowledge and to absorb the atmosphere of holiness and purposefulness which is found there. Those who do wish to become rabbis take a special course, which they begin only after several years of general yeshiva studies (p. 93). Some boys go to a yeshiva for a year between A levels and university, others for a couple of years after they graduate. Five years is about the average length of stay.

Higher Jewish education for girls is described in Unit 44.

ADULT EDUCATION

Education is so important in Jewish life that most synagogues run courses for adults of both sexes. The larger synagogues offer a wide variety of subjects at different levels. There are study groups for senior citizens too. Often a text such as Bible or Talmud is studied and sometimes there are lectures or discussion groups. To cater for all these projects a vast number of books have been published on Jewish topics, many in English. In traditional communities it is usual for men to devote several hours a week to studying Talmud and other texts with a companion (chavruta system).

This age-old ideal of learning from the cradle to the grave made the Jews a highly literate community even when most people in Europe could neither read nor write. Today, the latest educational media such as interactive videos and computerized learning are being used in Jewish studies.

THINGS TO DO

▶ Imagine two schools fairly near to one another. One is a comprehensive, the other is a Jewish secondary school. What differences would you expect to find?

▶ What is the purpose of studying in a yeshiva? What subjects are studied there? How does it differ from a university?

▶ You have been asked to organize a programme of adult education for your local synagogue. How would you go about it?

REFLECTION

'The chavruta system is very challenging because it's not possible to switch off in the way I've done in countless lectures and sessions of private study.'

(Mr B, North London)

FOR DISCUSSION

▶ In many places, the problems that dogged the Talmud Torah system are still experienced today, so that large numbers of Jewish children are receiving very little Jewish education. Discuss how this might be improved.

WOMEN AND MITZVOT

In the past, women's lives centred almost exclusively around the home and family. There were two reasons for this. First, in Jewish society, as in the world at large, women rarely took part in public activities or assumed leadership roles. Second, Judaism taught that marriage and motherhood were important for a woman's own personality development (p. 76).

Today, the feminist movement has achieved far-reaching changes in women's educational and career opportunities. Like other people, religious Jews welcome these changes. However, they believe that some feminists have confused the two issues mentioned above. While they are pleased that there are now opportunities open to women that were previously denied them, they strongly resent the notion, found in some feminist writings, that wifehood and motherhood are burdensome and restrictive. For Jews, raising and nurturing children is a privilege not an imposition.

So important is this, that the halakhah (p. 30) even frees women from those mitzvot which have to be carried out at set times, e.g. putting on tefillin (p. 87), saying the Shema (p. 18), counting the Omer (p. 52). Women are also exempt from the obligation to pray together with the community. Their time cannot be governed by such mitzvot nor by the time the community prays. Of course, many women do choose to carry out some of these mitzvot and attend communal prayers. However, they do these things out of personal choice rather than obligation.

EDUCATION FOR WOMEN

For many centuries, while boys attended school and yeshiva (p. 89), there was no such provision for their sisters. Most girls learnt their Judaism at home, by watching, listening and doing. Wealthy parents sometimes hired private tutors for their daughters, but the range of subjects they were taught was small. Nonetheless, there have been outstanding women throughout history who acquired formidable standards of Talmudic scholarship. Some are mentioned in the Talmud; in particular, Bruria in the second century CE, who was consulted by the rabbis of the day. A famous sixteenth century rabbi had such a learned wife that, when he was absent, she gave halakhic advice to the congregation. Such women, however, were the exception.

The first schools for Jewish girls were established by maskilim (p. 10) during the closing years of the eighteenth century. At these schools, set up in various German cities, girls were taught German and Hebrew, arithmetic, art and handiwork as well as some Jewish studies. However, the purpose of the maskilim was to prepare Jews for integration into German society (p. 10) and these schools often aided the process of assimilation. Rabbi Sampson Raphael Hirsch (p. 132) was the first person to open a secondary school for girls that provided a sound religious and secular education in a spirit of Jewish commitment.

While Jewish education was becoming increasingly available to women in Germany, there was nothing comparable for their sisters in eastern Europe. Sarah Scheneirer (1883–1935), a dressmaker from Cracow, Poland, observed how their lack of education left them exposed to secular culture without any anchor. In 1918 with scant resources, she started teaching a group of teenage girls. When they had learnt some basic Jewish subjects, she sent them out to teach others. Then she began with another group and another. She was a charismatic person who had the ability to inspire others and recognized the importance of having trained teachers to educate her students. By the outbreak of the Second World War, Bet Yaakov (House of Jacob), as her movement came to be called, had established hundreds of schools in eastern and central Europe, catering for over 80,000 Jewish girls. Today, there are schools and seminaries (places of higher Jewish education) for girls all over the world.

The study in a girls' seminary is more structured than in a yeshiva, (p. 89) and the range of subjects

A science lesson in a Jewish girls' school

is wider. There is no set age to start seminary; most girls go after GCSE or A levels. Some seminaries cater specially for women in their 20s and 30s. Students usually follow a three-year course, though many stay for only one or two years and there are examinations with diplomas at the end. The subjects studied include Hebrew, Bible, Midrash, Jewish literature, Jewish history, philosophy and Shulchan Aruch. The method of study is similar to that of a university. There are lectures, written assignments and research projects; the chavruta system of the yeshiva is also used. Most seminaries also offer career training. The most popular are courses in teaching and secretarial skills.

Today, many synagogues have study sessions for women in all subjects and at all levels. In the USA and Israel there are special institutes offering evening courses or short residential courses for women, some catering specifically for older women. Some of these offer courses at a very high academic standard and attract university graduates.

WOMEN IN THE SYNAGOGUE

Women are free to pray wherever they choose. Nor are they tied to the set times of prayer to the same extent as men. Men, on the other hand, have an obligation to take part in communal prayer at fixed times. For these reasons only men may make up a minyan, the ten worshippers needed for communal prayer (but see p. 143). Ten is the minimum number regarded as a communal unit. This is also the reason why most synagogues have a separate area in which men pray (but see p. 138). Women who choose to join the community in prayer, do so in the ladies' section. However, only those who are obligated to be there (i.e. men) will conduct the service, read from the Torah scroll (p. 85) and be called up to recite a blessing over the reading (p. 38).

In recent years, many women have come to feel that they want to take a more active part in the service and pray as a community in their own right. The first women's prayer group was formed in a north west London synagogue in 1992.

In essence, women's prayer groups are nothing new. Girls in seminaries and Jewish schools have been praying in groups for many years. What was new was that the north west London group was holding its prayer sessions in a room in a synagogue building at the same time as the main service. Some rabbis, while recognizing that prayer groups were a means by which women could deepen their religious experience, felt it important that women continue to participate in those prayers which can only be said together with a minyan. The Chief Rabbi ruled, therefore, that on synagogue premises women's prayer groups should take place at times other than when the main service was in session. There are now an increasing number of women's prayer groups. Women are also taking their place on synagogue management boards.

THINGS TO DO

▶ In what area of life were women mainly active in the past?

▶ What has the feminist movement done to change this? How do some Jews feel about feminism?

▶ Which kind of mitzvot are women exempt from? Give some examples.

▶ How did girls receive their Jewish education in the past. What changes did the maskilim bring about?

▶ What was Sarah Scheneirer's contribution to girls' education

▶ What subjects are studied in girls' seminary? How does the study differ from that in a yeshiva?

▶ What is a minyan? Why are men only included in it?

▶ Why did women start forming their own prayer groups?

'All who occupy themselves with the affairs of the community should do so for the sake of Heaven.'

(Ethics of the Fathers)

Jewish communities provide their members with a wide range of services. They do this through the various people who serve the community. Most are employed by the community; some are volunteers.

THE RABBI

Rabbi is a Hebrew word meaning 'my master' or 'sir'. It is a title given to the spiritual leader of a Jewish community (p. 25).

Rabbis in the past

In ancient times rabbis were not employed by communities. They earned their living as carpenters, shoemakers and blacksmiths; some were farmers, others merchants. The rabbis were wise and saintly men and people would turn to them for guidance on a wide range of issues. They were consulted mainly on questions of Jewish law and they gave public lectures.

These rabbis would gather a number of close disciples around them. Many of these disciples would go on to become rabbis themselves. The most outstanding scholars also lectured in the yeshivot (Talmudic academies, p. 89), where they might teach many hundreds of students. Sometimes they would be called upon to judge disputes. To do this they would join up with two other rabbis to form a bet din, a rabbinical court.

This changed in the fourteenth century, when the Black Death wiped out nearly a quarter of the population of Europe. Jews were massacred as they were blamed for having caused the plague (cf p. 9). After the plague, there was so much work to do to rebuild Jewish life that communities began to offer salaries to rabbis. This ensured that the rabbis would be able to devote their whole time to helping the community. At about the same time some rabbis began giving diplomas to their best students. Originally, these were simple letters stating that the student had reached a high standard of learning and that he was of good character. In this way communities could decide whom to employ. These diplomas, known as **semikha**, are still issued to rabbis today.

Rabbis today

A modern rabbi plays many roles. In the synagogue he sometimes leads prayers or reads the weekly **sidra**, the Torah portion (p. 38). He also conducts weddings and funerals. Standards of Jewish learning are generally much lower today than in the past, so rabbis are usually very involved in education. Part of a rabbi's day, in particular on Shabbat, will be spent conducting study sessions. In the larger towns, Jewish educational organizations run classes for children and employ trained teachers.

A rabbi usually has various pastoral duties in the community. He might be the Jewish chaplain to a local hospital or prison, which he will visit regularly. In a university town he will care for the Jewish students. Some rabbis are marriage guidance counsellors; most are consulted on a wide range of domestic and communal matters.

In traditional communities rabbis spend much of their day studying, teaching or deciding matters of Jewish law (like the rabbi in the photo). Sometimes they judge disputes between Jews who want to have their problems sorted out according to Jewish law rather than go to the civil courts.

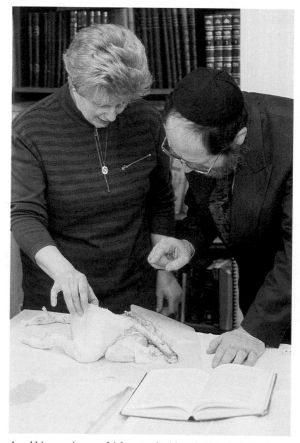

A rabbi examines a chicken to decide whether it is kosher

Training to be a rabbi

A rabbi's training is mainly in Jewish law, in particular kashrut (laws about kosher food, p. 68), Shabbat and festival observance and marriage and mourning customs. In yeshivot (Talmudic academies, p. 89) students only begin their rabbinical training after having completed several years of general Biblical and Talmudic studies.

Some rabbinical colleges are attached to universities. These usually require students to have a degree in Jewish studies before beginning a rabbinical diploma course. Some colleges also offer courses in Jewish philosophy or pastoral skills. Those students who do become rabbis are selected as much for their good characters as for their academic achievements.

Some rabbis choose to continue their studies in a **kollel**, an institute of higher rabbinical learning, before taking up posts with communities. They may spend several years in kollel. Some become lecturers in yeshivot.

Today, there are so many more fields of study than in the past. In the same way that doctors now specialize in certain areas of medicine or lawyers in certain areas of law, many rabbis chose to specialize in particular areas of halakhah (p. 32). Some specialize in halakhic questions relating to medical issues such as abortion, euthanasia, organ transplants; others in halakhic questions revolving around the use of electronic devices on Shabbat and festivals. Still others specialize in the halakhot relating to business and commerce. These rabbis must have a thorough working knowledge of their chosen field of study. Some take degree courses, others work together with specialists in the field.

THE CHAZAN

Many synagogues employ a **chazan** (cantor) to lead the congregation in prayer. He will chant certain parts of the prayers on Shabbat and festivals, but rarely during weekday services. He usually leads the service alone, but in some synagogues there will be a choir to help him. The chazan (plural **chazanim**) often assists the rabbi at weddings, funerals and memorial services. Many synagogues do not have a chazan and prayers are led by members of the congregation.

During his training the chazan will study music and voice projection. He has to learn the various chants for different festivals and the laws about the order of the prayers. Some chazanim will have attended yeshiva, but the majority have no rabbinic training. Apart from his duties in the synagogue, the chazan sometimes provides light entertainment at weddings or similar functions, by singing traditional Jewish songs.

TEST YOURSELF

Choose the correct answer for each of the following.

1 In ancient times rabbis earned their living by
   a telling fortunes
   b various trades
   c teaching
   d selling Jewish books.
2 Rabbinical students study
   a in a kollel
   b in a university
   c by correspondence course
   d in a yeshiva.
3 Rabbis are trained to
   a decide matters of Jewish law
   b take care of a synagogue
   c design a synagogue
   d represent Jews in a court of law.
4 Most rabbis
   a lecture in university
   b teach Jewish study groups
   c teach Jewish subjects in schools
   d lecture in yeshivot (Talmudic academies).
5 A chazan
   a leads the band at weddings
   b chooses people to lead the prayers
   c leads the service in the synagogue
   d teaches people to sing Jewish songs.

THINGS TO DO

▶ Imagine that you are a member of a synagogue committee about to appoint a new rabbi. Make a list of the questions you want to put to the candidates you are going to interview.

▶ How are rabbis trained? (You might wish to read p. 89 before attempting this question.)

THE GABBAI

A **gabbai** is a synagogue warden. The word 'gabbai' actually means 'collector' for in ancient times the gabbai took charge of charity collections. Today, the gabbai is responsible for the overall conduct of the services in the synagogue. He chooses people to lead those prayers not chanted by the chazan and asks members of the congregation to open or close the Ark (p. 84) or take out the Torah scrolls at the appropriate stages of the service. The gabbai also calls people to the reading of the Torah (p. 38). At the end of prayers on Shabbat morning the gabbai announces the times of forthcoming services or special communal events.

THE SHAMASH

The gabbai is assisted by the **shamash** (servant) who makes sure that people have siddurim (prayer books) and tallitot (prayer robes). Most people have their own tallitot, but every synagogue keeps some spares for those who do not. The shamash also sees to it that the rabbi or chazan has wine for kiddush (p. 37) or havdalah (p. 39) and that the siddurim are returned to their shelves at the end of the services.

OTHER SYNAGOGUE WORKERS

As well as those who actually run the services, synagogues have caretakers, sometimes resident, who see that the premises are kept clean, that the heating is turned on and that minor repairs are carried out. A board of officers, usually elected each year, manages the synagogue and runs its finances. Larger synagogues may have several committees to run their various communal and educational activities. These officers and committee members are volunteers.

THE SOFER (SCRIBE)

'One should not live in a town that has no sofer.'

(Talmud)

A sofer writes the Torah scrolls that are used in the synagogue (p. 85), the small scrolls that go into tefillin (p. 87) and also mezuzot (p. 66). He spends much of his time checking and repairing them. Whenever a get (document of divorce, p. 78) has to be written, a sofer will be called upon to do it. Soferim (plural of sofer) have very responsible jobs.

After several years of general yeshiva studies (p. 89), a boy may choose to become a sofer. He will study the necessary laws and will apprentice himself to a qualified sofer. Under his master's guidance he learns to prepare parchment from animal skins, to make ink and to cut quill or reed pens. It takes months of practice to perfect the lettering and he will have to learn the different styles of the Ashkenazi and Sephardi Jews.

He will also learn to open tefillin for inspection (p. 87) and the correct method of sewing them up again. Sometimes he will learn to make the tefillin. Under his master's eye he will also repair Torah scrolls for synagogues.

When an apprentice sofer has reached the required standard he takes an examination in scribal law. His master will then write him a certificate of competence. He is now free to practise as a sofer in his own right.

The sofer has a very responsible job. He must be totally honest for people have to rely on him to ensure that their mezuzot and tefillin are kosher. For example, we saw on p. 67 that mezuzot may only be written in order and that if a sofer spells a word wrongly he might have to erase several words and write over again. If he failed to do this no one would ever know. The community therefore expects soferim to be people of such integrity that their word is beyond doubt.

THE SHOCHET

A **shochet** is a slaughterer of animals. It is a very responsible job, because people rely on the shochet to make sure that their meat is kosher (p. 68).

Like the sofer, the shochet begins his vocational training after several years in a yeshiva. He too will undergo an apprenticeship. While he is studying the laws of shechitah (Jewish method of slaughter, p. 68), he will watch expert slaughterers at work and learn to take care of the special shechitah knife. He has to study the anatomy of animals and birds and learn how to inspect carcasses for defects.

Internal organs that are missing, deformed or diseased often make a carcass **treifah**, (not kosher, p. 68). The trainee shochet must be able to recognize these faults.

A sofer (scribe) writing part of a Torah scroll

The trainee usually starts by slaughtering poultry. He may choose to remain a shochet of poultry or he may progress to the more difficult shechitah of animals. Eventually, when he has reached the right standard and has passed an examination in the laws of shechitah, he will receive a certificate enabling him to practise shechitah. A shochet has to be a deeply religious person. Often he is the only one who knows whether or not he has slaughtered an animal properly. Like the sofer, his word must be beyond doubt.

THE MOHEL

The mohel is responsible for circumcising Jewish males. The details of his work and training are given on p. 73.

THINGS TO DO

▶ Why is the gabbai important in the synagogue?

▶ A synagogue is looking for a new shamash. Prepare an advertisement to put in a Jewish newspaper, outlining the duties the new employee will have to undertake.

▶ What do the sofer and the shochet do? Describe their training. Why is it important for them to be deeply religious people?

▶ What does a mohel do? You have a friend who wants to become a mohel. Read p. 73 and then write a letter, from him to you, describing his training.

MIKVEH ATTENDANTS

Visiting the mikveh after menstruation and childbirth is a very important part of Jewish family life (p. 77). A female attendant will be on hand to make sure that women prepare properly. A good mikveh attendant will go through a checklist with each woman before she immerses. Once in the water, the attendant will stand on the edge and see that she immerses herself correctly. Sometimes a woman's hair will float on the surface and the immersion will not be total. The attendant has to watch out for this.

Mikveh attendants are usually older women. They have to know all the laws about immersion. Above all, they must be kind and understanding. Brides and young wives sometimes feel a little awkward when they begin using the mikveh. They usually find the presence of a sympathetic older woman very reassuring and helpful.

SHATNEZ TESTING

The Torah forbids Jews to wear **shatnez**, wool and linen fibres, in the same garment (*Deuteronomy 22:11*, p. 64).

The prohibition of wearing shatnez is one of the chukim (p. 22) – no reason is given for it. Taking care not to wear shatnez is an act of faith. Observant Jews will have their suits and coats checked before wearing them. Large Jewish communities, such as those in London and Manchester, have shatnez testing facilities. There is another in Gateshead which tests suits for some of the large clothing manufacturers. Individual fibres are taken from selected parts of garments and examined under a microscope to determine what they are. Sometimes chemical tests are used. Shatnez usually takes the form of linen stiffening or internal stitching in woollen garments. When this is found the garment will be sent to a reliable Jewish tailor, who will replace the linen inserts with those of a different fabric.

Fibres as seen under the microscope

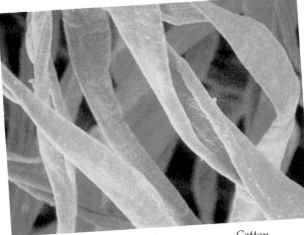

Cotton

Wool

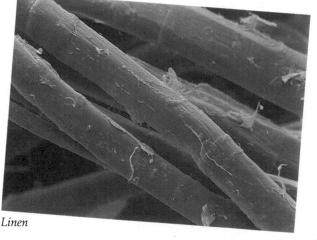

Linen

Silk

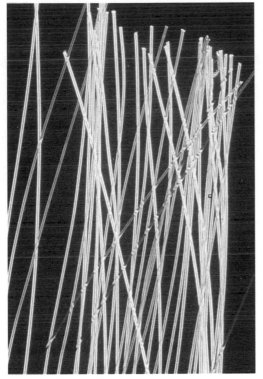

Nylon

THE BET DIN (RABBINICAL COURT)

In Jewish law there is no trial by jury, nor are there professional prosecutors and defenders. A bet din consists of a panel of judges who listen to people presenting their cases and question witnesses themselves. The judges then reach a verdict and give their decision.

In ancient Israel there were three types of bet din, one more senior than the other. Most ordinary cases were considered by three judges. For crimes where a person might receive the death penalty, 23 judges presided. When more than one person's life was at stake, e.g. in considering whether the country should go to war, the decision would be taken by the supreme court of 71 judges – the Sanhedrin. No Jewish court has carried out a death sentence since Roman times. Today, there is only the bet din of three judges.

Most towns with large Jewish populations have a bet din. London has four. The judges (dayanim) are usually very learned rabbis with a good deal of communal experience behind them. Sometimes Jews want to have their business disputes and similar matters judged according to Jewish law and will go to a bet din. Rabbinical courts today, however, are also concerned with divorces and conversions and the supervision of food products.

THE CHEVRA KADDISHA (BURIAL SOCIETY)

Chevra kaddisha means 'holy society'. It is the name given to the men and women who prepare bodies for burial. They are called by this name because Jews regard burying the dead as a holy responsibility. Taking care of the dead is also called 'true kindness' since the one receiving the kindness cannot repay it. A body is thought of as the garment which a soul puts on in order to carry out mitzvot (commandments, p. 22). A soul cannot do mitzvot by itself. For this reason, a body is treated with very great respect.

Members of the chevra kaddisha, who are usually volunteers, must know all the laws about preparing bodies. A Jewish body may not be made up with cosmetics nor dressed up and laid out in a plush casket. Instead, members of the chevra kaddisha wash it carefully, wrap it in a plain linen shroud and place it in a plain wooden coffin. In death, rich and poor are treated equally.

SUPPLIERS OF KOSHER FOOD

Jews are only permitted to eat kosher food (p. 68) and every community will have several shops that sell it. In Jewish areas, even the local supermarkets might have a kosher section. Shopkeepers do not require a licence to sell kosher food since the food products themselves will have a hechsher (seal of kashrut, p. 70) on them. Jewish butchers, bakers and restaurants do require a licence from a bet din (see above) because they prepare the food themselves or, in the case of butchers, sell food that has no distinguishing mark to show that it is kosher. The licence will usually be displayed in the window and the bet din that issued it will make periodic checks on what is being sold.

THINGS TO DO

▶ What does a mikveh attendant do?

▶ What is shatnez? How are garments tested for its presence?

▶ Why are dayanim important in a Jewish community?

▶ What is a hechsher? Why do butchers require one, but not grocers?

'It has been told to you, O man, what is good and what the Lord requires of you; only to do justice and loving kindness and walk humbly with your God.'

(Micah 6:8)

The details of Shabbat observance (p. 41), family purity (p. 77) and other mitzvot can be set down in clear terms of what Jews should or should not do. Indeed, this is what the shulchan aruch does (p. 32). The moral principles of Judaism are not so easy to set down. As we shall see in the pages that follow, the Torah gives guidelines for moral behaviour, but applying those guidelines is often up to the individual.

For example, how far should people tell the truth if it might lead to someone getting hurt (p. 100)? What should be the right blend of justice and compassion in dealing with a criminal? Clearly, we do not always arrive at decisions like these simply by weighing up alternatives and applying logic. What any individual decides will depend on how he or she reads a particular situation and that, in turn, depends on developing a moral sensitivity, i.e. on the kind of people we are. Judaism has important things to say about what constitutes a morally sensitive person.

MORALITY AND HOLINESS

Unlike some other religions, Judaism has no place for hermits – people who withdraw from human company to occupy themselves with their own spiritual progress. In Jewish thinking, holiness without active concern for other people is meaningless. The reverse is also true. Caring for other people while not observing the mitzvot is not true Jewish practice for it is possible to care for people solely out of humanitarian considerations. For Jews, moral behaviour is a way of serving God. Today, many people are moral without trying to progress spiritually. Jews would say that there is an important dimension missing in their morality. 'On three things the world stands,' says the Mishnah, 'On the study of the Torah, on worship and on deeds of kindness.' In Jewish terms, serving God requires time and effort in all of these areas.

These ideas go back to the very origins of the Jewish people. On page 6 we saw that the Jews' first ancestors combined their worship of God with acts of hospitality and that the Ten Commandments demand correct behaviour towards people as part of serving God (p. 26) Centuries later, at a time when people thought they could rob and oppress others as long as they brought their offerings to the temple, the

Learning to share one's possessions with others

prophet Isaiah told them that if they wanted God to hear their prayers, they would have to 'seek justice, relieve the oppressed, treat the orphan justly and help the widow' (Isaiah 1:17). The Mishnah summed it up, 'Anyone in whom people find pleasure, God can find pleasure; but someone in whom people can find no pleasure, God finds no pleasure.'

THE MITZVOT AND PERSONAL DEVELOPMENT

Look back to page 22. There it was explained that keeping the mitzvot leads to personal refinement. Everybody understands that the way we think and feel affects the way we behave. Jewish morality is based on the reverse principle – that the way we behave affects the way we think and feel. Morality is never a simple matter of keeping rules. However, observing the mitzvot consistently until they become second nature does affect the way people develop as individuals.

This is certainly true of the mitzvot Jews call 'between one person and another', i.e. the ethical mitzvot. People who respect their parents, help the poor and are careful not to steal even seemingly small things (like taking the extra change a shopkeeper has given you by mistake) will develop morally.

The mitzvot that Jews call 'between a person and God', i.e. the regular prayers and holy days also play a part in shaping the moral sensitivity of the people who observe them. For example, the Jewish prayers, most of which are in the plural (p. 47) make people aware of the needs of others. The Sabbath, when Jews are not permitted to do any work, is an opportunity to devote time to strengthening family ties, (p. 37). The Passover, when Jews celebrate their ancestors' release from slavery, is a time for reflecting on freedom; the Day of Atonement is an occasion for thinking about forgiveness; Purim, when Jews celebrate their deliverance from a cruel decree (p. 58) brings home the fate of those living under tyrannical regimes.

The destruction of the Jerusalem Temple, in the year 70 CE, is still remembered in many Jewish prayers and marked by several fasts throughout the year. The rabbis of the time saw the destruction as a punishment for the unfriendliness that then existed between one Jew and another. They taught that the time of the Messiah (p. 24), when the Temple would be rebuilt, could be brought nearer by acts of love and compassion towards other people.

The destruction also resulted in the dispersal of Jews throughout the world. The rabbis taught that although this was a punishment for the Jews' sins, it also opened up new opportunities for Jews to play their part in the general moral advancement of humanity. These fasts are particularly appropriate times for reflecting on these ideas.

THE MORAL INDIVIDUAL

In Jewish terms, a moral individual is one who combines personal spiritual progress with concern for other people. Such a person will, on the one hand, constantly be on the look-out for moral inspiration in his or her religious observance. At the same time, he or she will see moral behaviour as an essential part of serving God.

THINGS TO DO

▶ Isaiah, Jeremiah, Hosea and Micah are some of the prophets who preached morality. Use an encyclopedia to find out about their teachings.

FOR YOUR FOLDERS

▶ What is morality? Why are moral decisions not a simple matter of setting down possible alternatives and using logic?

▶ 'Love your neighbour like yourself.' (*Leviticus 19:18*) is one of the best known moral statements of the Torah. What do you think it means? Suggest realistic ways in which it might be put into practice.

▶ What is a hermit? Why do such people have no place in Judaism?

▶ Imagine that you are a rabbi, and that you have just given a talk on Jewish morality. Someone in the audience comments, 'Jews aren't really moral people, they just keep rules.' What would you say?

▶ The Jewish travellers' prayer (prayer for a safe journey) is always said in the plural even though one might be travelling alone. This is so that Jews can pray on behalf of all the other people who might be travelling at the same time. Why might people want to pray for a safe journey? Do you think the Jewish travellers' prayer has any moral value? Explain your answer.

▶ What are 'commandments between a person and God'? Give three examples. How might observing these commandments help a person's moral development?

▶ How did the destruction of the second Temple (p. 8) open up new moral challenges for Jews?

'O my God, guard my tongue from evil and my lips from speaking deceitfully.'

(Prayer Book)

The Midrash tells the story of a man who had a wise servant. One day he told his servant to go and buy the best meat in the market. The servant brought back a tongue. The next day he sent him to buy the worst thing in the market. Again, the servant returned with a tongue. When he asked the servant to explain what he had bought, he replied, 'Nothing is better than a good tongue, and nothing is worse than a bad one.'

Judaism has always stressed the importance of the spoken word. Jews are expected to be truthful, neither to humiliate nor mislead another person, nor spread rumours: the more influential the person, the greater the care he or she is expected to exercise when using words. 'Even the everyday speech of Torah scholars deserves study,' says the Talmud. Naturally, this also applies to words in writing or in print.

You never know who's listening!

CARELESS TALK COSTS LIVES

The power of the spoken word in a World War II poster. What is it trying to convey?

TRUTH AND FALSEHOOD

Being truthful is an important Jewish ideal. The Torah tells Jews to 'Keep far away from a false word' (*Exodus 23:7*), and again, 'That which goes out of your lips you shall keep and do' (*Deuteronomy 23:24*). The Talmud calls truth God's seal.

The difference between truth and falsehood is not always clear and simple. There are many situations where holding back some of the truth might be the nobler thing to do. For example, Jewish teaching disapproves of boasting. The Talmud permits people to withhold the truth when questioned about their achievements. It also recommends, when praising people, not recounting all of their achievements in front of them.

There can even be times when a lie is preferable to the truth. Elisha, one of the great Jewish prophets, was asked by a sick Aramean king whether he would recover. Elisha saw that he would die, yet to have said so would have been unnecessarily cruel. He told the king's messenger, 'Go, say to him "You shall certainly live".' (*II Kings 8:7–15*). Some see this as a classic situation of where telling the truth would have been morally wrong.

There have been many situations throughout history where people have had similar dilemmas. During the Holocaust (p. 16) there were instances where people put their lives at risk to hide Jews. Yet they knew that when they lied to the German soldiers, they were doing the right thing.

It is also possible to tell the truth, but to say it in such a way as to imply something that is not true. This happens fairly often in advertising. For example, a manufacturer of washing-up liquid might claim that its product contains no nitrates. This would be perfectly true, since washing-up liquids never contain nitrates! However, since the manufacturer wants people to buy its goods, it is using the truth in such a way as to make the product appear more environmentally friendly than its competitors. This might not be so at all. The Talmud calls this **genevat daat**, 'deception'. It is a practice Judaism strictly forbids.

There are other situations where truth becomes so critical that the slightest deviation from the truth, even unwittingly, becomes a sin. An example of this is an oath – a statement made with reference to God or some holy object as a means of declaring it to be true. The Talmud teaches that oaths are very serious things indeed and advises people to avoid making them. Many Jews, called to give evidence in a court of law, choose to 'affirm' that they will tell the whole truth rather than swear to it.

This does not mean that their testimony is suspect. Rather it means that, while taking truth very seriously, they recognize that memory can let them down or they might misunderstand something.

SPREADING RUMOURS

'Do not go about as a tale-bearer.'

(*Leviticus 19:16*)

One of the most serious offences for a Jew is **leshon hara**, literally, 'a tongue of evil'. Jews use this term to describe passing on unpleasant information about another person. The Torah strictly forbids this, even though the information might be true. It is all too easy to slip into this kind of talk. People do it even without thinking. For this reason the Talmud calls leshon hara a 'sin that a person treads underfoot'. However, this too is not clear cut. There are always circumstances when passing on unpleasant information is necessary and permitted. For example, it would be right to warn a shopkeeper to be careful about accepting cheques from a dishonest customer.

CAUSING EMBARRASSMENT

'Someone who humiliates another person in public has no share in the World to Come.'

(*Ethics of the Fathers*)

Unkind words can make people feel very uncomfortable. People who have been humiliated will sometimes continue to feel the discomfort whenever they think about it. This is what the Talmud means when it says, 'You can kill a person only once, but when you humiliate him, you kill him many times over.'

FIND OUT

▶ In English law, a person can be sued in court for libel, slander, perjury or violating the Trades Descriptions Act. Find out what these are. How far are they consistent with Jewish moral teachings?

THINGS TO DO

▶ Why is being truthful an important ideal in Judaism? When might Jews consider it preferable not to tell the truth?

▶ How might (a) a shopkeeper, (b) a journalist, (c) a detective, (d) a film critic and (e) an estate agent have to take care in order to live by the teachings discussed in this unit?

▶ What is genevat daat? Can you think of any examples apart from those given here? Why do you think Jews regard it as wrong?

▶ The Midrash tells the following story:

'One day Truth came into the world. She went to a big city expecting to be greeted with joy, but instead everyone turned their backs on her. The same thing happened in city after city; Truth was shunned everywhere. Saddened, Truth left the towns and sat down by the roadside. Along came Parable, and asked her, "Why are you crying?" Truth told him what had happened. "I just don't understand why people turn away from me," sobbed Truth. "But just look at you," said Parable. "You are naked. That's why no one wants to acknowledge you. Come, I will clothe you." So Parable clothed Truth and wherever she went people accepted her.'

Explain what you think the story means.

▶ A company offering package holidays abroad has asked you to help design their travel brochure. Write two drafts of the same paragraph, one which includes genevat daat and the other not. Which do you think the company will prefer? Explain your answer.

'Not to have known suffering is not to be truly human.'

(Midrash)

For anyone who believes that God is good, all-powerful and ever-present (p. 18), suffering raises obvious questions. Why do innocent people suffer? Why does a child have an incurable illness? For Jews today there is the agonizing question of the Holocaust (p. 16) – why were six million men, women and children murdered by the Nazis between 1933 and 1945? Many have asked, 'Where was God in the concentration camps?'

Jews have always recognized that there are no simple answers to these questions. Only the prophets (p. 7), who heard the voice of God, were ever able to pinpoint the reasons for particular calamities. Rather than try to give reasons for suffering, the rabbis formulated ways of approaching it. These were often based on the stories of the Tenakh.

SUFFERING IN THE TENAKH

The Tenakh describes the sufferings of people like Joseph, who was sold into slavery by his brothers (*Genesis 37:28*), Ruth, who endured young widowhood and poverty (*Ruth 1:2–5*) and King David, whose infant son died (*II Samuel 12:1–18*). We read of how they coped with their ordeals and came through them. The book of *Job* deals entirely with

suffering. It tells of a man who lost his home and family, endured appalling pain and torment, yet never once turned against God (p. 28).

Stories such as these offer ways of coming to terms with suffering. Sometimes suffering might be a punishment sent by God (e.g. *Judges 3:7–8*), a test of faith (*Genesis 22:1–2*) or God's way of prompting people to return to Him (*Leviticus 26:41*). There might be other reasons. But wherever we look in the Talmud, two points emerge: (a) suffering does not just happen, it is brought about by God; (b) since suffering comes from God it must serve some purpose.

TEACHINGS OF THE RABBIS

Based on these two ideas, the rabbis of the Talmud and Midrash offered some very important insights into suffering. They never tried to *justify* suffering. However, they did try to show that it is possible for some good to come from it. They taught people to see suffering as a call to repent, that people are responsible for one another and that good people sometimes suffer for the sake of the wicked; they taught that God only tests those who can stand up to a trial and that He never afflicts people beyond what they can endure; and they showed that suffering can help refine peoples' characters teaching them to be patient, humble, sensitive to the suffering of others, conscious of the brevity of human life and alert to its purpose.

They taught that suffering is many sided; it is

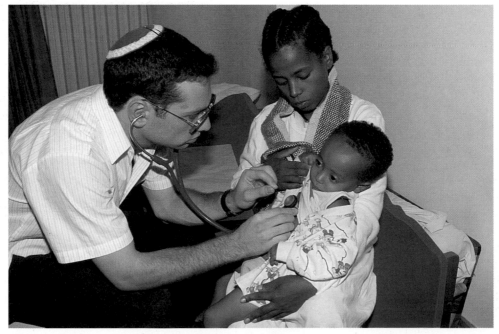

Relief of suffering is an important Jewish ideal

seldom solely a punishment or a test or a way of changing a person's outlook on life. Most important of all, they pointed out that if people are to come through suffering they have draw upon inner reserves of strength they might otherwise never have known they had. They can sometimes emerge as better people.

JEWISH PHILOSOPHY

The Jewish philosophers, taking a different approach, arrived at a further insight. For them, suffering was necessary so that people should have freedom of choice (p. 20). If God only showered us with blessings, we would have no choice but to love Him. As a result we would have to do good. Suffering makes it possible for us to reject God and do evil. Suffering is, therefore, important as it makes us totally free to choose between good and evil.

RELIEF OF SUFFERING

The rabbis were not content simply to show that suffering can have a purpose. They also taught that every effort should be made to avoid it (the Talmud contains a good deal of sound advice for avoiding illness and not taking unnecessary risks) and to relieve it. Jews have always regarded it as a religious duty to visit the sick, provide for the poor or comfort the bereaved. Since the earliest times Jewish communities have always set up organizations for providing for those in need (p. 118). The rabbis also pointed out the role of entertainment. The Talmud tells the story of a rabbi who wanted to see someone who had earned a place in heaven. He was shown two men in the market place. He ran up to them and asked, 'What is your occupation?' They replied, 'We are clowns; we try to lift people out of their sadness.'

EUTHANASIA

In Jewish thinking, killing people to put them out of their misery is murder. It is forbidden even if a sick person requests it. However, allowing people to continue suffering conflicts with the Jewish ideal of doing everything possible to bring relief. Although Jews may not actively terminate someone's life, therefore, the rabbis do permit withholding treatment from patients who are really beyond help, especially where the treatment is likely to cause pain or distress (e.g. chemotherapy), while keeping the patient as comfortable and pain-free as possible.

Switching off a life-support machine would also be murder if there was any possibility, however remote, that the patient might recover. If a patient no longer has any heart, brain or lung functions, the rabbis permit turning off the machine. Without these functions the machine is not *supporting* life – it is *providing* it.

FOR YOUR FOLDERS

▶ To what extent might their religious teachings help Jews to cope with suffering?

▶ Explain what the Jewish philosophers meant when they said that suffering is necessary so that we should have free choice.

▶ Write a letter from a Jew to the parents of a terminally ill friend. (Remember, they are suffering as well as your friend.)

▶ 'If God is all-powerful, He could stop people suffering. If he is all-good, He could not want them to suffer. Since people do suffer, God is either not all-good or not all-powerful.' How might a Jew respond to this view?

▶ The Mishnah (p. 30) states, 'A person must bless God for bad things – the same way as for good things.' What do you think this means? What might it do for people if they can bring themselves to thank God for suffering? How might it change their outlook on life?

▶ What is euthanasia? When do the rabbis permit a life-support machine to be turned off? What is their reason?

THINKING POINT

● Judaism teaches that the human body is God's creation and therefore his possession. How do you think this view has shaped the Jewish attitude to euthanasia?

'Keeping the body fit and healthy is part of serving God, for it is impossible to know or understand anything of the Creator's will if one is ill. Therefore a person should avoid whatever undermines bodily health.'

(Maimonides)

In Jewish teaching, keeping the body clean and healthy is a religious duty. This does not mean that Jews are expected to eat health-foods and do aerobics. It does mean that they are to treat the body sensibly, keep it clean and try to avoid harming it.

CLEANLINESS

The Talmud (p. 31) tells the story of Hillel, a first-century rabbi, who once told his students that he was going to carry out an important mitzvah (p. 22). When they asked him what he was going to do, he told them that he was going to the bath-house. 'Is that a mitzvah?' they asked. 'Yes,' he replied. 'See how the statues of kings which are set up in the theatres and arenas are scrubbed and kept clean by specially appointed officials. Should not we, who are created in the image of God (*Genesis 1:27*), have even greater regard for the cleanliness of our bodies?'

'A person must wash his face, hands and feet each day in honour of his Creator.'

(Talmud)

The Talmud also teaches Jews not to pray without having rinsed their mouths in the morning (except on fast days), and to wash their hands before meals and after leaving the lavatory. These are all religious duties. However, there have been 'fringe benefits'. For example, during the Great Plague of London (1665), when people were dying by the hundreds, hardly any Jews became ill.

HEALTH

Today, people are more health-conscious than in the past. However, even in ancient times, people were aware that there were simple ways of taking care of their bodies. The Talmud contains a good deal of sound practical advice for healthy living. For example, it advises people to eat and sleep at regular times but never to excess; and not to sit, stand or walk for long periods. It also points out that the body is affected by mental and spiritual health. 'Three things drain a person's health: worry, travel and sin.'

Jews are also commanded to avoid harming their bodies. The Talmud expressly warns people not to do things that could be dangerous, such as entering a derelict building, walking across a rickety bridge or drinking from a river at night (when one cannot see what one is drinking).

Today there are three widespread habits that are known to be harmful:

- drinking alcohol
- taking drugs
- smoking tobacco.

Alcohol

Jews are not forbidden to drink alcohol. Indeed, they use wine in various religious ceremonies (p. 37 and p. 39). However, Judaism strongly disapproves of consuming alcohol in large quantities.

'Do not be among the wine bibbers, or the gluttons who fill themselves with meat' (*Proverbs 23:20*). The Midrash warns: 'Wine enters, sense goes out; wine enters, secrets come out.'

In Jewish law, drinking even a small amount of alcohol is inadmissible for people with responsible jobs. A priest in the Temple (p. 7) or a judge who had drunk even one glass of wine would be considered unfit to officiate or pass judgement until a suitable time had elapsed.

Today, we know that heavy drinking can cause brain damage, liver damage and impair the blood-clotting process. Many Jews regard excessive alcohol consumption as being similar in principle to the harmful practices the Talmud forbids.

Drugs

Whereas drugs are useful when used medically to relive pain and suffering, their abuse leads to altered mental states, and sometimes to coma and death. Some young Jews are becoming addicted to drugs, though the problem is virtually unknown in religious families. A number of Jewish care organizations now run drug-counselling services (p. 119), and it has been suggested that drug education should be given in synagogue religion classes.

There are three halakhic (p. 30) objections to alcohol and drug abuse; (i) Jews are forbidden to break the laws of the country in which they live (p. 120) and most countries have laws against drunkenness and drug taking/peddling; (ii) consuming alcohol and taking drugs leads to loss of self-control, making it impossible to observe one's religious obligations while, at the same time leaving oneself open to transgressing God's commands; and

(iii) in Jewish teaching a person does not own their body and is therefore forbidden to inflict damage upon it; the body is God's creation (*Genesis 2:7*) and must be treated with respect (p. 97). This last consideration would also apply to smoking tobacco.

Tobacco

Tobacco smoking is a fairly recent habit, and over the years large numbers of Jews have taken it up. However, as it gradually became known that tobacco smoking was a major cause of lung disease, many Jews came to regard it as inconsistent with their religious teachings. Today, it is known that people can be harmed by breathing in other people's tobacco smoke, passive smoking – and in 1982, Rabbi Eliezer Waldenberg, a major authority on medical matters in Jewish law, wrote:

> *'There are sufficient grounds to forbid smoking according to the Torah. Similarly, when someone is smoking in a public place, those in the vicinity who are concerned about their health have a right to object.'*

Although the majority of rabbis have not wanted to issue an outright ban on smoking, many have tried to discourage it, urging parents not the let children take up the habit. Today, fewer Jews smoke than in the past and other rabbis are following Rabbi Waldenberg's lead. Some synagogues have now become no-smoking areas, setting aside one room for those who wish to smoke.

SUICIDE

In Jewish thinking, God is the giver of life, and the only one who has the right to take life away (*Deuteronomy 32:39*). Judaism only gives people the right to take life in self-defence, war (p. 122) or where a court of law passes a death sentence (p. 121). Suicide is regarded as such a serious sin that a Jew who does commit suicide is not buried together with other Jews, but in a separate part of the cemetary. However, this would not be carried out where the person committing suicide was mentally unbalanced or if there were grounds for thinking that they repented before dying (e.g. when someone who

took an overdose of drugs and was then overcome with remorse but unable to do anything about it).

THINGS TO DO

▶ Why do Jews regard cleanliness as a religious duty? According to a Talmudic expression, 'A rabbi with a stain on his clothes deserves to be put to death.' What do you think this saying means?

▶ Discussions about drinking and driving often revolve around the idea of a 'safe level' of alcohol consumption. What bearing might Jewish teachings have on these discussions?

▶ You are the secretary of a synagogue. The committee has voted to set aside a room for people who wish to smoke. Compose the letter you intend sending to all members, explaining the new rule.

▶ How far are Jewish people likely to agree with people who say that the use of drugs, alcohol and tobacco is up to individuals to decide?

▶ Why do Jews regard suicide a serious sin? How do they treat a person who commits suicide?

FOR YOUR FOLDERS

▶ What does the story of Hillel tell you about the importance of cleanliness in Judaism?

▶ Find out all you can about the Great Plague of London. How was it spread? Why do you think that very few Jews died in it?

*'If men fight and one injures the other . . .
He (i.e. the attacker) must make sure that he
(i.e. the injured man) is completely healed
[Exodus 21:19]. From here we see that it is
right for physicians to heal.'*

(Talmud)

Treating illness is an important Jewish ideal. In the Torah, God himself says 'I, the Lord, am your healer' (*Exodus 15:26*); and in their morning prayers Jews praise God as 'the healer of all flesh'. Since Jews are taught not to rely on miracles, they see doctors as the instrument through whom God heals the sick.

Medicine has always raised ethical questions. In the past, these were relatively uncomplicated questions, such as whether it was right to run away from a plague-ridden city or whether one should eat non-kosher food if a doctor had recommended it as a cure. The possibilities opened up by modern medical and surgical techniques raise much more difficult questions. Some of these problem areas are outlined in this unit.

AUTOPSIES

Autopsies (post-mortem examinations) raise a number of halakhic problems. Jews are forbidden to mutilate a corpse, derive benefit from one or delay burial. However, the all-important principle of preserving life overrides these considerations. The definitive statement was set down by Rabbi Yechezial Landau (1713–93) who permitted an autopsy where it would provide information that could cure another patient who was near at hand. Today, with instant communication and rapid global travel, many rabbis regard 'near to hand' to include anywhere in the world.

Rabbis have also extended this ruling to performing an autopsy on anyone suffering from an obscure, little understood disease (provided the patient consented to it previously) since other patients will benefit from the information gained. Where the patient has not given consent before they died, a group of rabbis may meet to authorize the autopsy, provided that the next of kin have given their consent.

An autopsy requested by a coroner has to be carried out by law. Naturally, Jews comply with this law.

ORGAN TRANSPLANTS

Organ transplants are of two types: those from a living donor and those from a dead one. Should a living person donate an organ, for example, a kidney to someone else? The question here is really whether one should endanger one's own life to save another. Most rabbis agree that it is permissible where the recipient's life is at risk (or could become so) and where the donor is in good health and has consented to the removal of an organ. However, a person cannot be compelled to endanger their life in this way.

Removing an organ from a dead patient, for example, heart, lung or cornea, raises all the issues mentioned above with regard to autopsies. Rabbis agree that these considerations may be set aside to save a life, i.e. where a particular patient is waiting for the organ . Many rabbis put eye transplants in the same category, since a blind person is constantly at risk of walking into life-threatening situations.

The most serious consideration in this kind of transplant is determining when the donor is dead. This is particularly important in heart transplants since a heart is only usable if it is removed fairly soon after the donor's death. Even though the recipient is waiting desperately for the organ, one may not murder one patient, no matter how hopelessly terminally ill he or she is, to save the life of another.

ABORTION

In Jewish thinking, abortion is more objectionable than contraception. The latter impedes God's will (p. 22); abortion actually destroys potential life. The destruction of a viable foetus is forbidden for Jews and non-Jews alike.

At the same time, Judaism does not give the foetus, which is only potential life, the same importance as the mother, who is actually alive. Abortion is therefore acceptable if a pregnancy becomes hazardous for the mother (or might become so), or if she is likely to be severely psychologically affected. Some rabbis permit abortion where a child is likely to be so retarded that it would never function as a human being. However, Judaism could *never* agree with terminating a pregnancy because it got in the way of holiday arrangements or because it might disrupt a woman's career.

An anti-abortion rally, USA. To what extent are such campaigns consistent with Jewish teachings?

INFERTILITY

Due to the great importance Jews attach to raising a family (p. 108), the rabbis have explored every means of helping infertile couples. They have permitted artificial insemination by husband (*never by donor*), though with strict safeguards to ensure that only the husband's semen is used. Some even permit masturbation (which is otherwise strongly disapproved of), where no other method is available for obtaining semen for sperm counts or insemination procedures.

In vitro fertilization (fertilizating an ovum in the laboratory and implanting it in a woman's womb) is still very new. Some rabbis have welcomed the procedure, though they insist that it too should be governed by safeguards. However, *none* agrees with implanting one women's fertilized ovum in another women's womb (surrogate motherhood). Paying a woman a fee to 'lease' her womb could lead to all sorts of abuses. Women could have children without the 'inconvenience' of being pregnant; others could turn pregnancy into a profitable business, knowing that they will not be tied down with a child afterwards. The possible psychological stresses on *both* women are completely unpredictable. The rabbis see this as destroying the sanctity of marriage and childbirth.

Many rabbis also regard it as morally wrong to freeze a husband's semen for use after his death, as this deliberately brings orphans into the world. This could only be sanctioned when a man is undergoing some treatment (e.g. for cancer) that might destroy his sperm, and he expects to be alive to raise his child.

Equally important is the spiritual help and moral boost that religious leaders have given in this area. Priests, prophets and rabbis have always given their blessings to childless couples (*see* II *Kings 4:14–16*). Today's rabbis often encourage couples to continue seeking medical help, even though they themselves have felt like giving up.

FOR YOUR FOLDERS

▶ 'A woman has the right to do what she wants with her own body.' How might Jews respond to this view?

THINGS TO DO

▶ In Jewish thinking, who heals – God or the doctor?

▶ Why do post-mortem examinations present problems for Jews? Under what circumstances do rabbis sanction it?

▶ What possible dangers do you think a blind person faces?

▶ What do Jews regard as the most important question relating to heart transplants?

▶ What is infertility? How do Jews deal with it?

The family is fundamentally important in Jewish life. It is the setting in which a husband and wife reach full maturity as personalities (p. 76), where children receive their earliest education (p. 64) and where the basis of their identity is formed. The Torah, and later the rabbis, laid down some ground rules governing the relationship between various family members.

HUSBAND AND WIFE

A husband's primary duty is to feed and clothe his wife and make her welfare his first priority. In the ketubah (marriage document, p. 77) every Jewish husband undertakes to support his wife 'even if I have to sell the coat from off my back.' The ketubah also makes provisions for the wife's maintenance in the event of the couple divorcing or the husband predeceasing her.

PARENTS AND CHILDREN

'Honour your father and your mother.'

(Exodus 20:12)

Judaism teaches that parents and children have responsibilities towards one another. Parents are expected to feed and clothe their children and show them how to live as Jews. They must also see that

Illustrated ketubah (nineteenth century)

they can support themselves. 'Teach your son a trade,' says the Talmud,' or you teach him to become a robber.'

The Talmud also recommends that parents teach children to swim, i.e. basic survival skills. In today's terms this would include such things as road safety and wariness of accepting lifts from strangers. While much of this is common sense, for Jews these things are religious obligations.

Children are expected to treat their parents with respect and take care of them. 'See that they eat and drink and take them where they need to go,' says the Talmud.

Naturally, parents are only human and they sometimes do wrong. Judaism insists that children have an obligation to point out their parents' shortcomings. However, it would be wrong for them to shout at their parents or be sarcastic. They must be as tactful as possible and try to avoid hurting their feelings.

THE EXTENDED FAMILY

In her book about the time she spent with a **Hasidic** family (p. 130), Lis Harris, a former editor of *New Yorker* magazine, wrote:

'. . . Bassy, the youngest, who was nineteen, was with her grandmother. Bassy, a slim, spirited girl who in the secular world would probably be taken for the captain of her field hockey team, had explained to me several hours earlier, as she hastily gathered a few belongings together and headed for the door, that she spent Shabbat (Sabbath) with her widowed grandmother who lived around the corner. "Sometimes she comes here for Shabbat but sometimes she likes to stay at home, so I help her prepare everything and I stay overnight to keep her company." When I said that most of the girls her age that I knew would not be eager to do that, she looked genuinely surprised.

"But I don't mind at all. It's no problem. You'll see when you meet Bubbe (Grandma). She's great. Actually I've spent every night with her since she

had to have one of her fingers removed because of cancer last year. It's really no big deal."

All the Bubbies' and Zeydes' (grandfathers') places in their families were secure, of course, because though personality conflicts were as common in the Hasidic world as anywhere else, the values of the older and the younger members of the family were the same. There was no generation gap.'

The importance of the family unit is a principle that affects others areas of Jewish practice too. For example, Jews place great stress on **tzedaka**, giving charity (p. 116) to those in need. However, they regard helping one's own brother or sister (or other close relative) as coming before helping others.

FOR YOUR FOLDERS

▶ What do the extracts from Lis Harris's book tell you about the place of the elderly in religious Jewish families?

▶ How do you think the point about the values of the old and young affects family relationships?

▶ Why do you think Jews regard family relationships as important?

▶ A Jewish teenager wants to go out with friends on a Friday night (Sabbath). The parents are very unhappy about this. Write out the conversation that might take place.

▶ If a parent tells a son or daughter to do something which is against the teachings of Judaism, what do you think the child ought to do? Try to give an example and explain the young person's dilemma.

'The Torah lists the forbidden sexual relationships and then says "You shall be Holy" (Leviticus 19:2). This tells you that even in a permitted relationship you must sanctify yourself.'

(Rabbi Moses ben Nachman, 1194–1270)

Judaism teaches that sexuality plays an important role in human relationships and has always taken a very natural view of it. The Talmud discusses sexual matters quite frankly, but always in an atmosphere of modesty. This is a way of recognizing that the sexual urge can generate very powerful emotions and that sexual behaviour should be carefully regulated.

ACCEPTABLE SEXUAL PRACTICE

In Jewish thinking, sexual activity is only acceptable within marriage – a stable relationship between one man and one woman. Through sexual intercourse husband and wife fulfil the first commandment of Torah, 'be fruitful and multiply' (*Genesis 1:28*). Bringing children into the world is regarded as a holy act – an act in which a man and woman become partners with God in creating new life. However, Judaism recognizes that this is not its only purpose. Through sexuality, two people who are sharing their lives can express their love for one another in a way that is deeply personal to them. For this reason it is considered natural and purposeful even beyond the age of childbearing.

FORBIDDEN SEXUAL PRACTICES

The Torah strictly forbids adultery (a sexual relationship with someone else's husband or wife) and incest. Incestuous relationships are those between brother and sister, father and daughter, mother and son, and other people related by family or marriage (*Leviticus 18:6–23*). The Torah also forbids a sexual relationship between one man and another. 'You shall not lie down with a man in the same way that you would lie down with a woman; it is an abomination.' (*Leviticus 18:22*). Lesbian sexual activity is not mentioned in the Torah, though the Talmud refers to it with disapproval.

In recent years, homosexual pressure groups have campaigned to make their sexual preferences acceptable. They often put forward the view that homosexuals are by nature different and cannot be other than what they are. No one has yet produced satisfactory evidence to prove this. In contrast, many people strongly believe that homosexuality can *develop* for a variety of reasons and that many of those with homosexual inclinations can, if they wish, be 'helped' by regular psychotherapy.

Of course, Judaism considers close friendships between people of the same gender as perfectly acceptable. Indeed, the rabbis held up the relationship between David and Jonathan (King Saul's son, p. 7) as an example of a pure, selfless friendship. It is specifically *sexual* activity between men that Judaism finds objectionable (but see p. 138). In Jewish thinking, a man feeling attracted towards another man is no different from him being attracted to someone else's wife. In both cases, allowing his attraction to lead to a sexual relationship is a sin. However, Judaism does not permit men or women with homosexual leanings to be persecuted or discriminated against.

Judaism also forbids prostitution – either becoming one or using the services of one. Jews have always regarded prostitution as cheapening sexuality by detaching it from its real context as part of a loving, husband–wife relationship and turning it into a commodity to be sold. They see it as a degrading, unclean practice. For this reason, prostitutes have always been regarded with disdain. Nonetheless, Jews can feel profound sympathy for a man or woman driven to prostitution through poverty and would want to bring them back to what they see as a respectable way of living.

Judaism is very strict in its laws regulating sexual behaviour. Jews disapprove strongly of the kind of lifestyle that involves having several sexual partners, whether heterosexual or homosexual. At the same time, however, they can feel sympathetic towards a man or woman who caught AIDS from a sexual contact. For Jews, there is no contradiction between disapproving of a person's lifestyle and feeling compassion for a human being who is suffering.

CONTRACEPTION

The Jewish writings teach that when 'God formed the world . . . He created it not to remain empty; He made it to be populated' (*Isaiah 45:18*). This is because of His desire that there should be people who will fulfil His will, bring holiness into the world and prepare it as His dwelling (p. 22). Contraception impedes this.

On the other hand, Judaism regards preserving life as of prime importance. Where it might be hazardous for a woman to become pregnant, the rabbis insist that contraceptives should be used. The same holds true where pregnancy might put a woman under severe psychological strain.

Temporary use of contraceptives is also acceptable in circumstances where a woman has just had a child and feels unable to cope with another. However, using contraception for the sake of convenience is not acceptable in Jewish teaching.

Where contraception is used, it is governed by halakhah (p. 30) and Jewish ethical principles. The rabbis felt it important that intercourse be as natural as possible. This makes methods that prevent fertilization preferable to barrier methods, i.e. methods that physically block the passage of sperm. The most halakhically acceptable method is oral contraception (commonly known as the Pill). For women who cannot safely use oral contraceptives (for example, women with heart disease or liver disease) a barrier method is permissible. As a contraceptive method the intrauterine device (IUD), commonly known as the coil, is acceptable to Jews. However, it often causes minor bleeding from the womb. This is of no medical significance but, according to the halakhah, such bleeding would make the woman nidah (p. 77) and require husband and wife to cease all physical contact until after she had visited the mikveh (p. 82), a minimum span of twelve days.

Where a barrier contraceptive is used the diaphragm is preferable to the condom. The latter is regarded as completely unnatural since it creates a barrier to complete bodily contact between husband and wife. Feminine condoms would be unacceptable for the same reason. These would only be acceptable in circumstances where a woman might be at risk if she become pregnant and no other method was available.

Vasectomy, cutting and tying the tubes that carry sperm from the testes is regarded as a form of castration. This is forbidden to Jews unless there are sound medical reasons for doing it. The same principle applies to sterilizing women.

THINGS TO DO

▶ Why do Jews regard sexual activity as only appropriate within marriage?

▶ The advertising industry often uses sexual imagery as a means of selling products. Find some examples in newspapers and magazines. Do you think using sexuality in this way is consistent with Jewish teaching? Explain your answer.

▶ Why do Jewish teachings place restrictions on contraception? According to British law, doctors can make contraceptives available to girls under the legal age of consent without having to inform the girls' parents. Write a letter from a Jewish mother to her doctor, giving her views on the subject.

▶ What is homosexuality? Explain the Jewish view.

▶ How would Jews behave towards someone with AIDS?

◇

FOR DISCUSSION

▶ Discuss the view that prostitution should be legalized. (Remember to include the Jewish attitude in your discussion.)

'The study of Torah together with an occupation is an excellent thing.'

(Ethics of the Fathers)

In Jewish belief people are put into this world to serve God (p. 22). To do this properly, Judaism teaches that they must work. Work is important not only because it enables people to earn their livelihoods, but also for developing the personality of the individual.

◇

WORK AND THE INDIVIDUAL

In Jewish teaching it is necessary for people to have an occupation. 'Idleness leads to immorality,' said one rabbi in the Mishnah; 'It leads to depression,' said another. A well-balanced person is one who has an occupation, with time set aside for Torah study (p. 65). All the rabbis of the Talmud had an occupation; among the most outstanding rabbis of that period was a blacksmith, a shoemaker, a farmer, a stonemason, a weaver and a merchant.

Work also elevates humans above the animals. The Talmud describes God driving Adam out of the Garden of Eden (*Genesis 3:17–19*). When God tells him that the ground will grow thorns and thistles, Adam is stunned at the thought that he will have to root around for food together with the animals. Then God says to him, 'By the sweat of your face you shall eat bread.' As soon as he hears this Adam is relieved. He realizes that he can earn his own food by working. To be human is to be able to work, to control one's environment and be responsible for it.

For Jews, work is also necessary for fulfilling God's will. Judaism has no place for hermits, people who withdraw from the world of work and human contact to spend their time in spiritual pursuits (p. 98). It teaches that people have to serve God by being active in the world, bringing God's will into every sphere of activity.

'Great is work. God's presence only rested upon the Jewish people when they began occupying themselves with useful work.'

(Midrash)

WORK AND THE COMMUNITY

Work is also vital for the health of the community. People need to feel valued through being productive. The Talmud tells the story of an old man planting fruit trees. A Roman officer, who happened to be passing, asked him why he was toiling when he would never live to enjoy the benefits. The old man replied, 'Just as my father planted for me, so I am planting for my children.'

A healthy community is one where every person is contributing to the common good. Unemployment is harmful to society, since in some cases it might lead to crime. 'Teach your son a trade,' says the Talmud, 'or you teach him to become a robber.' Jews are permitted to take up any occupation they wish, except those which are likely to bring harm to people physically (such as drug trafficking) or morally (like selling pornographic literature). Indeed, in Jewish thinking, such things are forbidden to non-Jews too.

BUSINESS ETHICS

Very often, business ethics depend on doing what is profitable. For example, a trader with a reputation for fair dealing is likely to attract more customers than one with a bad name. In other words, it pays to be honest.

In Jewish teaching such a view is not ethical at all because it takes no account of a person's *intentions*. It is all too easy for a business person to give a customer unsound advice or withhold information and still keep his or her good reputation. Jewish business ethics depends on fulfilling God's will in intention as well as in deed. For this reason almost every time the Torah lays down a rule about business conduct it adds, 'And you shall fear your God'. God knows what a person's intentions really are.

The Midrash tells the story of a man who approached a rabbi while he was praying, wanting to buy some goods. Not wanting to interrupt his prayer, the rabbi did not answer. The man thought that the rabbi wanted a higher price for the goods and offered more. Again the rabbi did not answer. Again the man raised his offer. At that point, the rabbi finished his prayer and said, 'My son, at the moment you approached me I made a quick mental agreement that I would sell and then put the matter out of my mind because I wanted to concentrate on my prayers. Since I agreed to accept your first offer I shall sell you the goods at that price.'

A Jewish summer camp: afternoon prayers in the open air

TRADE RELATIONS

Centuries before trade unions came into being, halakhah (p. 30) laid down guidelines for industrial relations. In Jewish law the relationship between an employer and an employee is a contract. Violating the contract is a sin. For this reason an employer is obliged to pay wages on time; not to do so is robbery.

Similarly, an employee is forbidden to use his working time to do something else. This, too, is robbery. The rabbis even allowed workers to say some of their prayers while up a tree or on a scaffold and also to say a short form of the grace after meals (p. 65), so that they would not be robbing their employers.

Employers, for their part, may not force employees to work longer hours than those agreed to in the contract. They must also honour local customs. For example, where it is the practice for employers to provide employees with a midday meal, they are obliged to do so.

LEISURE

Jews, like anyone else, spend their leisure time in various ways. Some might choose entertainment, others prefer to be active and still others have hobbies. However, there are certain things they may not do. First, Jews are forbidden to put themselves in danger unnecessarily. This rules out such activities as hang gliding or motor racing. Second, forms of entertainment that violate Jewish standards of modesty (for example, strip-tease) would also be forbidden to Jews.

The over-riding principle governing the way Jews spend their leisure time is that the regular practices of observing Judaism must be maintained. Many Jews make a point of taking their holidays where they can be sure of praying with a minyan (p. 65) and obtaining kosher food (p. 68). In Jewish summer camps, there are regular study sessions (p. 65). These are usually fairly short, for their purpose is simply to provide an opportunity for Jews not to let a single day go by without some Torah study.

THINGS TO DO

▶ What do you think the rabbis meant when they said (a) idleness leads to depression, (b) teach your son a trade or you teach him to become a robber?

▶ What kind of occupations are forbidden to Jews? Give some examples (apart from the ones above).

▶ What is meant by the term 'business ethics'? What is the basic principle of Jewish business ethics?

▶ Explain how Jews see employer/employee relations? What guidelines did the rabbis lay down to allow people to fulfil their religious duties while at work?

▶ You are organizing a holiday camp for observant Jews. What would you include on your programme and what would you avoid? Explain your answer.

The idea of human rights is based on the belief that individuals have worth. People did not always think like this. Those who kept slaves, for example, seldom thought of them as people. Aristotle, a Greek philosopher who lived over 2,000 years ago wrote, 'A slave is a human tool just as a tool is an inanimate [i.e. non-living] slave'. The serfs in the Middle Ages were not much better off; even a century ago in Britain, the aristocracy and upper middle classes were known as 'the quality'. Ordinary people had little value.

To a large extent, the notion that ordinary people had worth, and therefore rights, grew out of the teachings of the Torah and the prophets. It took root in western countries as those teachings found expression in Christianity.

◇

RIGHTS AND RESPONSIBILITIES

Judaism teaches that each human being is created for a purpose and has a place in God's plan (p. 22). It follows that people must be given certain basic rights and freedoms if they are to fulfil the purpose for which they were created. However, Judaism also teaches that rights depend on responsibilities. The Torah tells the story of a time when people had become so wicked that there was 'only evil the whole day' (*Genesis 6:5*). Literally, this means that no one, anywhere, at any moment of the day was doing a single good deed. Those people were no longer fulfilling any of their responsibilities, i.e. any part of the purpose for which God had put them in the world. They therefore lost the most basic of human rights, the right to live. God destroyed them with a flood.

Today, we live in a society where we hear a lot about people's rights. For example, trade union leaders speak about the 'right to strike'. We hear far less about responsibilities – those same trade union leaders usually say very little about the small traders whose businesses they might ruin when their members go on strike. In Jewish thinking rights and responsibilities are inseparable. We would normally respect a person's right to his or her own lifestyle. However, it would be wrong to claim that someone has the *right* to hold noisy parties or do other things that cause distress to neighbours.

THE SOURCE OF HUMAN RIGHTS

In Jewish thought, human rights are the basic principles people have to accept about themselves and others so that they can carry out their part in God's plan. Some of the most basic rights are embedded in the Noachide Laws, which Jews see as applying to all humanity (p. 20). For example, the Laws forbid murder. By commanding people not to take life, it affirms the right to live.

For Jews life is sacred because it is given by God (*Genesis 2:7*) and only God may normally take it (*Deuteronomy 32:39*). The rabbis expanded on this and taught that living is a positive duty. 'Against your will you must live' (*Ethics of the Fathers*). Judaism teaches that human life is necessary because every person has something to contribute to fulfilling God's desire for a dwelling among low creatures (p. 22). For this reason Judaism disapproves strongly of suicide and euthanasia (p. 103). A foetus also has the right to live, since each child born is another person with a part to play in God's plan. Judaism usually only permits abortion if there is any possible risk to the mother's life.

The Noachide Laws also forbid theft. In Jewish teaching, theft includes kidnapping (e.g. taking hostages). This prohibition therefore affirms the right of individuals and institutions to own possessions and of people to go about their daily lives unhindered.

The prohibition of sexual malpractice implies the right not to be abused. No one has the right to force himself or herself on another person. With regard to adultery, the Laws affirm that individuals have the right to the unique love and care of their spouses. Even a casual flirtation with someone else's wife or husband would be a violation of this right.

The final requirement of the Laws is the setting up of a legal system. Judaism recognizes the right of governments to make laws for the benefit of their citizens and to enforce them. 'The law of the land is the law,' says the Talmud. By imposing upon people the responsibility to abide by the laws of the country in which they live, the Laws, in effect, give everyone the right to be protected by those laws.

On the other hand, Jews do not regard laws which violate human rights as binding. Among such laws would be those passed by the Nazi government of Germany in the 1930s (p. 16) or the laws enforced today in some South American dictatorships. Similarly, Jews do not consider themselves bound by laws which were aimed at preventing them observing Judaism. The Maccabean revolt (p. 56) was a struggle against just such a system of laws.

The United Nations General Assembly

THE UNIVERSAL DECLARATION OF HUMAN RIGHTS

In 1948 the Universal Declaration of Human Rights was drawn up. In 1966 the General Assembly of the United Nations began to turn the terms of the Declaration into international law. These took effect in 1976 and are now legally binding for the 45 countries (including Britain) that accepted them. Among the terms of the Declaration are:

- No one shall be subjected to arbitrary arrest, detention or exile.
- Everyone charged with a penal offence has the right to be presumed innocent until proven guilty.
- Everyone has the right to freedom of movement. Everyone has the right to leave any country.
- Everyone has the right to work, to free choice of employment, to just and favourable conditions of work and to protection against unemployment.
- Everyone has the right to a standard of living adequate for health and well-being. Motherhood and childhood are entitled to special care.

Jews strongly approve of the Declaration. Many of its terms have their roots in the Tenakh and other Jewish teachings about morality.

THINGS TO DO

▶ What is meant by the term 'human rights'? What might the world be like if no one believed that there should be human rights? Why are these rights important for Jews?

▶ How do Jews relate rights to responsibilities?

▶ What basic rights emerge from the Noachide Laws?

▶ Friedrich Nietzche, a German philosopher of the last century, wrote:

'For those who are strong and independent, destined and trained to command . . . religion is an additional means for overcoming resistance . . . to the majority of people, who exist for service and general utility, religion gives invaluable contentment with their lot . . . justification of all the commonplaceness, all the meanness, all the semi-animal poverty . . .'

How far does this accord with Jewish teaching?

CLASS DEBATE

▶ Discuss *either* the view that abortions should be carried out on demand *or* the rights and wrongs of euthanasia. Bear in mind the human rights issues involved.

'Who is rich? He who is satisfied with what he has.'

(Ethics of the Fathers)

Jews believe that each Rosh Hashanah (New Year, p. 44) God decides what a person's financial position shall be. Striving after wealth is, therefore, pointless. On the other hand, Judaism also teaches that people have to provide the means by which God may bless them.

WEALTH

Although Judaism strongly discourages materialism, it recognizes that material possessions are necessary if people are to serve God properly. 'Where there is no flour there is no Torah,' declares the Mishnah. According to the Talmud, 'a pleasant home, nicely furnished' is important for a person's psychological well-being. Judaism has always encouraged people to steer a middle path between striving after wealth and shunning it.

'Give me neither poverty nor riches . . . in case I become too full and deny, and say "Who is God?", or in case I become poor and steal . . .'

(Proverbs 30:8–9)

The Torah warns people not to become caught up in materialism, for it can lead them away from God.

'Take care not to forget the Lord your God...in case when you have eaten and are satisfied, and have built fine houses and live in them, and when your herds and flocks increase, and your silver and gold and all that you have has increased, then your heart be lifted up and you forget the Lord your God.'

(Deuteronomy 8:11–14)

Wealth has no real value other than what people use it for. 'When a man leaves the world, neither silver nor gold nor precious stones nor pearls accompany him, but only the Torah he has learnt and the good works he has carried out,' says the Mishnah.

POVERTY

Although Judaism rejects materialism, it never went to the other extreme and turned poverty into an ideal. 'Poverty is worse than fifty plagues,' says the Talmud. Throughout the Talmud and Midrash, the poor person is variously described as miserable, crushed or in a rut.

In Jewish thinking, it is not just up to the poor to find their means of sustenance; those who are better-off have a responsibility to help them. All Jews are required to give at least a tenth part of their earnings to charity. In fact, Judaism teaches that this tenth does not even belong to the individual. It is just put into a person's hands so that he or she can decide which charity to give it to. To keep all of one's wealth to oneself is, in effect, robbing the poor.

Although very poor people are excused from giving a tenth, they are expected to contribute something. In Jewish thinking, everyone has a responsibility to help people in need – even those who are themselves in need.

Jews are also expected to set aside money for celebrating the Sabbath and other holy days. Poor Jews often cut down on their weekday expenses in order to make the Sabbath a special experience.

CHARITY

Judaism distinguishes between two kinds of charity; giving of one's *material* means and giving of *oneself*. For the former, Jews use the word tzedaka ('righteousness').

One can give to the poor in many ways. The rabbis taught that some ways are preferable to others. Putting money into a poor person's hand is an act of tzedaka, but it may cause embarrassment. Judaism teaches that it is important to preserve human dignity and so considers it far better to give in such a way that the giver does not know who receives and the receiver does not know who has given (p. 59).

An even better way of giving tzedaka is to regard the donation as an indefinite, interest-free loan. In this way the person who receives the money does not need to feel embarrassed. Of course, the giver does not seriously expect the loan to be repaid, but the receiver has the face-saving feeling of intending to repay 'some day'.

The trouble with most methods of giving tzedaka is that the poor person remains poor and may soon need more help. The best possible form of tzedaka is helping a poor person to become self supporting. This preserves the poor person's sense of human dignity.

The same consideration governs the Jewish attitude to famine-stricken countries. Gathering starving refugees in relief centres gets food to large numbers of people as quickly as possible. But looking beyond the actual emergency situation, Jews are far happier with relief programmes that provide farmers with tools and tractors and teach them to use fertilizers and pesticides. In this way they can eventually help themselves and so preserve their self-respect.

Giving of one's own time and effort is called **gemilut hassadim**, good deeds. In Jewish communities people rally round to look after the sick, to take care of children when families are in difficulties and to comfort mourners. Giving tzedaka is something the wealthy can do with the greatest effect, but rich and poor alike can take part in gemilut chassadim.

Many Jewish homes keep **pushkes**, collection boxes for various worthy causes. People put in small change left over after shopping and the pushkes fill up surprisingly quickly. Pushkes are regarded as a part of the home.

Jewish children are encouraged to put part of their pocket money in the pushke. In Jewish kindergartens, children often make their own pushkes and bring a few pennies each day to put in them. This trains them from the earliest age to share what they have with others.

THINGS TO DO

▶ What is materialism? Why do you think this might lead people away from God? How might a religious Jewish cabinet minister try to influence government employment policy?

▶ Explain why in Jewish thinking some ways of giving charity are preferable to others.

◇

REFLECTION

'I was in hospital having Esther when my husband was rushed in with appendicitis. My neighbours were fantastic. All my children were fixed up with places to stay and there was a rota of helpers ready for when I came home. By the time my sister arrived from Melbourne there was really nothing for her to do.'

(Mrs W, North London)

FOR YOUR FOLDERS

▶ A shabby young man is sitting on a street corner, holding a piece of cardboard with 'Homeless and hungry' written on it. What dilemmas might this create for a Jew who is serious about living by Jewish values? What might he or she do?

▶ The following is from Shakespeare's play, *The Merchant of Venice*:

'If you repay me not on such a day, In such a place, such sum or sums as are expressed in the condition, let the forfeit be nominated for an equal pound of your fair flesh, to be cut off and taken in what part of your body pleaseth me.'

(The Merchant of Venice, Act 1, Scene 3)

The speaker is Shylock, a Jew who has agreed to lend money to a Venetian merchant on these inhuman terms. Literature like this has done much to sustain the belief that Jews will do anything for money. How does such a stereotype fit with what you have learnt in this unit?

No home to go to: poverty in a city of plenty

'Regard the needy as members of your household.'

(Ethics of the Fathers)

In classical Jewish literature, the welfare of the disadvantaged has always been a major priority. God himself is described as caring for them.

'The Lord gives food to the hungry, the Lord frees those imprisoned, the Lord opens the eyes of the blind, the Lord raises up those that are bowed down, the Lord takes care of strangers, He supports orphans and widows.'

(Psalm 146:7–9)

The Talmud urges people to take God's example.

'Just as God visits the sick, feeds the hungry and clothes the naked, so you do the same.'

SPECIAL NEEDS

The disadvantaged have special needs and these have always been a major concern of the rabbis. They frequently permitted people with disabilities to do things that would have been forbidden to others. For example, on the Shabbat, Jews are forbidden to carry any object from the house into the street or vice versa. However, the rabbis permitted someone with walking difficulties to go out with a walking stick or on crutches.

The use of machinery is also forbidden on Shabbat although heart pace-makers and similar appliances are always permitted, since people's lives depend on them – preserving life over-rides the Sabbath. However, machinery not directly connected with saving life does not. Jewish scientists, working closely with rabbis, have helped design hearing-aids and hospital lifts which may be used on Shabbat.

CARE ORGANIZATIONS

Judaism insists that it is not only up to the poor and people with disabilities to find the help they need. Disadvantage is everyone's problem. The Talmud and Midrash tell many stories of people who went to great lengths to help others in need.

However, helping the disadvantaged is not only up to individuals, it is a responsibility for the whole community. Since ancient times, wherever Jews have settled they have set up organizations to care for those in need. In the past, these were mainly concerned with distributing food and money to the poor as well as those who could not easily support themselves, such as widows and orphans. Jewish committees used to impose a tax on their members so that they could provide these things. The elderly always received special treatment. The rabbis explained the directive, 'Honour your father and mother' *(Exodus 20:12)* to mean respect for any elderly person. The Talmud

Helping out at an old age home

warns that those who no longer have their full mental faculties are to be treated with dignity.

Today, there are several, highly professional Jewish care agencies in Britain. Among them are:

- Norwood Child Care, which began in 1795 as a Jewish orphanage in South London with 20 children. Today, it provides a complete range of social services for Jewish children. Norwood also helps families in difficulty, in particular those who have children with a disability. It also offers help to those trying to cope with unemployment and drug and alcohol dependence. Some families just need some extra cash to buy clothes for their children. Others need a holiday they could not otherwise afford. The organization always makes children its priority and offers various kinds of help, including counselling, residential foster care and financial assistance. At Norwood's residential homes, trained staff care for young people who have grown up with violence or neglect, those on drugs or suffering from anorexia.
- Jewish Care was formed by a merger of the Jewish Welfare Board, the Jewish Blind Society (both nearly 300 years old) and the Jewish Association for the Physically Disabled. It runs housing schemes providing elderly, disabled or blind people with sheltered flats. This enables them to be independent while knowing that help is near at hand. The organization also runs residential homes for mentally frail people and hostels, group homes and a health care centre for people with mental health problems. It sends trained care staff to help house bound people with dressing, washing and feeding. Jewish Care also runs day centres, providing elderly people with companionship, hot meals, activities and outings.
- Chai-Lifeline is a Jewish agency that supports cancer patients and their families through the traumas of terminal illness. It offers counselling, alternative therapies and runs a well-woman clinic.

There are many care agencies such as these. One very popular organization supported by British Jews is the Magen David Adom, the Israel ambulance service.

CARING FOR THE CARE ORGANIZATIONS

A few Jewish care projects receive local council grants, the majority do not. The bulk of the money these organizations need has to be raised from voluntary contributions. Jews provide the finance required in a variety of ways – through fund-raising events, sponsored walks and appeals in the Jewish press. Many Jews have collection boxes in their homes (p. 117), some remember the care organizations in their wills. All these ventures are expressions of the Jewish ideal of tzedaka (p. 116) – helping others with one's money. Judaism also teaches the importance of gemilut chassadim, i.e. donating one's own time and effort. This ideal has enabled the care organizations to rely on the help of volunteers to work alongside the trained staff. These volunteers do the things that require no special expertise – help serve meals in old-age homes, take people with disabilities on outings or simply be on hand to chat to people.

Jews do not only support the specifically Jewish care organizations. Judaism teaches them to contribute to any deserving cause that comes their way.

THINGS TO DO

- ▶ Name three charities you would like to support. Give your reasons for choosing them. Would a Jewish person necessarily support them for the same reasons as you do? Explain your answer.
- ▶ What help is available in the Jewish community for (a) the elderly, (b) children who have a disability, (c) families with someone dying of cancer?
- ▶ Why do you think rabbis and Jewish scientists work together to design aids that people with disabilities may use on Shabbat?
- ▶ You are the secretary of a Jewish youth club. A local hospital is looking for people to play with the young patients on the children's ward. Write a letter to club members asking them to volunteer.

FOR YOUR FOLDERS

- ▶ Give three ways in which organizations can help the disadvantaged more effectively than individuals.

'Pray for the welfare of the government; if it were not for the fear of it, men would swallow each other alive.'

(Ethics of the Fathers)

THE ROLE OF GOVERNMENT

The Talmud illustrates the difference between good and bad government by telling the following story of Alexander the Great's visit to King Katzia.

Katzia offered his royal visitor silver and gold, but Alexander told him that he only wanted to see how justice was carried out in his country. At that moment two men came before King Katzia. One of them said, 'Your majesty, this man sold me a field. When I began to dig in it I found a treasure. I want him to take the treasure back because I only bought the field from him.'

The other man responded, 'No, your majesty. I sold him the field, and therefore anything he finds in it belongs to him.'

King Katzia turned to the first man and said, 'Do you have a son?' 'Yes,' he replied. Katzia turned to the other man. 'Do you have a daughter?' 'Yes.' 'Then let your son marry your daughter and give them the treasure as a wedding present,' ruled the King.

King Alexander started to laugh. Katzia turned to him. 'What would you have done?' he asked.

'I would have killed them both,' replied Alexander, 'and taken the treasure for myself.' Katzia was shocked. 'Does it rain in your country?' he asked. 'Yes,' replied Alexander. 'Are there cattle in your country?' 'Yes'. 'Well,' said King Katzia, 'if that is the way you carry out justice, then the rain surely falls only for the benefit of the cattle. The people do not deserve it!'

THINKING POINT

- What does the above parable tell you about good and bad government?

THE LAW OF THE LAND

In Biblical times, almost all Jews lived in the part of the world now known as Israel. The law of the land was the Torah and Jews obeyed it because they understood it to be God's will (p. 104). By the fifth century BCE Jews had begun to migrate and towards the end of the first century they were scattered throughout the known world. Jews found that they had to live by two systems of law at the same time: the laws of the Torah and the laws of the country in which they lived. This could sometimes present difficulties, e.g. where the laws of the country required people to do something which the Torah disallowed or vice versa. To meet this difficulty, the rabbis ruled that 'the law of the land is the law'.

Naturally, they never applied this principle when the law of the land actually compelled Jews to violate the commandments of the Torah. For example, in the second century BCE, a Greek–Syrian king tried to force the Jews in his empire to change their religion (p. 56). At first, the Jews just disobeyed him. Eventually, however, he began to persecute them. They rose in armed revolt and fought for their right to worship as they wished.

JUSTICE

'You shall appoint judges and officers in all your towns . . . and they shall judge the people righteously.'

(Deuteronomy 16:18)

From the earliest times, Jews were commanded to set up a system of justice. This consisted of law courts, where judges would try offenders, settle disputes and issue rulings on religious matters. The Jewish legal system comprised three levels of bet din or court. Ordinary trials were conducted by a bet din of three judges. They questioned the witnesses themselves and, after considering the evidence, gave a verdict. When someone was standing trial for an

Discussing a case in the London Bet Din

offence that carried the death penalty, a bet din of 23 judges tried the case. Matters of national importance required a Sanhedrin, a court of 71 judges (p. 97).

In Jewish law, the death penalty was sometimes used for offences that were regarded as particularly serious, such as murder, raping a married woman or violating the Sabbath. This was not only a punishment and a deterrent to others, it was also an atonement for the offender.

Circumstantial evidence was never admissible. A person could only be executed if witnesses had given a warning, pointing out the possible punishment and had then actually seen the crime carried out in front of them almost immediately. If people had heard a scream and then rushed into a building to find a man standing over a body holding a knife that was dripping blood, there was no way that the death penalty could be enforced. No one had actually witnessed the crime.

Although the death penalty was always there as a possibility, it was rarely carried out. It was, in effect, a way of indicating which crimes were the most serious. The Mishnah even states that a bet din that executed a person once in 70 years was a 'destructive bet din'. No Jewish court has carried out a death sentence since Roman times.

Nor is there any place for mutilation in Jewish law. The often misunderstood verse, 'an eye for an eye' (Exodus 21:24) is taken in the Talmud to refer to monetary compensation. It teaches that if someone's eye is injured, they may only claim the value of an eye as compensation, i.e. no more than the value of an eye for an eye.

Nowadays, there is only the bet din of three judges. They are very learned rabbis with many years of communal experience. There are several such rabbinic courts in England, four of them in London alone. They are concerned mainly with divorce cases, conversions and business disputes between Jews.

The workings of the bet din depend on the careful examination of witnesses by impartial judges. Very high standards of truth and reliability are expected of both judges and witnesses. It is easy to be disqualified. For example, people with criminal records may not appear as witnesses in a bet din; nor may dishonest traders or gamblers.

A judge, too, may be disqualified if there is the slightest risk that he might be partial. The Talmud tells the story of a rabbi who was getting into a boat.

A man standing nearby put his hand out to help him. As the rabbi thanked him, the man mentioned that he was due to appear before him in court. 'In that case,' said the rabbi, 'I am disqualified from being your judge.'

FOR YOUR FOLDERS

▶ Do you know of any good or bad governments today? How might a Jew decide which governments are good?

▶ How do you think the ruling 'the law of the land is the law' helped Jews?

▶ Here are some Jewish teachings about government and justice. What do you think each one means? What do they teach you about justice and government in Jewish thought?
   a 'A habitual borrower cannot be a judge' (Talmud).
   b 'A government can be brought down because of a single injustice' (Rabbi Israel Meir Kahan, 1839–1933).
   c 'The laws of governments are determined by everyday life; the laws of God determine everyday life' (Rabbi Joseph Isaac Schneersohn, 1880–1950).

▶ What do you think 'atonement' means? Try to find out. How might punishment be an atonement for a criminal?

▶ What do people sometimes take an 'eye for an eye' to mean? How do Jews understand these words?

THINGS TO DO

▶ What arguments might Jews put forward in a discussion on capital punishment?

'The world stands on three things, on justice, on truth and on peace.'

(Ethics of the Fathers)

PEACE AS AN IDEAL

Shalom, peace, is the standard Jewish greeting and parting. Jews have used it from Biblical times to the present day (*II Kings 4:26*). It is more than just a greeting. Jews have always hated war and shalom expresses the hope that one day all humankind will live in peace. This does not mean that Judaism teaches total pacifism. Although it regards war as evil, it recognizes that there are times when someone has to fight. Nonetheless, it teaches that they must go to great lengths to avoid war (e.g. *II Kings 6:21-23*).

OBLIGATORY AND OPTIONAL WARS

Jews have no concept of a 'just war'. Wars are either **milchemet mitzvah** (obligatory war) or a **milchemet reshut** (optional war).

After Moses died, his successor, Joshua, led the Israelites into the Promised Land. However, the land was not empty and the Israelites were going to have to fight for it. God commanded Joshua:

'. . . rise up, cross over this River Jordan, you and all this nation . . . Every place where the sole of your foot treads I will give to you . . . be strong and courageous, for you will lead this people to take possession of the land which I have promised to their ancestors . . .'

(Joshua 1:2-6)

That war was a milchemet mitzvah – one which the Israelites were commanded by God to fight. There are three other kinds of milchemet mitzvah.

Jews regard it as a religious obligation to defend their lives and the lives of their families (e.g. *Exodus 17:8–13*). A war fought in self-defence is therefore a milchemet mitzvah.

An Israeli soldier at the Temple site: prepared for war but praying for peace

An extension of this is the pre-emptive war – attacking an enemy who is about to strike, in order to avoid being attacked. In the summer of 1967, Israeli intelligence discovered that Egypt and Syria were about to launch an attack. The Israeli air force attacked those countries' airfields and destroyed most of their aircraft while they were still on the ground. As a result, the war was over in six days and thousands of lives, both Jewish and Arab were spared.

Milchemet mitzvah also covers going to the aid of a country that is under attack, to prevent war reaching one's own country. In 1939, when Germany invaded Poland, Britain had a pledge to help the Poles if they were attacked. The British government realized that if the German armies were not halted, they would eventually invade Britain and so it declared war on Germany. In Jewish terms, this would be regarded as an obligatory war.

A milchemet reshut is an optional war. It can only be undertaken if there are sound reasons for fighting, diplomacy has failed (*Judges 11:12–33*) and if the Sanhedrin, the supreme rabbinical council, approves it (though, in practice, there has not been a Sanhedrin since Roman times). For example, by the time of King David, in the tenth century BCE, hostile neighbours had been attacking Israelite border towns for three centuries. They had plundered, killed and taken captives. David decided that the only way to put an end to the problem was to subdue them by force of arms. The court gave its approval and David secured a lasting peace.

Fighting any other kind of war, whether to build an empire, colonize or to take revenge, is forbidden to Jews.

A NON-MILITARY HERITAGE

As a result of their long-standing hatred of war, Jews do not have a military heritage. There is no Jewish equivalent of the European knight or the Japanese samurai. Even today, Jews do not bring up their children to glorify war. The earliest Israelite army was conscripted for the express purpose of taking possession of the Holy Land (p. 7). The tribes were called to arms whenever there was a need to defend their land, but as soon as the battles were over the men went back to their farms.

The rabbis of the Talmud saw war as an avoidable evil. They taught, 'The sword comes to the world because of delay of justice and through perversion of justice.' Where justice was practised, the need for war should never arise.

MARTYRDOM

Although Jews place great value on life, Judaism teaches that sometimes life must be set aside. In Jewish thought, martyrdom is called **kiddush Hashem**, sanctifying the Name of God. Judaism expects Jews to surrender their lives rather than commit one of the three cardinal sins: murder, idolatry or sexual immorality. In times of religious persecution, for example Hanukkah (p. 56), this requirement is extended to other violations too.

During the Holocaust, six million Jews were killed simply because they were Jews. Jews call such people kedoshim, holy ones. There are many stories of Jews who, during that period, faced death calmly and inspired others to die singing God's praises. Even so, attitudes to martyrdom differed widely. One famous Jewish leader, Rabbi Elchonon Wasserman, was shot by the Nazis in 1941. As he faced his executioners he addressed the Jews who were going to be killed with him and told them:

> '. . . we must repent right now, the time is short, and we must bear in mind that if we repent we will become better sacrifices . . . no wrong thought must enter anyone's mind for this can spoil the sacrifice . . . we are now going to perform the greatest mitzvah . . .'

Another famous leader, Rabbi Menachem Zemba, felt differently about it. Just before the Warsaw Ghetto uprising in April 1943, he proclaimed:

> 'There is absolutely no purpose nor any value in kiddush Hashem, in the death of a Jew. Kiddush Hashem in our present situation means the will of a Jew to live. This struggle for life is a mitzvah.'

PEACE

The Jewish ideal of peace is not just a situation where people are not fighting one another. Peace means friendship and co-operation. It means achieving such a degree of harmony between nations that taking up arms becomes unthinkable.

> 'And I will give peace to the land . . . so that the sword will not even pass through.'

(Leviticus 26:6)

Jews believe that universal peace will finally come about in the Messianic Age (p. 24), when 'They will beat their swords into plough shares and their spears into pruning hooks, nation shall not lift up sword against nation nor shall they train for war any more'

(Isaiah 2:4). For this reason Jews praise efforts to reduce tensions anywhere in the world, particularly negotiations that lead countries to dismantle their nuclear weapons. They see each move towards peace as a step nearer to the time of universal peace.

THINGS TO DO

▶ For what reasons have Jews been prompted to go to war?

▶ Why do you think martyrs were called 'kedoshim'? Does Judaism encourage martyrdom?

▶ Benjamin Franklin, a famous American statesman, once said, 'There never was a bad peace or a good war.' How might a Jew respond to this view?

FOR YOUR FOLDERS

▶ Here are some Jewish teachings. What do you think each one means? What do they tell you about the Jewish attitude to peace?
  a 'Seek peace and run after it' (*Psalm 34:15*).
  b 'Peace is the vessel for receiving God's blessing' (*Mishnah*).
  c 'The Torah was given to establish peace' (*Midrash*).
  d 'Peace is to the world what yeast is to dough' (*Talmud*).

▶ Think of three wars you have learnt about in history. Explain whether Jews would regard them as milchemet mitzvah, milchemet reshut or neither.

FOR DISCUSSION

▶ Some Jewish parents do not allow their children to play with toy guns. Can you suggest why? Do you think they are right?

'A righteous man pays attention to the needs of his animal.'

(Proverbs 12:10)

Consideration for animals occupies an important place in Jewish moral teachings. The prohibition of cruelty to animals is part of the Noachide Laws (p. 20) which Jews see as binding on all humanity.

In its opening chapter, the Torah describes the creation of animals:

'Then God said, "Let the water team with swarms of living creatures, and let birds fly above the earth . . ." and God made the animals according to their kinds, the beasts according to their kinds and all the things that creep upon the earth'.

It then tells us that God created humans to 'have control over the fish of the sea and the birds of the sky, over the animals and over the whole earth.' *(Genesis 1:20–26)*.

Jews derive two important principles from these verses:

- Animals are God's creatures and must be treated as such.
- Animal life can never have the same value as human life.

Animals are our helpers. They work for the benefit of people (more so in the past than today) and provide us with certain raw materials. Most important of all is the part they play in maintaining a balanced ecology, making this planet a fit place for humans to live.

In the Torah, one of the reasons for resting on Shabbat (p. 36) is so that beasts of burden might also rest *(Deuteronomy 5:14)*. At harvest time, the horse or ox pulling the wagon was not to be muzzled, so that it could eat its share of the crop as it worked *(Deuteronomy 25:4)*. A farmer (in ancient times) was not permitted to have an ox and an ass pull his plough at the same time *(Deuteronomy 22:11)* since the greater strength of the ox would put unnecessary strain on the ass. Earlier in the same chapter, there is an express command to help an animal that is stumbling under its burden. Two verses further on, Jews are told that if they want to take eggs from a bird's nest, they must first of all shoo the mother bird away. The rabbis of the Talmud ruled that a farmer was to feed his cattle before sitting down to his own meal and that he should not buy more animals than he could afford to feed properly. They even relaxed the very strict Sabbath laws to help an animal that had fallen into a pit.

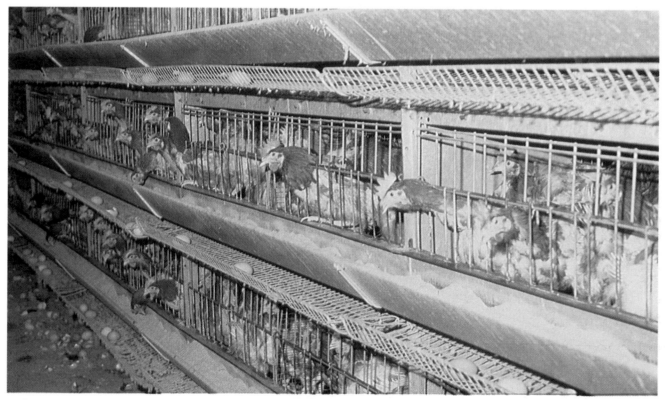

Battery hens: how not to treat animals

Teachings such as these have created a Jewish sense of morality in which kindness to animals occupies a major part. Jews today feel repelled by cruelty to animals.

ANIMALS FOR FOOD

Apart from one specific annual sacrifice (which does not apply today as there is no Temple), Jews are nowhere commanded to eat meat. They may become vegetarians if they wish. Indeed, according to the Talmud, the earliest humans were vegetarians. Judaism insists, however, that if people choose to eat meat, they must slaughter animals in a pain-free way. For Jews, that means shechitah. Shechitah has been shown to be one of the most painless methods of slaughtering animals. It is explained on page 68.

EXPERIMENTS ON ANIMALS

Judaism takes two principles into consideration when looking at the rights and wrongs of experiments on animals. First, inflicting unnecessary pain on an animal is strictly forbidden in Jewish law. It is also forbidden in the Noachide Laws (p. 20). Second, Jews do not regard animal life as being of the same value as human life. They believe that animals may be used to further human needs.

Bringing these two principles together rules out experiments for the production of cosmetics. There is no way that blinding rabbits to test eye shadow can be thought of as 'furthering human needs'.

Jews regard medical experiments as different. Finding cures for diseases, or perfecting surgical techniques, are extremely important human needs. Killer diseases such as diphtheria and smallpox, which were widespread in Britain earlier this century, have been more or less wiped out due to experiments that involved animals. So has polio, which once left children paralysed. Surgeons have learned to transplant hearts, kidneys and livers by operating on animals before trying the techniques on people.

Nonetheless, Jews would only condone experiments on animals if no other means of combating a disease are available, and if the experiment is carefully controlled to minimize the pain as much as possible. For the same reason, Judaism forbids cruel sports such as bullfighting or cockfighting.

THINGS TO DO

▶ What raw materials do we obtain from animals? (Remember to include insects and marine creatures.)

▶ What is meant by 'a balanced ecology'? How might animals help to maintain it?

▶ How might thinking of animals as God's creations affect the way we treat them?

▶ How do Jews justify the fact that they may eat animals when Jewish teachings mention avoiding inflicting pain on them?

▶ You read a report in the newspaper about a group of people poisoning food in a supermarket as part of their campaign for animal rights. A Jewish person writes a letter to the editor giving their opinion. Write that letter.

▶ Write a short conversation between two people who are arguing over whether it is right to keep animals in zoos. Alternatively, make this the topic of a class discussion. What might Jews think about it?

▶ You are a Jewish head teacher. Someone rings you up to tell you that two of your pupils have drowned a kitten in a nearby canal. What would you say or do to those pupils? What would you say at school assembly?

CLASS DEBATE

▶ 'This house believes that animals should never be used for experiments.' Remember to include some of the things mentioned in this unit in your discussion.

'The earth, and everything that fills it, is the Lord's.'

(Psalm 24:1)

GOD'S PLANET

The first chapter of the Torah describes the stages in which God fashioned planet earth for us to live on – how He formed a climate, separated the land masses from the oceans, created plant life and then animal life, first in the sea, then in the air and finally on land. Only after He had brought about a world suitable for humans to live in did He create the first human pair (p. 20).

The Torah tells us that human beings are put on this planet 'to work it and to look after it' (*Genesis 2:15*). The importance of this becomes clear in terms of the Jewish belief – that God wants people to serve Him and make this world a place where He can one day dwell (p. 22). This means that it is God's planet, not ours and that we have to use the world's resources wisely. This places a tremendous responsibility on people.

DO NOT DESTROY

The Torah, Talmud and later Jewish writings all give guidelines for using the planet's resources. One of the most important is the principle of not destroying anything unnecessarily. The Torah's basic statement is:

'When you lay siege to a city . . . you must not destroy its trees by taking up an axe against them; . . . for the tree of the field is man's life . . .'

(Deuteronomy 20:19)

In ancient times, an army attacking a city would lay siege to it – they would build a wall around the city so that no one could get in or out. Jews were commanded not to cut down fruit trees for their siege walls. In the oral Torah (p. 25) this is taken as a directive not to waste things in general. Judaism forbids the purposeless destruction of anything.

CONSERVATION

Jews believe that it is important for people to live decently so that they can serve God properly. This means that conservation measures must lead to the benefit of the people. One such Jewish conservation measure is the **migrash** – an area of open land surrounding towns (*Numbers 35:2*).

In some ways, the migrash resembles today's 'green belt'. However, unlike the green belt (which is sometimes the site of golf courses, cemeteries or rubbish tips), the migrash was to be preserved as open land. No one was permitted to grow crops or set up a business there. It provided the town with a light, airy and pleasant setting, where people could sit, stroll or picnic. The migrash also limited the size of the towns since no building development could take place there. This prevented the growth of huge sprawling cities (called megalopolis) with its millions of inhabitants and impersonal lifestyle.

In ancient times all the cities of Israel had a migrash. Jews also used to enhance the beauty of their towns by surrounding them with a ring of fruit trees. In modern Israel, planting trees is a priority – it prevents soil erosion and helps remove pollutants from the atmosphere. The Jewish National Fund,

Cutting down rain forests in Brazil: development or destruction?

originally set up to buy land (p. 146) now funds a variety of conservation projects. Its slogan is 'Working for a greener Israel'.

POLLUTION

Pollution is an unavoidable fact of life. Every time you throw away a sweet wrapper or turn on a gas cooker you are causing pollution. However, we can control our pollution by disposing of waste responsibly, recycling it when we can and not wasting energy. Judaism teaches that controlling pollution has a moral dimension, the main consideration being people's health and well-being. These always come before commercial interests. For example, the Talmud insists that businesses that cause annoyance or that produce harmful substances must be kept at a suitable distance from towns and always away from the prevailing winds.

Today, it is not simply a matter of keeping industrial plants away from towns. The problem is much more complicated.

Manufacturing processes always produce waste, much of it toxic. It might be given off as smoke, poured into the sea or buried in landfills. Whichever way, it is sooner or later absorbed by fish, or seeps into the soil and finds its way into plants and the animals that feed on them. Eventually, it enters our own food chain. There is no simple way of preventing these substances from reaching people. Applying the Talmud's principles to today's conditions, Judaism would consider it essential for *all* factories to have waste treatment facilities *before* they started operating.

THE MORAL DIMENSION

A few years ago, a zoologist in Africa allowed himself to be charged down by a white rhino rather than use his rifle to shoot a member of an endangered species. Some time later a British motorist was killed when another driver swerved to avoid a swan that was crossing the road. At that time, the AA issued a warning telling drivers not to endanger human life for the sake of animals.

These incidents reflect a trend that is growing out of our present day concerns about the environment – people are beginning to regard themselves as just another part of the ecosystem. In Jewish thinking, such a trend is misguided and dangerous. It leads to the view that people are, in effect, no more important than dandelions and dragonflies.

For Jews, environmental concerns have to take into account the supreme value of human beings and their special place in creation. In other words, they have to have a *moral* dimension.

For example, should Brazilian rainforests be cut down to make room for farms? In Jewish terms it is not simply a matter of balancing the amount of carbon dioxide being given off into the atmosphere against the amount the trees can reabsorb. It is also a *human* question. If the trees are cut down, the forest dwellers lose their home and their way of life; if they are not, there will be insufficient farmland for a poor country with a growing population. There are no easy solutions. But, for Jews the human dimension is a central part of any discussion of these issues.

FIND OUT

▶ Find out what you can about the work of the Jewish National Fund.

THINGS TO DO

▶ How do you think seeing the planet as God's world affects a person's attitude to the environment?

▶ Make a survey of the environmentally friendly products used by members of your class. Imagine some Jewish pupils are designing a poster to promote the use of such products. How might they word it?

▶ When coal is used to produce energy it gives off a number of environmental pollutants. However, closing down the world's coalmines and turning to cleaner sources of energy would result in massive unemployment and hardship for thousands of people. How would you expect a Jew to respond to the problem?

▶ Imagine that a religious Jew has just been appointed Secretary of State for the Environment. What steps do you think he or she might take: (a) immediately, (b) as long-term projects?

WHAT IS ORTHODOXY?

For centuries, Jews have understood their religion in terms of a covenant with God (p. 22) and that they were to keep their part of it by observing the mitzvot. During the late eighteenth and early nineteenth centuries, assimilated German Jews wanted to make changes in Judaism (see Unit 67). They began calling Judaism as it had always been known, by a new name – 'Orthodox Judaism'.

Today, the term 'Orthodox' might refer to Jews who are fully observant as well as to those who hardly ever attend a synagogue. Many Jews find the term meaningless and would prefer not to use it at all. Loosely put, 'Orthodox' might describe those Jews who accept that traditional Jewish practices are important, even if they do not observe them themselves. In this, and the following two units, we shall focus on those styles of Judaism which have become models for all orthodox attitudes.

THE RISE OF LITHUANIA

Jews have always valued learning (p. 88). In the past, most people hoped that their sons would go to a yeshiva (Talmudic academy) and become learned men. During the early seventeenth century, the largest Jewish population in Europe was in Poland; so were some of the most famous yeshivot.

In 1648 disaster struck the Polish Jews. Cossack hordes poured in from the Ukraine, slaughtering Jews and Poles alike. No sooner were they beaten back than Russia invaded Poland, bringing death and destruction to the Jews. Moreover, the Poles suspected the Jews of being in league with the Russians and, as their forces retreated, they wiped out one community after another. The following year an epidemic killed many more. By the end of the seventeenth century, the horrific loss of life and the economic ruin of those Jews who survived heralded the end of Poland as a centre of Jewish learning. Lithuania now began to emerge as the new Torah centre of Europe.

Rabbi Elijah of Vilna

More than any other person, Rabbi Elijah of Vilna (1720–97), known as the Vilna Gaon (the genius of Vilna) put his stamp on Lithuanian Orthodoxy. Following the decline of Polish Jewry, he set out to re-establish Jewish life on a solid foundation of Torah scholarship. His students became teachers and rabbis and spread Torah knowledge throughout Lithuania and beyond (Torah in the broadest sense of the word, see p. 26).

Rabbi Elijah's method of Talmud study involved clear understanding of each passage together with broad knowledge of the whole literature as well as using the science of his day. Above all, Rabbi Elijah became a role model. Devoting himself day and night to Torah study, he embodied what every young Talmudic scholar wanted to become, a **lamdan** – a man with unparalleled understanding of the Talmud and its associated literature (commentaries, codes etc., p. 31).

In 1803, Rabbi Elijah's foremost disciple, Rabbi Chaim, established a yeshiva in Volozhin. Only the most able students were accepted there and it achieved high standards of scholarship. It established a pattern followed by other Lithuanian yeshivot and, indeed, for much of Lithuanian Jewry. In Lithuania, Jewish life revolved mainly around Talmudic study. Every synagogue had its study group and even ordinary shopkeepers, tailors and cobblers saw learning as their principal way of serving God. Young men trained in Lithuania became rabbis for Jewish communities all over the world. Wherever they went, they aimed to replant the Lithuanian model, establishing yeshivot and setting up study groups.

THE MUSAR MOVEMENT

'Studying Musar [religious ethics] is like putting oneself under a microscope.'

(Rabbi Israel Lipkin of Salant)

During the late eighteenth century, the maskilim (followers of Haskalah, p. 10) wanted to change the Jews' language, dress and manners and have secular subjects taught in Jewish schools. The Hasidim (see Unit 64) were bitterly opposed to Haskalah and it had no success in Poland. However, its effects were felt in Lithuania. Also, by the mid-nineteenth century two political movements were gaining ground in Russia. These were the Bund, a Jewish socialist movement (p. 11) and Zionism (p. 144). Both believed that the way forward for Jews was not to be found in Judaism, but in taking political control of their own destiny. The Bund wanted to have the Jews of Russia officially recognized as a self-governing national group. The Zionists wanted to create a Jewish homeland in Palestine.

These movements introduced new ways of thinking about Judaism and the new ideas even penetrated the yeshivot. Students read political pamphlets, classics or scientific books in their rooms, or hid them inside their copies of the Talmud. As a result many drifted away from Jewish observance.

Rabbi Israel Lipkin of Salant (1810–83)

The person mainly responsible for reviving Torah values in Lithuania was Rabbi Israel Lipkin of Salant. In about 1842 he set up a **chevrat musar** (society for studying religious ethics) in Vilna. They republished several mediaeval works on ethics (p. 33) and encouraged people to study them. He also opened a **musar shteibel** (ethics room), a place where people could spend time reflecting on the quality of their lives.

These moves failed to attract businessmen who were already set in their ways and Rabbi Lipkin turned to the yeshivot. Through his efforts many Lithuanian yeshivot introduced the study of musar.

WHAT MUSAR IS ABOUT

Musar is a way of helping people to improve their character traits and become more careful in serving God. Musar writings examine pride, envy, greed and sloth and explain why these prevent a person serving God properly. They point out the importance of humility, love, compassion and zeal and give advice as to how these might be developed. The musar teachers gave lectures on character improvement and spent time talking to individual students. They taught their pupils to analyse themselves and to apply the lessons of the musar books.

By the 1880s the Musar movement had produced a new generation of yeshiva graduates dedicated to traditional Judaism. These Jews brought high standards of morality and religious observance to their business and professional lives. Musar had given them the strength of character to resist being influenced by the secular movements. Today, musar is studied in most yeshivot and girls' seminaries, though the methods vary from one place to another. The works of the mediaeval teachers are widely studied, as well as those written by the successors of Rabbi Lipkin. Most institutions employ a sensitive person to give individual guidance to the students. In synagogues too rabbis use their sermons to guide and encourage people in their character development and Jewish observance.

THINGS TO DO

▶ What happened to the Jews of Poland during the eighteenth century?

▶ What is a lamdan?

▶ Why do you think Rabbi Elijah saw Torah scholarship as important?

▶ What is musar?

▶ Imagine that you are showing a friend round a yeshiva. You arrive when the students are studying musar. How would you explain to your friend what they were doing and why they were doing it?

▶ Why do you think Rabbi Lipkin's attempt to set up a musar shteibel (ethics room) was unsuccessful? Do you think this idea would be any more successful today? Explain your answer.

Yeshiva students studying in pairs (chavruta system)

'If a person is attached to God then he is truly alive.'

(Rabbi Israel Baal Shem Tov)

Unit 63 looked at the calamities that overtook Polish Jewry during the second half of the seventeenth century and how Poland fell into decline as a centre of Jewish learning. The Jews who survived were mainly poor people who worked long hard hours to eke out a meagre living. There was hardly any opportunity for learning. By the 1730s, three generations had grown up with little Jewish education.

There was also widespread dejection. Although the Polish Jews prayed and recited psalms with devotion, they felt that without Torah study they were deficient as Jews. In addition, the Torah scholars in Lithuania (p. 128) tended to look down on them. Many felt that they were diminished in God's eyes.

RABBI ISRAEL BAAL SHEM TOV (1698–1760)

The religious revival of the Jews in Poland was brought about by Rabbi Israel Baal Shem Tov ('Master of the Good Name', i.e. the Name of God). In his earlier years he had joined the **nistarim** (hidden mystics) who travelled round Jewish communities to encourage the ignorant villagers to improve their standards of Jewish observance. By about 1734, he realized that the work of the nistarim was no longer adequate and began to teach and preach openly. His teachings brought new hope to the ignorant majority and he rapidly gained an enormous following.

Rabbi Israel drew upon the kabbalah (p. 33) and simplified it for ordinary people. He taught that the purpose of serving God is attachment to Him. This could be achieved by praying with sincerity and carrying out the commandments with enthusiasm, as well as through Torah study. For Rabbi Israel, God loved the simple Jew who read the psalms with sincerity as much as the most learned scholar. He taught the poor that their simple humility even gave them an advantage over the scholars, whose path to God was often obstructed by feelings of pride. Above all, he stressed the importance of joy in serving God. For ordinary Jewish people, teachings such as these were like a breath of fresh air. They began to feel that God really could love them and felt inspired to pray and carry out mitzvot with enthusiasm and joy.

THE HASIDIM

Although Rabbi Israel is best known for inspiring the masses, his main teaching was to the learned. Many scholars liked his approach. He showed them that kabbalah was a way of illuminating their Judaism. In particular, they were attracted to his way of serving God with joy and the love he showed to the ordinary people. His followers became known as **Hasidim** (pious ones).

Other scholars, particularly in Lithuania, were opposed to the Hasidim. Two generations earlier a certain Shabtai Zvi had claimed to be the Messiah (p. 24) and had disrupted Jewish life in eastern Europe. These scholars were worried that Rabbi Israel might be another false messiah. They were also worried because some Hasidim seemed to make serving God with joy the centre of their Judaism rather than Talmudic study. These scholars became known as **mitnagdim** (opponents).

Habad Hasidim conducting a children's rally on Lag b'Omer (p. 62)

THE MOVEMENT EXPANDS

When Rabbi Israel died, his foremost disciple, Rabbi Dov Baer of Mezritch became leader of the Hasidim. He gave special attention to a handful of close disciples who were to become the future leaders. The movement spread to many other areas of eastern Europe. By the time Rabbi Dov Baer died in 1772, his disciples had established centres right across settled Poland, Galicia, White Russia and Ukraine.

The towns where they settled became the new centres of the Hasidic movement. Those who lived in or near these towns turned to the **Rebbe** (Hasidic leader) for guidance on general as well as on Jewish matters. They would seek the Rebbe's blessing for many things, from bringing up children to starting a business. The first Hasidic community outside Europe was established in 1778, when a group of Hasidim settled in the Holy Land.

The **Rebbeim** (plural of Rebbe) turned to educating the masses. Study groups, lectures and eventually yeshivot were established. By the mid-1930s there were several million Hasidim in Eastern Europe.

HASIDIM TODAY

During the Holocaust (p. 16), the Hasidim suffered terrible losses. Towns which had once been major Hasidic centres were all but wiped out. Those who survived fled to the west and to Israel (then Palestine) and re-established their traditional pattern of life.

Today, there are Hasidic communities in Jerusalem, London, New York, Antwerp, Melbourne, Rio de Janeiro and many other cities. They live in close-knit communities, with their own schools, synagogues and yeshivot. Many still wear the traditional dress of their Polish forebears – long black coat, large black hat, knee length breeches and fur hat (streimel) on the Sabbath and festivals – and speak the same dialect of Yiddish. Hasidic women dress very modestly.

Hasidim are very strict in observing the mitzvot and serve God with great joy. Their synagogues are lively places and they sometimes sing during prayer – not the orchestrated singing of a choir under a choirmaster, but the warm singing of people who feel happy and privileged to be serving God. Marriage partners are usually selected from within the community or from another Hasidic group, and the divorce rate is exceptionally low. Families stay close together, and members of a community share in each other's joys and sorrows.

One group, the **Habad** Hasidim (also known as Lubavitch, the name of the Russian town where the movement grew up) is different. Whereas most Hasidim prefer minimal contact with the world at large, Habad Hasidim are deeply concerned with the spiritual welfare of all people, Jews and non-Jews. They usually wear western clothes and speak the language of the country in which they live. Habad runs the largest Jewish educational network in the world, with centres in over 20 countries and has played a significant part in re-vitalizing Jewish observance in the UK (p. 134).

THINGS TO DO

▶ Draw a time chart to illustrate the history of the Hasidic movement. Include any information you have been able to find in other books.

▶ What were the main features of Rabbi Israel Baal Shem Tov's teachings? From where did he draw his ideas? Why do you think these teachings brought renewed hope to the masses?

▶ Discuss the advantages and disadvantages of religious people having minimal contact with the world at large.

▶ Who were the mitnagdim? What were their main concerns?

▶ What is a Rebbe? How does a Rebbe differ from a rabbi?

▶ Describe Hasidic dress. What language do many Hasidim speak? What would you expect to find if you watched Hasidim at prayer?

'The Jew will never frown at any art, any science, any culture . . . the more firmly he stands on the rock of his Judaism . . . the more ready he will be to accept whatever is true and good.'

(Rabbi Samson Raphael Hirsch)

Unlike the Jews of eastern Europe who, throughout the nineteenth century were regarded by Poles, Russians and Ukrainians as aliens, those in the west had begun to enter European society. The Haskalah (p. 10) had encouraged Jews to shed their distinctiveness. Many, particularly in Germany, had become so assimilated that they could hardly be distinguished from the non-Jews around them. Some had even converted to Christianity. These changes led to the emergence of the Reform movement (p. 136). Its leaders believed that traditional Judaism was incompatible with modern life and had to be changed. They shortened the prayers and introduced the organ into the synagogue; some abolished circumcision and moved Shabbat to Sunday (see Unit 66).

Far from welcoming these changes, traditional rabbis saw Reform as yet another step towards assimilation and tried to oppose it. They were unsuccessful and the Reform movement spread rapidly. However, many western Jews felt they were committed to traditional Judaism and wanted to see that it was compatible with modern European life. Neo-Orthodoxy emerged in response to this need.

RABBI SAMSON RAPHAEL HIRSCH

During the early nineteenth century, some rabbis in Germany looked at ways of bringing Judaism and secular culture together. However it was Rabbi Samson Raphael Hirsch (1808–88) who gave the neo (new) Orthodoxy its direction. Rabbi Hirsch saw the difficulties of living as a Jew in a free society, but he did not accept that Judaism had to be refashioned to fit people's lifestyles. In one famous passage he wrote, 'It is Jews who need reforming, not Judaism.' He believed that Judaism contained the highest ideals of religion and morality. If Jews were to be part of European society, they had to elevate themselves to live by the ideals of Judaism, not dismantle Judaism to make it fit the way that assimilated Jews had chosen to live (as he accused the reformers of doing).

In 1836 Rabbi Hirsch published his *Nineteen Letters on Judaism*. It took the form of a correspondence in which a young German–Jewish intellectual discusses his problems with a traditional Jew. Written in beautiful German, the *Nineteen Letters* explains how

Rabbi Samson Raphael Hirsch

Judaism is perfectly compatible with modern culture and leads to the loftiest virtues to which a cultured person should aspire. The book made an immediate impact among young German Jews. Many began looking to Rabbi Hirsch for clear-sighted leadership.

In 1851 Hirsch became rabbi of an Orthodox congregation in Frankfurt. There he established three schools, including a high school for girls – almost unheard of in traditional communities at that time (p. 90). In these schools, Hebrew language and traditional Jewish subjects were taught alongside German, mathematics and science. In the synagogue, Hirsch gave sermons in German and introduced a choir and communal singing.

However, it was in his writings that he developed and spread his ideas. Hirsch's ideal was the *Jissroel-mensch* (Israel man) – the educated and cultured Jew who observed the mitzvot fully. A *Jissroel-mensch* was one who was committed to seeking God in both the Torah and nature. Like nature, the Torah was to be investigated honestly and fully; and like nature, the Torah was not within human power to change.

Rabbi Hirsch took a saying from *Ethics of the Fathers*, 'Torah im derech eretz' ('Torah with a worldly occupation'). He reinterpreted this as 'Torah together with secular education'. This became his slogan. He wrote a great many books, including a translation of the Five Books of Moses into German with a commentary and other works explaining the ethical ideals of Judaism.

RABBI AZRIEL HILDSHEIMER

Another important leader of Orthodoxy in Germany was Rabbi Azriel Hildsheimer (1820–99). Like Hirsch, his background included traditional Jewish and secular studies, having studied Talmud under the most outstanding scholars in Germany before attending Berlin University. In 1869 Hildsheimer became rabbi of an Orthodox congregation in Berlin. Four years later, he founded a seminary for training rabbis. Here, he went further than Hirsch, seeking to show that not only was Judaism compatible with modern culture, it was also compatible with the critical scientific study of the classical Jewish texts.

Some rabbis felt that Hildsheimer had gone too far, in particular for agreeing to train non-Orthodox leaders (p. 136) in his seminary. However, the Lithuanian yeshivot (p. 128) were mainly concerned with studying Torah for its own sake; they were not actually training rabbis. On the other hand, the non-Orthodox institutions were. Hildsheimer felt that, in spite of opposition, it was necessary to equip rabbis with the skills they would need in modern communities. Forty years after Hildsheimer founded his seminary, an historian wrote:

'However much opinion amongst Jews might differ . . . when we consider what was the position of Torah-true Judaism in western Europe, we must admit that the founding of the Rabbinical Seminary constituted one of the chief measures towards the presentation and salvation of the traditional teachings amongst the Jews.'

Today, Jews' College in London is the spiritual heir to Hildsheimer's seminary, as is Yeshiva University in New York and Bar Ilan University in Ramat Gan, Israel.

NEO-ORTHODOXY

The Judaism taught by Rabbis Hirsch and Hildsheimer became known as neo-Orthodoxy. It was a way of bringing together traditional Jewish values with German culture. Those who followed it accepted the authority of the Shulchan Aruch (p. 32) in all things and were very strict in their observance of mitzvot. At the same time they spoke German, wore western clothes, believed that secular studies had a place in the education of modern Jews (Hirsch

himself had studied at Bonn University) and that women should be educated too. Hirsch always insisted that it was possible to lead a full Jewish life in a non-Jewish environment. To achieve this one had to be totally committed to Judaism and to regard art and science as tools for serving God.

During the 1930s many neo-Orthodox Jews fled from Germany and settled in Britain, the USA and other countries. They set up their communities and established school and synagogue systems where the ideals of Hirsch and his successors continued to be taught. Through the rabbinical seminaries, neo-Orthodox ideas became very influential in shaping modern centrist Orthodox communities (see Unit 66).

THINGS TO DO

▶ Define neo-Orthodoxy. Why did it emerge as a movement?

▶ What did Rabbi Hirsch mean by the term *Jissroel-mensch*? What was his contribution to Jewish education?

▶ Rabbi Hirsch believed that secular studies should be used as tools for serving God. Choose three subjects you are studying and explain how they might help a religious person in his or her observance.

▶ What did Rabbi Hildsheimer do? Why do you think some people disapproved of his work?

CLASS DEBATE

▶ 'Secular studies must lead a person away from religion.'

Two speakers should defend the motion and two should oppose it before it is thrown open for general discussion.

In the past, the three styles of Orthodoxy described in Units 63–5 had little connection with one another. They belonged to fairly well-defined geographical areas and, to an extent, even regarded each other with suspicion. Today, this is no longer true. Over the years, they have all influenced each other in many ways and, although most Hasidic groups still keep largely to themselves, they have all moulded British Orthodoxy.

Orthodoxy in Britain, as elsewhere, falls roughly into two groups – 'centrist' and 'right-wing' Orthodoxy. These are rather imprecise terms referring to the extent to which people feel they want to be involved with secular culture. Generally speaking, centrist Orthodox families would not necessarily send their children to a Jewish school or, if they did, would choose one that combined Jewish studies with a wide secular curriculum. Right-wing families would only opt for a Jewish school that put its stress on the Jewish curriculum. However, it would be wrong to think of centrist and right-wing Orthodoxy as comprising of two distinct groups. Rather, they are tendencies that merge into one another as individual Jews express their commitments in different ways.

THE GROWTH OF ORTHODOXY

We saw on page 12 how, during the first half of the twentieth century, most Jews growing up in Britain had little interest in Jewish observance. This began to change towards the end of the 1960s. There were three reasons for this. First, the handful of religious communities had been growing steadily. They were building schools, synagogues, community centres; by 1962 they had established a newspaper, some had even begun taking part in local government. They were more numerous, more confident and more noticeable than they had been in the past. Second, during the years following the Holocaust and the establishment of the State of Israel, an increasing number of Jews who had not had a religious upbringing were beginning to take an interest in their heritage (p. 13). They were better educated and more open-minded than their parents' generation and were willing to make the effort to find out about Judaism. The stage was set for building bridges between these sections of the Jewish community.

Finally, there came the Six-Day War. In June 1967 several Arab countries, led by President Nasser of Egypt, launched a war against Israel (p. 63). Within six days, Israel had defeated them and the war was over. But Jews everywhere were shocked at the world's silence. For many it was almost like the Holocaust over again – Israel had been threatened with annihilation yet, with the exception of the United States, no one condemned the aggression; no one helped. Some countries, Britain included, even held up supplies of arms (already paid for) when Israel desperately needed them. Jews suddenly realized just how alone they were. British Jews, like those elsewhere in the diaspora, turned to their own development as Jews strengthened their ties with Israel.

THE NEW FACE OF BRITISH ORTHODOXY

There were far-reaching changes. Whereas previously, the United Synagogue (the largest Synagogue organization in Britain) had only accepted university graduates as rabbis, they now began taking men with yeshiva backgrounds. In the main, these were from Lithuanian-type yeshivot (p. 128), though many of these young men had obtained university degrees. Hasidim (p. 130), with the exception of Habad Hasidim (see below) did not become communal rabbis in centrist Orthodox congregations.

There was a renewed concern for Jewish education. More and more people wanted to send their children to Jewish schools; in particular to Jewish nurseries and primary schools. Study groups opened up in synagogues, businessmen took time off to attend 'lunch and learn' sessions.

From 1967 on, Habad Hasidim, at the direction of their leader, Rabbi Menachem Mendel Schneerson (1902–94) began a series of campaigns to teach people about the mitzvot. Over the following years, they established Habad houses, regional learning centres in various parts of the country.

Other Orthodox Jews launched Project Seed, a nation-wide learning drive where people were supplied with individual teachers to explain beliefs and practices or take them through classical Jewish texts. The Tenakh, Mishnah, Midrash, Talmud and later Jewish writings began appearing in new English translations. New works also began appearing, not only books explaining Jewish beliefs and practices, but Jewish novels and children's literature – even Jewish picture books for toddlers.

During the same period, rabbis began applying themselves to new social and technological problems. Organizations like the Institute for Science and Halakhah in Jerusalem published works on topics like the use of electricity on Shabbat (p. 40) and running a modern kosher kitchen. Rabbis began specializing in modern technological fields or were helped by scientists and doctors to address contemporary issues (p. 93). People began to see that the halakhah was being seriously applied to modern questions (p. 32); popular journals appeared (in English) where they could read about these developments.

ORTHODOXY TODAY

Today, there are about 300 Orthodox synagogues in Britain, each one affiliated to one of four synagogue organizations. At the head of the largest is the Chief Rabbi. In the larger towns, Jewish observance and commitment are flourishing as never before. There are new schools, yeshivot (p. 89) and seminaries (p. 90) where young people can develop their Jewish knowledge and youth movements where they can develop their Jewish identities. In London, Jews' College now provides yeshiva graduates with the pastoral skills necessary for becoming communal rabbis. There is, today, an increasing demand for kosher food and new kosher shops and restaurants have opened up; the demand for new mikvaot is a sign that more couples are keeping family purity (p. 77) than in the past.

HOW ORTHODOX JEWS SEE THEMSELVES

Orthodox Jews see themselves continuing the ancient traditions of Judaism in a modern context. For them, the Torah is the eternal will and wisdom of God which they must live by in the social and technological conditions of the twentieth century as their ancestors lived by it in their day. This does not mean changing or diluting their religion; it means reapplying it to today's world (p. 32) and adjusting their lifestyles to the Torah's demands. Sometimes, there are difficulties, e.g. finding jobs where they can take off Shabbat and festivals, finding kosher food (p. 68) or praying with a minyan (p. 65) when they are out and about, or finding a mikveh (p. 82) when they are away on holiday. Orthodox Jews see these as part of the discipline of living as Jews – to change these things for the sake of comfort or convenience would be a betrayal of their heritage. Ultimately, they see themselves serving God in the fullest possible way and that is what makes life meaningful for them.

HOW OTHERS SEE THEM

Sometimes, members of non-Orthodox movements (see Units 67–70) think Orthodox Jews are making life hard for themselves by keeping what they see as outmoded laws. They feel that they could live more easily by changing Judaism, as they have done (p. 138). They call right-wing Orthodox Jews 'fundamentalists' (a term which means someone who thinks the Torah is the word of God), which they use as a derogatory term. Above all, they are displeased that Orthodox Jews do not recognize many of their practices as valid nor their leaders as rabbis.

Prayer time in Bnei Akiva, an Orthodox youth movement

THINGS TO DO

▶ What is meant by 'centrist' and 'right-wing' Orthodoxy?

▶ A British Jew goes to sleep in 1935 and wakes up in 1995. What changes would he see? (You might want to read page 13 before answering this question.)

▶ What are some of the difficulties of living as Jews in Britain? How do Orthodox Jews approach these problems?

▶ What is a fundamentalist? Why do you think some people use this word as a derogatory term?

A minority of Jews in Britain are members of non-Orthodox movements. There are three of these: Reform, Liberal and Masorti. These movements are all founded on the belief that God did not give the Torah to the Jewish people on Mount Sinai (p. 26). They all maintain, in their different ways, that Jewish beliefs and practices may be altered or given up in order to allow Judaism to adapt to today's society. Orthodox Jews, however, do not recognize these movements as teaching authentic Judaism.

The first non-Orthodox movement to emerge was the Reform movement.

HOW THE REFORM MOVEMENT BEGAN

Read page 10 before beginning this section.

The creation of a movement for Reform was neither planned nor was it anyone's decision. Rather, it was a tendency that developed gradually in the minds and hearts of assimilated German Jews during the last quarter of the eighteenth century and first found expression with relatively small-scale changes in the synagogue service. Only later did thinkers and leaders emerge to develop consciously the tendency into a movement.

We saw on page 10 how the maskilim wanted to change the way Jews lived so that others would grant them emancipation. In 1778 a school was opened in Berlin offering secular education to Jewish children. It was the first of many. In the years that followed, armed with a secular education and knowledge of German that their parents had not known and wanting to be accepted into German society, young Jews began drifting away from Jewish observance. They became so German in lifestyle and outlook that Judaism seemed alien to them. Many had themselves baptized into Christianity (p. 15).

Others did not want to go that far. They felt that if they made changes in the synagogue service, modelling it on the Lutheran Church, Germans would find Judaism worthy of esteem. The first attempt was made at Seesen in Hanover in 1810 where Israel Jacobson founded a school. In it, Jewish children were taught secular subjects (by that time, quite common) and services were held with songs and sermons in German as well as an organ, as in the church. Similar services began taking place elsewhere. In 1818 the Hamburg Temple, regarded as the first Reform synagogue, was opened. In the years that followed different communities introduced different changes ranging from those who used German for their prayers in part of the service and sung to organ accompaniment to others where they abolished circumcision and moved Shabbat to Sunday. However, the most significant change was the growing belief that people could alter Judaism to suit their needs.

LEADERSHIP

The reforming tendency spread. In communities where large numbers of Jews favoured it, they began to feel dissatisfied with their existing rabbis. They wanted leaders who thought like themselves. The new Reform communities also began looking for people to employ as rabbis.

Those who were offered rabbinic posts in the reforming communities had little or no traditional background. They were in the main, assimilated German–Jewish intellectuals whose approach to Judaism had been moulded in the critical study programmes of the universities rather than the sanctity of the yeshivot (p. 89). These men provided the reforming tendency with a theoretical underpinning and forged out the direction Reform was to take. Among the most prominent were Samuel Hirsch (1815–89) and Samuel Holdheim (1806–60). For Hirsch (no relation to Samuel Raphael Hirsch, p. 132) the mitzvot were merely symbols of divine truths. He taught that when people's lives changed so that the truths were no longer conveyed through the symbols, the symbols (i.e. the mitzvot) could be discarded. Holdheim saw the mitzvot as the laws and customs of the ancient Jewish state destroyed by the Romans nearly 2,000 years earlier. This made the mitzvot obsolete and Holdheim criticized the rabbis for teaching people to live by what he regarded as the laws of a long dead state.

Abraham Geiger

The most influential of all was Abraham Geiger (1810–74). Like other assimilated Jews of his day, he felt perfectly at home in Germany and had no wish to follow a messiah to the Holy Land (p. 24). He therefore taught that Jews were a religious community rather than a nation. On this basis, he saw no need to pray for the restoration of a Jewish state.

Geiger developed a kind of theory of evolution of Judaism. He taught that Judaism had always changed to suit new circumstances; the mediaeval rabbis had remodelled the Judaism of the Talmudic period, just as the rabbis of the Talmud had adapted the Judaism of Biblical times. On this basis, he believed, it was reasonable for modern rabbis to remodel Judaism again. Geiger believed that Judaism could be reduced to 'ethical monotheism' – belief in one God coupled with high standards of moral behaviour. For him the only mitzvot that had any value were those that led to this ideal. Other mitzvot might have been meaningful in an earlier age but since, as Geiger taught, nothing was eternally binding, they could be abandoned.

These men all produced justifications for Reform and their ideas made it possible, in theory, for people to change the Jewish religion in almost any way they wanted.

OPPOSITION AND EXPANSION

Rabbis in Germany and abroad opposed these changes. They were afraid the reformers would destroy the unity of the Jewish people by creating a separate community. They preached against the reformers, wrote letters denouncing them and even tried to persuade the German authorities to close down their synagogues. However, most rabbis did not have a university education and were unable to oppose the reformers on their own terms. The only one who did so successfully was Rabbi Samson Raphael Hirsch (p. 132). He was able to uphold Torah-true Judaism in such a convincing way that he even won the admiration of Geiger.

Meanwhile, Reform grew from a tendency to a movement. It spread, first throughout Germany, the Netherlands and other European countries. It reached the United States in 1824, though the first Reform synagogue was not built there until 1841. Reform began in Britain in 1842, when some members of the Bevis Marks Synagogue in London broke away to form the West London Synagogue.

REFORM CONFERENCES

Between 1844 and 1871 the Reform leaders held a number of conferences. Here the beliefs and practices of the new movement were worked out, for while the men who attended held diverse opinions, they all wanted to reach some form of agreement as to the direction Reform should take.

Seeing themselves as part of German society with no desire to leave Europe, they discontinued prayers for the restoration of the Holy Land and the rebuilding of the Temple (p. 24). They gave up the belief in the coming of a messiah and reinterpreted it to mean hope for a messianic age. They also decided that the dietary laws (p. 68) should no longer be binding and that they would abolish the second day of festivals (p. 48). Other topics discussed were the status of women and redefining the meaning of 'work' on Shabbat. These conferences laid the foundation for the Reform movement as it is today.

THINGS TO DO

▶ What is meant by the term non-Orthodox?

▶ An historian described the beginning of reform as 'the leadership of well-intentioned laymen'. What do you think he meant?

▶ What changes did the early reformers make in Judaism?

▶ Why was Abraham Geiger an important figure in Reform history?

▶ How did the conference of the mid-nineteenth century help to bring direction to the new movement?

Today, the largest number of Reform congregations is in the United States. American Reform is also more left-wing than that in Britain, being closer to the Liberal movement here (see Unit 69). It is only during the last 30 years that Reform has grown in the UK.

During the first half of this century, British Reform was mainly concerned with dignity and decorum in its three synagogues. It played little part in people's lives. From the 1960s on, it expanded. Today, it has 18 synagogues in the Greater London area and a further 22 in the rest of Britain. Its leaders now concern themselves to a much greater extent with education and youth activities and teach a more positive view of Israel than in the past. Reform Synagogues of Great Britain (RSGB), founded in 1942, is the overall co-ordinating body. However, individual synagogues have considerable freedom to do as they choose.

REFORM PRACTICE

The synagogue

The conduct of services varies from one Reform synagogue to another, but there is some basic uniformity. Prayers are shorter than in Orthodox synagogues and some might be read in English. There is no mention of a return to the Holy Land, nor of rebuilding the Temple. On Yom Kippur (p. 46) the order of the Temple service with its sacrifices is read, but only for its historical value.

In all Reform synagogues men and women sit together. Women may carry the Torah scrolls to and from the Ark and are called to recite blessings before and after the reading. Girls often celebrate their Bat Mitzvah by reading from the Torah. Some Reform synagogues have women as rabbis. The wearing of teffilin (p. 87) was once abandoned, but it has recently been making a comeback in some synagogues.

Shabbat

In traditional Judaism, Shabbat has always started at sunset on Friday (p. 37). In Reform communities, however, people commence Shabbat and light the candles at any time on Friday evening. Nor do they see Shabbat observance in terms of 39 melachot (p. 41). For them 'work' means literally going into the office or factory, or working for profit.

Members of Reform communities often drive their cars on Shabbat, especially to attend synagogue or visit members of their family, and also use electrical appliances. Festivals are observed in a similar way and Reform communities do not observe the 'second day' of festivals associated with the diaspora (p. 48).

Marriage and divorce

The marriage ceremony in Reform synagogues is basically traditional but, the laws of 'family purity' (p. 77) are not followed.

There are two types of divorce procedure. One follows the traditional giving of a get (p. 78). The other, used when the husband refuses to give a get, consists of the Reform bet din issuing a document which dissolves the marriage. This document is accepted as a get in Reform and Liberal congregations (p. 141), although for traditional Jews, this raises the possibility of mamzerut (p. 79).

The dietary laws

Reform leaders once abandoned kashrut as a matter of principle. Crab, prawns and other shellfish (p. 70) were served at the opening of the Reform Hebrew Union College in America in 1883. Nowadays, however, a number of Reform homes observe kashrut to some extent. Catering is officially kosher on synagogue premises, though there is no rabbinical supervision (p. 70) to ensure that it is so.

Sexual matters

In Reform communities, contraception and abortion are not regarded as religious issues to the same extent as among the Orthodox. These issues are approached mainly from a medical or social point of view. Reform leaders have accepted homosexuality (p. 110) as a valid alternative lifestyle.

Death and mourning

Some traditional mourning customs, such as saying kaddish, are observed in Reform communities, though they do not practise tearing of garments (p. 80) nor, necessarily, keep the full week of shiva. In Reform communities it is regarded as acceptable to cremate bodies if the individual requested it.

Conversion

On page 23 it was explained that the Orthodox conversion procedure consists of circumcision for males, immersion in a mikveh and accepting the mitzvot. Immersion was not part of the Reform conversion procedure until 1980, but Reform congregations recognize those who underwent the earlier form of conversion as Jewish.

Orthodox Jews do not recognize Reform conversions as valid. They believe that it is meaningless for people to undertake to observe the mitzvot when they do not regard them as binding.

Zionism

Early Reform thinkers rejected the idea of being in exile. They thought of themselves as loyal Germans or Americans and did not see Jewish destiny as being bound up with homeland in Palestine. For them, the dispersion of Jews throughout the world was not a punishment for sin, but God's way of bringing Jews together with other people so that they could work towards a better world (p. 99). In 1845 German Reform leaders agreed to discontinue all prayers for the restoration of a Jewish state. The Pittsburgh Platform of American Reform (1885) includes the statement:

> 'We consider ourselves no longer a nation, but a religious community, and therefore expect neither a return to Palestine . . . nor the restoration of any of the laws concerning the Jewish state.'

By the mid-twentieth century, Reform leaders were beginning to take a more positive attitude to the ancient Jewish homeland. Today, although they still do not pray for a return to Zion, most Reform congregations do pray for the welfare of Israel.

HOW MEMBERS OF REFORM SEE THEMSELVES

RSGB has as its slogan, 'Rooted in the past, responding to change'. Many of its members see themselves as observing a modernized form of Judaism which is responding to the needs of time. Others attend Reform synagogues because they like to pray in English or sit together as a family. Some are acutely aware of the two problems that have preoccupied the Reform movement since it began: finding a satisfactory balance between authority and independence and developing a consistent philosophy of Reform.

In traditional Judaism the authority of the rabbis is based on the written Torah (p. 24). However, the Reform movement teaches that the Torah is not the revealed word of God. For Reform Jews, therefore, the question is how can a rabbi teach people how to observe Judaism and expect them to follow what he says when he has no real authority?

Claude Montefiore, one of the founders of the Liberal movement (see next unit) solved this problem by dispensing with all rabbinic authority and making observance depend on each individual's conscience. Reform leaders, not wanting to go this far, have never really solved the problem.

Second, Reform thinkers have not been able to work out a satisfactory basis for changing or abolishing Jewish practices. Some early reformers maintained that Biblical laws were not to be altered whereas Talmudic laws could. When they began changing Biblical laws, they decided on a new distinction – that 'ceremonial' laws could be abolished whereas moral laws could not. This too proved unsatisfactory, for Reform leaders retained Shabbat and some festivals, which were clearly ceremonial practices. Today, a RSGB leaflet gives the current position as, 'We follow tradition unless there are religious or ethical reasons for departing from its practice'.

HOW OTHERS SEE THEM

The Orthodox tend to look on Reform as a watered-down Judaism. They also see it as a vehicle for assimilation since it includes within its ranks many converts whom the Orthodox do not recognize as Jewish. Of greatest concern to the Orthodox is the split in the community brought about by Reform adopting a different definition of Judaism.

THINGS TO DO

▶ How do girls celebrate their bat mitzvah in a Reform synagogue?

▶ How might Shabbat be observed in a Reform household?

▶ Explain the Reform attitude to Israel.

▶ Describe Reform procedures for (a) divorce, (b) conversion. Why do you think these are the cause of great concern to Orthodox Jews?

▶ How do Reform communities view rabbinic authority?

CLASS DEBATE

▶ 'This house believes that people have the right to change their religion to suit their needs.'

Two people should propose the motion and two should oppose it.

'. . . Liberal Jews who in happy and serene freedom stand above the facts and above the sources ready to pick and choose to accept and reject . . .'

(Claude Montefiore)

The Liberal movement in Britain began during the early years of the twentieth century as a result of the work of Lily Montagu and Claude Montefiore. It was a response to the feeling that the Reform movement made too many demands on people and that greater changes in Judaism were needed.

LILY MONTAGU (1873–1963)

Lily Montagu's liberal approach to Judaism developed during her years as a social worker among poor immigrant families. Seeing them struggling to make a living and going through torments over working on Shabbat (p. 12), she began to feel that Judaism should be changed to make it easier for them to observe. In 1902 together with Claude Montefiore, she founded the Jewish Religious Union, the forerunner of the present Union of Liberal and Progressive Synagogues.

CLAUDE MONTEFIORE (1858–1938)

Although Claude Montefiore was a member of a Reform congregation, he felt that the kind of Judaism it taught was too demanding. Also, he believed that the ethical teachings of Christianity were superior to those of Judaism. Montefiore wanted to develop a kind of Judaism which would dispense with the beliefs of the past and yet lead to what he regarded as a higher morality. To achieve this he developed the notion of 'the enlightened consciousness'. By this, Montefiore meant that people should study Jewish beliefs and practices and then choose what they wanted to keep.

LIBERAL BELIEFS

Liberal beliefs are based on Montefiore's view that God did not reveal himself to Moses at Sinai nor to any other of the prophets in a literal sense, but that He makes Himself felt in the consciousness of each individual. Montefiore used this idea to give the Liberal movement its basic approach to Judaism. In Liberal thinking, observing mitzvot is a matter of personal choice. Some people might feel they need mitzvot for their moral development, others might not. For example, eating kosher food (p. 68) is regarded as a moral discipline for those who want it. Those who wish to achieve moral discipline in some other way, however, are free to do so. Jews who follow the Liberal movement's teachings regard both as equally valid and consider people fully observant if they follow whatever practices they have chosen.

Like other Jews, the movement's leaders have been troubled by the Holocaust (p. 16), especially by the question of how God could have allowed it to happen. Some have come to believe that God is not all-powerful (p. 18) and that, like humans, He too struggles to overcome evil.

LIBERAL PRACTICE

Although the Liberal view is that individuals can observe Judaism however they choose, certain practices are common to most of the 29 Liberal congregations in Britain.

Claude Montefiore

The synagogue

Prayers are similar to those of Reform synagogues. Men and women sit together and men pray bareheaded if they wish. Liberal synagogues also hold confirmation ceremonies for boys and girls at the age of sixteen. In these ceremonies young people accept their moral responsibilities. They usually take place on Shavuot.

Sabbaths and festivals

As in the Reform movement, members of Liberal congregations do not necessarily start Sabbaths and festivals at sunset (p. 37), and often choose to light Shabbat or festival candles later. Certain practices, such as lighting the Hanukkah lamp (p. 56), blowing the shofar on Rosh Hashanah (p. 45) and fasting on Yom Kippur (p. 46) have been retained. On Pesach, members of Liberal congregations eat matzah (p. 50) but would not necessarily buy 'kosher for Passover' foods. Tisha b'Av (p. 60) and other fasts are not observed. Shavuot (p. 52) is regarded as having symbolic significance only, since Liberal Jews do not believe that the Torah was given at Mount Sinai (p. 6).

Marriage

In the marriage ceremony in Liberal synagogues the groom says, 'With this ring you are sanctified to me . . .' (p. 77). The bride also makes a similar statement to the groom. Both respond to the English questions 'Do you take this man . . .?, Do you take this woman . . .?' The ceremony takes place under a huppah (p. 76).

Divorce

There is no Liberal divorce procedure and no get. A divorce which has been carried out in the civil courts is accepted as valid in Liberal congregations. For Orthodox Jews this creates the possibility of a woman remarrying without a get from her former husband, causing her children to be mamzerim (p. 79). The movement's religious leaders do not regard this as important, though some might suggest to a divorcing couple that they contact the Orthodox authorities to arrange a get.

Mourning

In Liberal congregations the seven-day mourning period (shiva) is optional. Some people observe only one day. Some bodies are buried in plain wooden coffins (p. 80), others are cremated. Kaddish is recited on Friday night, as they do not hold regular weekday services.

Who is a Jew?

On page 76 it was explained that the Jewishness of a child is determined by its mother. If she is Jewish, so is the child; otherwise the child is not. In the Liberal movement a child is regarded as Jewish if either of the parents is a Jew. Any person brought up as a Jew (e.g. a non-Jewish child adopted by Jewish parents) is also considered to be Jewish, provided the child was under seven years of age when he or she was adopted. Similarly, if the child of a Jewish mother was raised in another faith, Liberals would regard him or her as a non-Jew.

Life after death

Liberal leaders long ago rejected belief in a bodily resurrection (p. 24) and have removed all references to it from their prayer book. Many believe that the soul is immortal. However, some have also rejected this notion, believing instead that immortality consists only of being remembered by future generations.

THINGS TO DO

▶ How would the seating in a Liberal synagogue differ from the one shown on page 84?

▶ Why would the fasts connected with the destruction of the Temple (pp. 60–1) not be observed in Liberal congregations?

▶ How do Reform and Liberal Jews differ from one another in their attitudes towards eating kosher food (p. 68), the giving of a get (p. 78) and the question of who is a Jew?

Whereas the Liberal movement emerged out of the feeling that Reform had not gone far enough, Masorti was founded on the view that it had gone too far.

MASORTI ANCESTRY

The Assembly of Masorti Synagogues, the youngest non-Orthodox movement in the UK, was established in 1991. However, the religious views it teaches go back to the early days of German Reform, in particular to Zacharias Frankel (1801–75). Like many German Jews of his day, Frankel felt that the emancipation of the Jews and their adoption of western culture (p. 10) called for some changes in Judaism. However, he could not agree with the extreme reforms of Geiger, Holdheim and the others (p. 136). His approach, which he termed 'historical-positive', was that Judaism had always changed to suit new circumstances and that slight changes could be beneficial. His views formed the basis of the Conservative movement in the USA, of which Masorti is the British equivalent.

MASORTI BELIEFS

In a sense, the Masorti movement began with a book published in 1957 by Dr Louis Jacobs, then rabbi of the (Orthodox) North West End Synagogue. In this book, he argues that God did not give the Torah at Mount Sinai (p. 6) but that Judaism had grown out of people's religious experiences. He explains his views by quoting an American Conservative thinker who writes:

> 'Revelation is not the communication of infallible information . . . nor is it the outpouring of 'inspired' sages and poets . . . Revelation is the self-disclosure of God in his dealings with the world. Scripture is . . . a story composed of many strands and fragments . . . it is the story of the encounter of God and man in the history of Israel.'

According to this view, the Torah is made up of documents written in different times and places, in which a variety of authors describe how they thought they were experiencing God. What distinguishes the Torah from other, similar, ancient writings is that Jews have always seen God's presence within it.

Dr Louis Jacobs

In 1963 Dr Jacobs left Orthodoxy and set up an independent synagogue. This congregation became the base from which the Masorti movement grew.

Masorti teachers believe that the halakhah is not related to the actual words of the Torah since, for them, these are not God's words. They prefer to relate the halakhah to the Torah's ideas. This type of reasoning creates a problem since the rabbis of old did indeed derive halakhot from the words of the Torah, sometimes even from unusual spellings (see p. 30). If those rabbis were mistaken, as Masorti thinkers maintain they were, it raises the question whether their halakhot should apply any longer.

Dr Jacobs' answer is that it does not matter how the halakhot came into being; what does matter is that the various laws and customs have 'all contributed to the ennoblement of Jewish life and the elevation of the Jewish spirit'. Simply put, this means that since the mitzvot have long been the Jewish people's way of serving God, they have acquired a kind of sanctity. However, they do not regard the mitzvot as being actual divine commands. Masorti leaders call this 'non-fundamentalist halakhah', i.e. halakhah without a basis in direct divine revelation.

MASORTI PRACTICE

The synagogue service

Masorti services follow the order of those in Orthodox synagogues. However, customs vary among its seven synagogues. Some have separate seating for men and women (p. 84), others follow Reform practices such as mixed seating, calling up women to the reading of the Torah or counting them as part of a minyan (p. 91).

The dietary laws

Masorti members are encouraged to observe certain areas of kashrut, e.g. meat and fish (p. 70). However, they would not insist on other things, such as kosher wine.

Conversions

Masorti requires circumcision for male converts and immersion in a mikveh for both men and women. There is also a formal acceptance of the mitzvot. They accept Reform converts who went through a conversion procedure after 1980 (when the Reform movement reintroduced immersion, p. 138) but would require immersion for those who converted previously. They do not recognize Liberal conversions. However, the Orthodox authorities do not accept Masorti conversions as valid.

Marriage and divorce

These follow traditional practice. Marriage takes place under a huppah and divorce includes the giving of a get. Masorti does not recognize Reform and Liberal divorce procedures as valid. Masorti marriages are not recognized by the Orthodox authorities.

Zionism

While Masorti is positive about Zionism (p. 144), its members do not look forward to the rebuilding of the Temple nor do they regard the land of Israel as holy in the generally accepted sense. For them sanctity means the collective prayers and hopes of the Jewish people over centuries directed towards Israel, rather than any holiness in the land itself.

HOW MEMBERS OF MASORTI SEE THEMSELVES

Masorti stands for (as they describe it) 'non-fundamentalist halakhah'. Its leaders claim to 'maintain the laws and practices of the past as far as possible' while believing that the Torah is not the actual word of God. They see themselves as committed to preserving the halakhah in ways that Reform is not. Members are taught that their movement offers them an Orthodox style of Judaism without what they see as outdated beliefs.

HOW OTHERS SEE THEM

Orthodox leaders are not convinced by Masorti's claims to maintain the laws and practices of the past. They point out that Masorti has already moved away from these laws and practices by allowing mixed seating in its synagogues and counting women in the minyan. Also, by choosing to believe that the Torah is the work of people who thought they were having some sort of religious experience rather than a direct communication from God, Masorti provides no anchor for the laws and practices it currently maintains and leaves the way open for unlimited change.

They are also worried that Masorti is a kind of Reform in slow motion and point to the Conservative movement in the USA, with which Masorti claims kinship. During the early years of the twentieth century the Conservative movement's practices were also largely traditional, but without the anchor of belief in divine revelation. Then in the 1930s, young men, with less sympathy for the traditions of the past than their forbears, came to the leadership. As a result, the movement started to move away from traditional practice. Since the early 1940s, it has been co-operating more and more with the American Reform movement. It has abandoned the second day of festivals (p. 48), has permitted the use of electrical appliances on Shabbat and has brought its divorce procedure closer to that of the Reform.

THINGS TO DO

▶ Write a short conversation between someone from an Orthodox, a Liberal and a Masorti congregation, discussing their views on halakhah.

▶ How does the conduct of a Masorti service differ from an Orthodox service?

▶ What is the Masorti view on Reform conversion?

'Accordingly, we, the members of the National Council, representing the Jewish people in Palestine . . . hereby proclaim the establishment of the Jewish State in Palestine, to be called Israel.'

(Israel's Declaration of Independence, May 1948)

Zion was originally another name for Jerusalem, though some Jews applied it to the whole of the Holy Land. Zionism is the belief that Jews should have a national homeland on their ancestral soil. During the nineteenth century the Zionist movement worked for and secured a Jewish homeland in Palestine. Today, it gives support to the State of Israel.

THE ORIGINS OF ZIONISM

Three factors led to the emergence of the Zionist movement:

- the Jews' centuries-old hope for a return to their homeland
- the rise of nationalism during the nineteenth century
- anti-semitism.

The hope for a return

Jews have always believed that the Land of Israel was their special possession. In the Bible God promised Abraham, 'I will give this land to your descendants' (*Genesis 12:7*), and repeated this promise to Isaac and Jacob. God warned the Jews that if they sinned, they would be driven out of their land. But He also promised them that their exile would only be temporary (*Leviticus 26:33–45*). The prophets repeatedly assured them that they would one day return (*Amos 9:14–15*).

As the centuries went by, the Jews were indeed scattered among the nations, although there was never a time when the Land of Israel was entirely without Jewish inhabitants. Hope of a return always remained alive. For nearly 2,000 years Jews prayed each day for God to restore their homeland to them.

The rise of nationalism

During the Middle Ages many wars were fought across Europe. National boundaries changed frequently. Sometimes people of different origins and cultures were thrown together; sometimes groups that were related were divided up. Towards the end of the eighteenth century, people began taking an interest in their own history, literature and music. They wanted to create nation-states in which people would be bound to each other by race and language. Germany and Italy became unified; the Irish attempted to free themselves of British rule. Similar moves were taking place elsewhere.

Nationalism affected the Jews too. Many Jews, particularly the younger generation who no longer shared the religious feelings of their parents (p. 128), began to think of having their own state. Some began looking to Palestine (then under Turkish rule) for a Jewish homeland.

Anti-semitism

The feelings of nationalism that were spreading through Europe had disastrous results for Jews. In many areas, creating a state on racial lines meant restricting or removing the rights of those of a different race. The Jews were a prime target and a wave of anti-semitism (hatred of Jews) spread through France, Germany and Austria. This came as a profound shock to the Jews of these countries who were largely assimilated and had come to regard themselves as loyal French or German citizens.

In Russia an outbreak of vicious pogroms (anti Jewish riots) began in 1881, bringing death and destruction to 160 Jewish communities (p. 15). One year later, the Tsarist government passed the notorious May Laws, which placed impossible business restrictions on the Jews and brought many to economic ruin. As a result of all this many Jews became convinced that there was no place for them in Europe. Some emigrated to Britain (p. 12), the USA and South Africa. Others turned their attention to Palestine, where the Hovovei Zion (lovers of Zion) were already supporting settlements.

HIBAT ZION (LOVE OF ZION)

During the latter half of the nineteenth century, Jews in Russia and Romania began forming societies with the aim of sending Jews to Palestine. They gained the support of a few wealthy Jews and founded a settlement in 1874. They had no political programme – they did not think of establishing a Jewish state. They simply wanted to build settlements in Palestine and support existing ones. In reality, they had neither the funds nor the influence to achieve this, except on a very small scale. Nor did they have organization or leadership until Dr Pinsker came on the scene.

At about the same time there was a move to revive Hebrew as a spoken language. It had been the language of prayer and of scholarship since the fall of the Roman Empire, but it was only spoken in oriental communities.

Y L PINSKER

Yehuda Leib (Leon) Pinsker (1821–91) was a doctor living in Odessa in the southern tip of the Pale of Settlement (p. 15). He believed that Jews should adopt Russian culture and assimilate into gentile society. It was the wave of pogroms that began in 1881 and the obvious anti-semitism of the Tsarist government that changed him. He came to believe that anti-semitism was due to the fact that Jews were always aliens. In 1882 he wrote, *Autoemancipation*. In this book he argued for the establishment of a Jewish homeland, though he did not specify where. He reasoned that if Jews had a homeland like other nations, there would be no further need for anti-semitism.

The Hovovei Zion applauded his book and invited Dr Pinsker to take part in a conference to elect a committee which would work to build settlements in Palestine. Public gatherings were forbidden in Tsarist Russia, so they met in Kattowitz (at that time in Germany) in 1884. He was elected head of the new committee and began travelling abroad to raise money to send Jews to Palestine. One of his supporters was Baron Edmund de Rothschild of Paris.

After the Jews were expelled from Moscow in 1891, the Hovovei Zion sent more people to Palestine. However, the Turkish authorities stopped immigration. At the same time, the Hovovei Zion ran out of money and lost some of the land they had purchased. Dr Pinsker began looking for other alternatives, including settling Jews in Argentina but died before he could carry out any of his plans.

THINGS TO DO

▶ Why has the Land of Israel always been important for Jews?

▶ What is meant by 'nationalism'? Why do you think nationalist leaders in Italy and Germany wanted to bring the separate states together? How did Jewish nationalism differ in its aims and how was it similar?

▶ Why do you think Jewish nationalism originally took root mainly among those Jews who were less committed to Judaism?

▶ What were Dr Pinsker's views on anti-semitism?

▶ What difficulties did the Hovovei Zion face?

▶ You find a letter written by a Russian Jew in 1884 to friends in New York. The letter finishes with the words, 'I hope to bring my family over very soon.' What might the rest of the letter have said?

The Kattowitz conference in 1884. Dr Pinsker is in the centre of the front row. Sitting on his right is Rabbi Mohilever (p. 148)

'If you will it, it is no idle dream.'

This was said by Theodor Herzl, the man who took a loosely co-ordinated Hibat Zion movement with limited aims and, almost single-handedly, turned it into an international movement whose objective was to create a Jewish state.

THEODOR HERZL (1850–1904)

Herzl was an Austrian journalist. In 1895 he was sent to Paris to report on the trial of Alfred Dreyfus, a Jewish officer in the French army. Dreyfus had been accused of treason (p. 15). The trial triggered off a wave of anti-semitism throughout France and the government declared the Jews themselves responsible. When the Paris mob began shouting 'death to the Jews', Herzl turned to another journalist and asked how such a thing could happen in a civilized country. 'They are rejoicing in the degradation of a Jew,' the other replied.

The Dreyfus trial affected Herzl deeply. Like Pinsker before him (p. 145, whose work he did not discover until years later) Herzl came to the conclusion that anti-semitism was unavoidable. It was the hatred of the stranger and would continue until Jews had a land of their own. He became consumed with a desire to make this happen and devoted his few remaining years to this ideal.

He first approached wealthy Jewish philanthropists (people who helped others) but they did not take him seriously. After several rebuffs, he decided to set down his ideas in writing. In 1896 he published a pamphlet, *'Der Judenstaat'* ('The Jewish State'). In it, he says that anti-semitism is a fact of life and argues that Jews can only preserve themselves if they have their own territory in which to settle. He recommended setting up a Society of Jews to represent the Jewish people and a Jewish Company to arrange finance. With this, land could be purchased, either in Palestine or Argentina and the wholesale resettlement of the Jews could start.

Herzl's ideas were rejected by assimilated Jews who felt completely at home in western Europe (p. 136), by religious Jews (for reasons explained in Unit 72) and by western Hovovei Zion, who thought it was too ambitious. However, east European Hovovei Zion acclaimed its bold plan and hailed Herzl as their leader. Herzl began organizing an international congress of those who supported his ideas. It was held in Basle, Switzerland, in August 1897 and became known as the First Zionist Congress. It adopted a resolution to create a home for the Jewish people in Palestine, secured by public law.

From then on, Herzl began meeting heads of state (including the Sultan of Turkey, who ruled Palestine at that time) and other influential people, to gain their support for his ideas. He was rebuffed time and again. Only in Britain did he achieve some success. In 1902 he began negotiating with British government officials. Joseph Chamberlain, the Colonial Secretary, put forward a plan for Jewish settlement in Uganda. At first, Herzl rejected this suggestion, but later decided to accept it as a stepping stone to acquiring land in Palestine. He thought that by co-operating with the British government, he would stand a better chance of achieving his ideal. However, the idea was strongly rejected at the next Zionist Congress. The Jewish homeland had to be in Palestine.

THE BRITISH MANDATE

In 1900 the World Zionist Organization set up the Jewish National Fund to buy land in Palestine. This fund, which was to be the property of the whole Jewish people, was based in London. The first modern Jewish city, Tel Aviv, was founded in 1909 on land purchased by the Fund. In 1917 after consultation with President Wilson of the United States, the British government pledged its support for a Jewish homeland in Palestine. The pledge was given to Lord Rothschild, the president of the English Zionist Federation. It read:

Foreign Office,
November 2nd, 1917.

Dear Lord Rothschild,

I have much pleasure in conveying to you, on behalf of His Majesty's Government, the following declaration of sympathy with Jewish Zionist aspirations which has been submitted to, and approved by, the Cabinet.

'His Majesty's Government view with favour the establishment in Palestine of a national home for the Jewish people, and will use their best endeavour to facilitate the achievement of this object, it being clearly understood that nothing shall be done which may prejudice the civil and religious rights of existing non-Jewish communities in Palestine, or the rights and political status enjoyed by Jews in any other country.'

I should be grateful if you would bring this declaration to the knowledge of the Zionist Federation.

Yours sincerely,

Arthur James Balfour

This letter became known as the 'Balfour Declaration'.

One month after the letter became public, General Allenby brought Palestine under British control. Three years later, Britain accepted the Mandate of Palestine. Under the terms of the Mandate, Britain was to help establish a home in Palestine for the Jewish people.

THE STATE IS BORN

By the end of the Second World War there was an urgent need to resettle thousands of Holocaust survivors (p. 16). Many of them tried to make their way to Palestine. For political reasons, the British forces in Palestine were ordered to restrict immigration and turned back the refugee ships. Some of the ships were old and barely seaworthy. They had limped to Palestine but sank on the return journey. Thousands of Jews who had survived the Nazi death camps were drowned. Jewish resistance movements in Palestine began attacking British military targets. The Arabs, who did not want large-scale Jewish immigration, also attacked.

In 1947 the United Nations voted to bring the British Mandate to an end and to partition Palestine into separate Jewish and Arab states. On 14 May 1948, the day before the last British troops left, the Jews of Palestine proclaimed the State of Israel.

FIND OUT

▶ Ze'ev (Vladimir) Jabotinsky and Joseph Trumpeldor were very influential in the struggle for a Jewish state. Find out what you can about them.

THINGS TO DO

▶ What did Herzl say in '*Der Judenstaat*'? Why did some Jews reject his ideas?

▶ Make a list of the things the 'Balfour Declaration' said, point by point.

▶ What was the purpose of the Jewish National Fund? What was its first major achievement?

▶ Why did the Holocaust make the need for a Jewish state more urgent than before?

▶ When the British Royal Navy was ordered to turn back the refugee ships, the Jews in Palestine began attacking British military targets. Why do you think they reacted in this way?

14 May 1948. David Ben-Gurion declares the State of Israel

From the very start, Hibat Zion and Zionism presented a dilemma for religious Jews. On the one hand, the return to the Holy Land was an age-old hope that religious Jews had prayed for over many centuries. On the other, it was being brought about by secular Jews, many of whom actually despised the practices of Judaism. Responses varied from religious support for Zionism to religious opposition.

RELIGIOUS ZIONISM

Rabbi Shmuel Mohilever (1824–98)

Religious Zionism really began with Rabbi Shmuel Mohilever. After the pogroms of 1881, Rabbi Mohilever felt that the Jews fleeing Russia should settle in Palestine. Although many rabbis did not support Hibat Zion because most of its followers were irreligious, Rabbi Mohilever shared their ideal. He was made Honorary President of the Kattowitz conference of 1884 (p. 145). In his speech he used Ezekiel's vision of the dry bones in the valley joining together and coming alive again (*Ezekiel 37*) to illustrate the renewal of Jewish life in the Holy Land.

Rabbi Mohilever tried to persuade other Orthodox people to join the movement. He believed that this would help to ensure that the new Jewish settlements in Palestine would be run along religious lines. At a meeting of Hovovei Zion in 1893, he argued for the establishment of a committee to ensure that Torah values would be upheld. This later gave rise to the Mizrahi movement.

The Mizrahi movement

A number of rabbis supported the early Zionist ideal. One of these was Rabbi Yitzhak Reines (1839–1915) who tried to spread the idea of a return to Palestine among his colleagues. Reines was dismayed by the Zionist movement's desire to undertake cultural activities. He believed that the movement should concern itself solely with securing a Jewish homeland in Palestine and should leave cultural activities to religious people. In 1902 he founded the Mizrahi movement, an organization of religious Zionists.

The Mizrahi ideal was to secure the future of the Jewish people through study of the Torah, observance of the mitzvot and return to the ancient homeland. In 1920 Mizrahi moved its headquarters to Jerusalem and the World Zionist Organization made it responsible for Jewish education in Palestine (a situation that continued until 1953). The following year, it established Rabbi Avraham Yitzhak Kook as the first Chief Rabbi of Palestine (see opposite). In 1956 it merged with a religious labour movement, to form the National Religious Party (NRP).

The Mizrahi movement fought long battles with the secular Zionists to preserve the Jewish character of the State of Israel. Due to its efforts, Shabbat is now an official day of rest where no public transport runs and Israeli soldiers are provided with kosher food. Mizrahi also set up a Ministry of Religions to ensure that peoples' religious needs would be met from public funds. It also kept marriage and divorce in the hands of the rabbis.

Rabbi Avraham Yitzhak Kook (1865–1935)

Rabbi Kook, the first Chief Rabbi of Palestine, criticized both the World Zionist Organization for concerning itself only with the secular needs of Jews and Mizrahi for not giving religious Zionism a theoretical basis. For him, the return of Jews to their ancient homeland was **athalta di'geulah**, an Aramaic phrase meaning 'the beginning of the Messianic redemption' (p. 24). He believed that the establishment of the Chief Rabbinate would lead to the restoration of the Sanhedrin (p. 30).

Rabbi Avraham Yitzhak Kook

Rabbi Kook was troubled by the fact that the return to the homeland, essentially a religious ideal, had been brought about mainly by irreligious Zionists. However, he believed that it was possible (as he put it) to do God's work without realizing it. For him, the most irreligious person was fulfilling God's will just by rebuilding the Holy Land. He maintained that the Zionists' sense of justice and commitment to the Jewish people would lead them to a deeper spiritual awareness.

For Rabbi Kook, Jewish nationality was not like that of other people, whose ties to their homeland was based on historical association with that land and sharing a common language and culture with those who lived there. Jewish nationality was divinely ordained. It was not the Jews, led by the Zionists, who had chosen to settle in the Holy Land; it was part of God's plan.

RELIGIOUS OPPOSITION TO ZIONISM

During the nineteenth century, many rabbis in eastern and central Europe disapproved of the Hovovei Zion and the Zionist movement. First, they believed that the return to Zion was to be brought about by the Messiah (p. 24) and that the Jews had to wait and pray for his coming. Second, they felt that a movement led and supported by secular Jews could only result in a weakening of Jewish values and practices. Indeed, Pinsker had formerly believed in total assimilation into Russian society (p. 145), his closest associate Moshe Lilienblum was a former yeshiva graduate who had abandoned religion. Even Herzl had once believed that the Jewish question (p. 15) should be solved by having all Jews converted to the Roman Catholic faith. In '*Der Judenstaat*' (p. 146) he had built up his case for a Jewish homeland without any reference to religion. His vision was of a Jewish state where the rabbis would remain in their synagogues and houses of study while the rest of the people led secular lives. Although many individual rabbis and Hasidic Rebbeim felt unhappy about Zionism, organized opposition came from Agudat Yisrael (Union of Israel), an association of Orthodox Jews formed in 1912 to counter assimilation and Reform. Its aim was to reinstate the authority of the rabbis as the supreme guiding factor in Jewish life.

Although Agudat Yisrael never actually obstructed the work of the Zionist movement, it objected to religious Jews co-operating with secular Zionists. Indeed, they found the very idea of a secular Jewish state in the Holy Land unacceptable. In their view, a state not run according to the teaching of the Torah could not be called a 'Jewish' state.

When the Nazis came to power (p. 12) Agudat Yisrael changed its position in order to help save Jewish lives. From 1937 it began co-operating with the World Zionist Organization, working for the establishment of a state where Jews could settle, while still refusing to call it a Jewish state.

THINGS TO DO

▶ Why did Zionism create dilemmas for religious Jews?

▶ Why did Rabbi Mohilever join the Hovovei Zion?

▶ List the achievements of the Mizrahi movement.

▶ How did Rabbi Kook think of Zionism?

▶ What is Agudat Yisrael? Describe its relationship with the Zionist movement.

Israel today is, in many ways, much like other modern democracies. Like other countries it has cities, factories, farms, schools, hospitals and universities; it has a police force and ambulance service; it has museums, art galleries and a national orchestra. And like other countries, it also has social problems – crime, unemployment, drug addiction and domestic violence. However, Israel also has features that are uniquely its own because it is a Jewish state.

A JEWISH STATE

Although the majority of Israeli citizens are Jews, it would be wrong to think that they all observe Judaism. Israel is mainly a secular country. There are even Israelis who are hostile to Judaism. They see Judaism as something that held Jews together in the past and which may still serve some purpose in the diaspora (p. 8), but is no longer needed for those who live in Israel. For religious Israelis, the reverse is true – Israel provides opportunities for observing Judaism in ways not possible in the diaspora. Naturally, these opposing views sometimes lead to confrontations. Thankfully, such confrontations are usually verbal. On the other hand, when the country has been at war, religious and secular Israelis have fought for – and died for – one another.

Judaism is the official religion of Israel, though other faiths are recognized and their holy places are protected. Marriage and divorce are largely in the hands of the rabbis. Secular Israelis do not always like this, but it does decrease the risk of mamzerim (p. 79). Except for marriage and divorce, Israeli law is based mainly on British law from the Mandate period (p. 147). There have been several attempts to introduce Jewish law and some elements of it are now finding their way into the Israeli legal system.

The Israeli flag depicts two horizontal blue stripes on a white background. Only when it is turned around so that the stripes are vertical does it become obvious what the flag really is – a tallit (p. 86). In the centre of the flag is a blue Magen David, a six pointed 'Star of David'. No one knows how it originated. However, over the years it came to be a symbol of Judaism. It can be seen on synagogue walls, on Rosh Hashanah greetings cards (p. 44), Jewish wedding invitations and elsewhere. During the Holocaust (p. 16), Jews were required to wear the star on their clothing.

KIBBUTZIM AND MOSHAVIM

The smaller townlets and villages of Israel are either **kibbutzim** (singular **kibbutz**) or **moshavim** (singular **moshav**). Most are agricultural settlements, though some have light industry.

Kibbutzim originated with the ideals of total social equality held by some of the early Russian Zionists. They are collectives, settlements where there is no private ownership. Everything belongs to the kibbutz which, in turn, takes care of its members' needs. All its members, in effect, work for the benefit of the whole kibbutz. People joining a kibbutz hand over all their personal belongings (they receive them back if they leave).

In kibbutzim, meals are taken together. There is a communal laundry, barber, clinic and clothing store. However, not all kibbutzim are the same. Some carry through the collective ideal even to having children brought up together and taking their meals together, meeting their parents at regular times. Others cater for individuality, for example in room decoration. Some kibbutzim are religious, most are not.

In moshavim, people own their own property.

ISRAEL AND THE DIASPORA

Since the beginnings of Hibat Zion (p. 144) Jews in the diaspora have provided funds for resettlement projects in Palestine, later Israel. Today, there are fund-raising agencies all over the world as well as departments for aliyah. **Aliyah** literally means 'going up'. Jews use the word to mean settling in Israel.

Israelis differ in their views about the diaspora. At one time, many Israelis felt that there should not be a diaspora at all and that all Jews should go to Israel. Today, most Israelis think positively about the relationship between Jews in Israel and those outside of it. However, some are beginning to resent the diaspora's role as provider of funds. They think Israel should stand on its own feet like any other country. For many non-religious Jews, giving money to Israel is sometimes their only way of expressing their attachment to the Jewish people.

Israel itself provides a haven for Jews anywhere in the world facing persecution. One of the first laws the Knesset (Israeli Parliament) passed was the Law of Return, stating that every Jew has the right to settle in Israel and be granted citizenship. In the past, Israel air-lifted entire communities from Yemen and Ethiopia (p. 5). Today, it is experiencing an influx of Russian Jews, many of whom suffered terribly under the former Soviet regime.

PILGRIMAGE

In ancient times, Jews used to take regular offerings to the Temple (p. 48). This type of pilgrimage ceased when the Temple was destroyed (p. 8). Today, pilgrimage, in the sense of a religious duty does not exist in Judaism. However, when modern Jews visit the ancient Biblical sites and other holy places, it gives them a sense of attachment to the whole of Jewish history. Some sites have a special significance for Jews and those who visit them feel a sense of personal pilgrimage.

The Western Wall (Hakotel Hamaaravi)

This is the last remaining wall of the second Temple and Judaism's holiest site. For centuries, Jews would go there to pray and mourn the Temple's destruction, resulting in it being called the Wailing Wall. From the armistice of 1948 until the Six-Day War in 1967 it was in Jordanian hands and no Jew could visit it. Now, regular services are held there every day. On festivals its forecourt is packed with thousands of worshippers. Some go there just to kiss the sacred stones. In recent years, boys from various countries have celebrated their bar mitzvah (p. 74) at the Wall.

Yad Vashem

This is the Holocaust memorial in Jerusalem. It has been described on page 62.

The tombs of great people

Maarat Hamachpelah in Hebron is the tomb of Abraham and Sarah, Isaac and Rebecca, Jacob and Leah. According to tradition, Adam and Eve are also buried there. It is in territory occupied by the Arabs who take care of the tomb, since they also claim descent from Abraham (through Ismail, *Genesis 16:15*). Rachel, Jacob's second wife is buried near Bet Lechem. Jews like to visit these tombs and pray there.

RELIGIOUS ATTITUDES TO ISRAEL TODAY

In the past, Zionism created dilemmas for religious Jews. Now that the State of Israel exists, there are real challenges. On the one hand, religious Jews are pleased that yeshivot (p. 89) and seminaries (p. 90) flourish there with even more students than in the heyday of the Lithuanian yeshivot (p. 128). They are pleased that all Jews have free access to pray at Judaism's holiest sites and that it is a haven for Jews anywhere in the world living under persecution. On the other hand, they are saddened by the secularism of Israeli life. They feel strongly about crime and prostitution on the holy soil of Israel; they are upset by the open sale of pork in some Israeli restaurants and they are deeply hurt when secular Israelis ridicule Judaism.

Usually, religious Jews look away from these things and focus on the positive aspects of having a Jewish state. While some prefer to have minimal contact with secular Jews, others try to reach out and build bridges of understanding between one Jew and another. After all, as we saw right at the beginning of this book, Jews are a family.

Prayers at the Western Wall

THINGS TO DO

▶ Sum up the attitudes of religious Jews to Israel today.

▶ What is (a) a kibbutz, (b) a moshav? How do they differ?

▶ What is a pilgrimage? Does the word have any meaning for Jews today?

▶ What is the Law of Return?

▶ How do Jews in Israel view the diaspora?

▶ What does the flag of Israel symbolize?

▶ Write a brief conversation between a religious and a secular Israeli.

GLOSSARY

Most words in this glossary are in Hebrew, the language of the Tenakh, the Mishnah and many Jewish written works. Today, Modern Hebrew is the official language of Israel and is spoken by many Jews around the world. Some parts of the Tenakh are written in Aramaic, a very ancient language closely related to Hebrew. Most of the Talmud is too. Jews do not speak Aramaic today.

Yiddish is a language rather similar to German. It was spoken by European Jews for many centuries. Today very few young Jews use Yiddish, though it is still the spoken language in Hasidic communities (p. 130). Many yeshivot (p. 89) teach in Yiddish.

Try to learn the correct pronunciation of the words in this glossary. The part of the word printed in bold shows you where to put the stress.

Please note: whenever you see 'ch' in the words that follow, it is not to be pronounced as in the English words 'chop' or 'much'. 'Ch' represents a Hebrew sound between k and h, made at the back of the throat. This sound does not exist in English. If you know the correct pronunciation of the Scottish 'loch' or the Welsh 'bach', you are fairly near to the Hebrew sound.

Afikomen (*A'fee'koo'***man**) 'Dessert'. Name given to the matzah eaten at the conclusion of the seder meal at Pesach (Passover)

Agadah (*A'ga'***dah**) A branch of Jewish learning that shows how particular beliefs and practices are related to Biblical verses

Agudat Yisrael (*A'gu'***dat** *Yis'ra'***el**) Lit. Union of Israel; an organization of Orthodox Jews whose aim was to restore the authority of the rabbis and Torah scholars in Jewish life

Agunah (*A'gu'***nah**) A woman whose husband is missing but not known to be dead

Aleinu (*A'***lay**'*nu*) The concluding prayer in each service in the synagogue

Aliyah (*Al'i'***yah**) 1. Being called to recite a blessing over the Torah reading in the synagogue 2. Going to settle in Israel

Almemar (*Al'***may**'*mar*) The raised platform in a synagogue where the Torah is read (see also Bimah)

Amen (*Ah'***men**) Response to a blessing, declaring that the blessing is true

Anti-Semitism Hatred of Jews

Aravot (*A'ra'***vot**) Branches of willow used in prayer during the festival of Sukkot

Arba'at haminim (*Ar'ba'***at** *ha'mi'***nim**) 'The four kinds' i.e. the four plants (palm branch, citron, myrtle and willow) used in prayers during Sukkot

Arvit (*Ar'***vit**) The evening service

Asarah b'Tevet (*A sa'***ra** *be'***te** *vet*) The 10th Tevet, a fast marking the day the Babylonians laid seige to Jerusalem in 587 BCE

Ashkenazim (*Ash'ke'na'***zim**) Western Jews

Athalta di'geulah (*At'hal'***ta** *de'ge'u'***lah**) Aramaic. Lit. The beginning of the redemption, i.e. the dawning of the messianic age

Av Fifth month of the Jewish Year (roughly corresponding with July/August)

Avel (*A'***vel**) A mourner (see also Onan)

Avelim (*A've'***lim**) Plural of avel

Avodah zarah (*A'vo'***dah** *za'***rah**) 'Alien worship', the worship of anything other than God; idolatry in general

Avraham Avinu (*Av'ra'***ham** *a'***vee**'*noo*) Our father Abraham; the term by which Jews refer to Abraham, the first Jew

Bar Kokhba (**Bar** *kokh'***ba**) A Jewish revolutionary leader who rebelled against the Romans in the year 132

Bar mitzvah (**Bar** *mitz'***vah**) 'Son of the commandments', the term used to refer to a boy when he reaches Jewish adulthood at the age of thirteen

Baruch shepatarani (*Ba'***ruch** *she'pa'ta'***ra**'*ni*) The declaration made by the father of a boy or girl, declaring that they are now responsible for their own actions

Bat chayil (**Bat** *chay'***il**) 'Daughter of excellence', a graduating ceremony for girls over the age of twelve

Bat mitzvah (**Bat** *mitz'***vah**) 'Daughter of the commandments', the term used to refer to a girl who reaches Jewish adulthood at the age of twelve

Bedikat chametz (*Be'dee'***kat** *cha'***metz**) The search for leaven (risen bread), carried out the evening before Passover

Bemidbar (*Bemid'***bar**) Hebrew name for the Biblical Book of Numbers

Bereshit (*Be'ray'***shit**) The Hebrew name for the Biblical Book of Genesis

Bet din (*Bet* **din**) 'House of justice', a Jewish court of law

Bet din hagadol (*Bet* **din** *ha'ga'***dol**) 'Great house of justice', the supreme Jewish court in ancient times

Bet ha Knesset (*Bet hak'***ness**'*et*) 'House of assembly', the Hebrew name for a synagogue

Bimah (*Bee'***mah**) The raised platform in a synagogue where the Torah is read (see also Almemar)

Birchat eirusin (*Bir'chat ey'roo'***sin**) 'Blessings of bethrothal', the first blessings recited at a wedding

Birchat nisuin (*Bir'chat nis'oo'***in**) 'Blessings of marriage', the final blessings recited at a wedding

Blech Yiddish for 'tin', a sheet of tin or aluminium placed over a cooker on Sabbaths, so that saucepans can be moved to hotter or cooler parts without being lifted

Brit Covenant

Brit milah (*Brit mee'***lah**) Covenant of circumcision

Challot (*Cha'***lot**) The special loaves of bread used on Sabbaths and festivals

Chametz (*Cha'***metz**) Leaven

Chamesh Megillot (*Cha'***mesh** *me'gi'***lot**) 'The five scrolls', the Biblical books of Esther, Song of Songs, Ruth, Lamentations and Ecclesiastes

Chamishah chumshei Torah (*Cha'mi'***shah** *chum' shei To'***rah**) The five books (lit. five fifths) of the Torah – Genesis, Exodus, Leviticus, Numbers, Deuteronomy

Chatan Bereshit (*Cha'***tan** *Be're'***shit**) The person called to the reading of the first Torah portion of the new cycle on Simchat Torah

Chatan Torah (*Cha'***tan** *To'***rah**) The person called for the reading of the last Torah portion of the old cycle on Simchat Torah

Chaver (*Cha'***ver**) Companion/member: a person with whom one studies the Torah or Talmud

Chavruta (*Chav'roo'***ta**) 'Companionship', a system of learning where two people study together

Chazan (*Cha'***zan**) The person who leads the prayers in the synagogue

Chazanim plural of chazan

Cheder (*Che'***der** but it is often also pronounced like 'raider') 'A room', a term originally meaning the room where Jewish children studied, now used to mean Jewish religious classes

Chevra kaddisha (*Chev'***ra** *ka'dee'***sha**) Aramaic for sacred society, the people who prepare a body for burial

Chevrat musar (*Chev'***rat** *mu'***sar**) Ethics group, a group of people who meet to study Jewish ethical teachings

Chol hamoed (**Chol** *ha'mo'***ed**) 'The ordinary days of the festival', the middle days of the festivals of Passover and Sukkot, during which some work is permitted

Chukim (*Choo'***kim**) Laws for which no reason is given; keeping these is regarded as a test of faith

Chumash (*Chu'***mash**) Short for chamishah chumshei Torah; a printed book of the Torah (the Five Books of Moses)

Chumashim (*Chu'ma'***shim**) Plural of chumash

Cohen (*Co'***hen**) A priest

Cohanim (*Co'ha'***nim**) Plural of cohen

Dayan (*Da'***yan**) Judge in a rabbinical court

Dayanim (*Da'yan'***im**) Plural of dayan

Devarim (*De'var'***im**) Hebrew name for the Biblical Book of *Deuteronomy*

Dreidle (*Drei'***dle**) (Yiddish) A spinning top with Hebrew letters used in a children's game during the festival of Hanukkah

Eichah (*Ei'***chah**) The Biblical book of Lamentations

Ellul (*El'***lul**) Sixth month of the Jewish year, roughly corresponding with August/September

Etrog (*Et'***rog**) Citron, one of the four plant species used during prayers in the festival of Sukkot

Etz chaim (*Etz cha'***yim**) 'Tree of life', the wooden poles to which the ends of the Torah scroll are stitched

Falashas (*Fa'lash'***as**) Ethiopian Jews

Gabbai (*Ga'***bai**) Person responsible for the running of the synagogue service

Gaon (*Ga'***on**) Head of one of the Babylonian academies which functioned from the third to the eleventh century

Gaonim (*Ga'on'***im**) Plural of gaon

Gemara (*Ge'ma'***ra**) Aramaic for 'learning', the name by which Jews call the Talmud

Gemilut hassadim (*Ge'mil'***ut** *ha'sad'***im**) 'Acts of kindness', giving of one's own time and effort to help others (see also Tzedaka)

Genevat daat (*Ge'ne'***vat** *da'***at**) Deception (lit. stealing the mind)

Get A document of divorce

Habad (*Ha'***bad**) A word composed of the initial letters of the Hebrew words Hachmah (wisdom), Binah (understanding), Daat (knowledge); name of a school of Hasidic thought founded by Rabbi Shneur Zalman of Liadi in the eighteenth century

Hadassim (*Ha'da'***sim**) 'Branches of myrtle', one of the four plant species used in prayer during the festival of Sukkot

Haftarah (*Haf'ta'***rah**) A portion from one of the Books of the Prophets read on Sabbath morning after the Sidra. Plural haftarot

Hagadah (*Ha'ga'dah*) 'Telling', the book read and discussed during the seder meal on Passover

Hagadot (*Ha'ga'dot*) Plural of hagadah

Hakafot (*Ha'kaf'ot*) 'Circuits'; during the festival of Simchat Torah, the Torah scrolls are carried round the synagogue seven times

Hakotel Hamaaravi (*Ha'ko'tel Ha'ma'a'ra'vi*) The western wall of the Temple

Halakhah (*Ha'la'khah*) 'A going', the name for Jewish law, also used to mean a particular law

Halakhot (*Ha'la'chot*) Laws, plural of halakhah

Hallel (*Ha'lel*) 'Praise', a recitation of *Psalms 113–118*

Hanukkah (*Cha'noo'kah*) 'Dedication', an 8-day festival commemorating the rededication of the Temple in Hellenistic times

Hanukiah (*Cha'noo'kee'ah*) A nine-branched oil- or candle-holder lit during Hanukkah (see also Menorah)

Haroset (*Ha'ro'set*) A mixture of apples, wine, nuts and cinnamon (some use other ingredients) eaten during the seder meal on Passover

Hasid (*Ha'sid*) A member of the Hasidic movement

Hasidim (*Ha'sid'im*) Followers of the Hasidic movement

Hasidic movement (*Ha'sid'dic*) A Jewish revivalist movement that began during the seventeenth century

Haskalah (*Has'ka'lah*) Enlightenment, a movement started by Jews who wanted to get rid of the differences between Jews and non-Jews

Havdalah (*Hav'da'lah*) 'Separation', a ceremony performed at the end of the Sabbath and festivals

Hechsher (*Hech'sher*) A stamp or label certifying that a food product is kosher

Hibat Zion (*Hi'bat Zi'on*) Love of Zion, a political movement which aimed to settle Jews in the Holy Land

Hillel (*Hi'lel*) Important rabbi of the first century

Hoshanah Rabbah (*Ho'sha'nah ra'bah*) The seventh day of Sukkot

Hovovei Zion (*Ho'vo'vei Zi'on*) Members of Hibat Zion

Huppah (*Hoo'pah*) 'Covering', the canopy beneath which a Jewish couple are married

Hurban (*Hur'ban*) Destruction

Iyar (*I'yar*) Second month of the Jewish year, roughly coinciding with April/May

Jissroel-mensch (*Yis'ro'el mench*) German. Israel-man, a term coined by Rabbi Samson Raphael Hirsch to mean a pious, cultured Jew

Judenfreige (*Yu'den'fra'ge*) German. The Jewish question

Judenrein (*Yu'den'rine*) German. Empty (lit. clean) of Jews

Kabbalah (*Ka'ba'lah*) Jewish mysticism

Kaddish (*Ka'dish*) Prayer said by a mourner praising God

Kaparot (*Ka'pa'rot*) 'Forgivenesses', a ceremony performed on the eve of the Day of Atonement

Kashrut (*Kash'rut*) State of being kosher; also study of the laws relating to kosher food

Kedoshim (*Ke'dosh'im*) 'Holy ones', Jewish martyrs

Ketubah (*Ke'too'bah*) Marriage certificate

Ketuvim (*Ke'too'vim*) Hebrew name for the Hagiographa, the third section of the Hebrew Bible

Kibbutz (*Ki'butz*) A collective settlement where there is no (or almost no) private ownership. Opposite of moshav

Kibbutzim (*Ki'butz'im*) Plural of kibbutz

Kiddush (*Ki'dush*) 'Sanctification', blessing recited over wine at the start of Sabbath and festival meals

Kiddush hashem (*Ki'dush ha'shem*) 'Sanctification of the name of God', sacrificing one's life for God

Kiddush levanah (*Ki'dush le'va'nah*) 'Sanctification of the moon', blessing recited during the first part of each Jewish month

Kinot (*Ki'not*) 'Dirges', poems recited in the synagogue on Tisha b'Av

Kippah (*Ki'pah*) Skull cap worn by Jewish males, also called a kupple

Kittel (*Ki'tle*) White, smock-like garment worn by Jewish men on the Day of Atonement

Knesset (*K'nes'et*) Israeli Parliament

Kohelet (*Ko'hel'et*) Biblical Book of Ecclesiases

Kollel (*Ko'lel*) College of advanced rabbinical studies

Kol Nidrei (*Kol ni'drey*) Annulment of vows made before the Day of Atonement service

Kosher (*Ka'sher*, often pronounced **Ko**'sher) 'Fitting, appropriate' food which a Jewish person is permitted to eat

Kupple (*Ku'ple*) See Kippah

Kvatter (*Kvat'er*) Yiddish. One of the people who carry a baby boy to and from his circumcision

Lag b'Omer (**Lag** *b'O'mer*) 33rd day of the counting of the Omer (the period between Passover and Shavuot)

Lamdan (*Lam'dan*) Torah scholar

Leshon hakodesh (*Les'hon ha'ko'desh*) Lit. the holy tongue

Leshon hara (*le'shon ha'ra*)   Lit. a tongue of evil; slanderous talk

Lulav (*Lu'lav*)   Palm branch, one of the four plant species used in prayer during the festival of Sukkot

Maarat hamachpelah (*Ma'a'rat ha'mach'pe'lah*) Cave where the Patriarchs and Matriarchs are buried

Machazit hashekel (*Ma'chaz'it ha'she'kel*)   'Half a shekel'. The temple tax in ancient times, the term now refers to a donation towards the upkeep of the synagogue, made during the Fast of Esther

Magen David (*Ma'gen Da'vid*)   Shield of David, a six-pointed star emblem

Mamzer (*Mam'zer*)   A child born of an adulterous relationship. Plural mamzerim

Mamzerut (*Mam'ze'rut*)   The condition of being a mamzer

Mashiach (*Ma'shi'ach*)   The Messiah

Maskil (*Mas'kil*)   A follower of haskalah

Maskilim (*Mas'kil'lim*)   Plural of maskil

Matzah (*Matz'ah*)   Unleavened bread

Matzot (*Matz'ot*)   Plural of matzah

Megillah (*Me'gil'lah*)   'Scroll', name used to refer to the Biblical Book of Esther

Melachah (*Me'lach'ah*)   'Work', one of the 39 types forbidden on the Sabbath

Melachim (*Me'la'chim*)   The Biblical Book of Kings

Melachot (*Me'lach'ot*)   Plural of Melachah

Menorah (*Me'nor'rah*)   The candelabrum in the Temple, also used for the oil- or candle-lamp lit during Hanukkah (see also Hanukiah)

Mezuzah (*Me'zu'zah*)   'Doorpost', small parchment scroll fixed to the right-hand doorpost of every room in a Jewish house (except bathroom and toilet)

Mezuzot (*Me'zu'zot*)   Plural of mezuzah

Midrashim (*Mi'drash'im*)   Jewish works which contain teachings illustrated with stories or parables

Migrash (*Mig'rash*)   Open land surrounding a town

Mikvaot (*Mik'va'ot*)   Plural of mikveh

Mikveh (*Mik'veh*)   Immersion pool

Milah (*Mee'lah*)   Circumcision

Milchemet mitzvah (*Mil'chem'et mitz'vah*) Obligatory war

Milchemet reshut (*Mil'chem'et re'shut*) Optional war

Minchah (*Min'chah*)   The afternoon service

Minyan (*Min'yan*)   'Required number', ten males over the age of 13 required if certain prayers are to be said

Mishnah (*Mish'nah*)   A work in 63 volumes compiled by Rabbi Judah the Prince in about the year 200, containing all the major rabbinical opinions of his day

Mishnah Torah (*Mish'nah To'rah*)   A Jewish code of law written by Rabbi Moses ben Maimon (Maimonides) in the thirteenth century

Mitnagdim (*Mit'nug'dim*)   'Opponents', those who opposed the Hasidic movement

Mitzvah (*Mitz'vah*)   Commandment

Mitzvot (*Mitz'vot*)   Plural of mitzvah

Mizrahi (*Mitz'ra'chi*)   Movement of religious Zionists

Modeh ani (*Mo'deh a'ni*)   'I thank you . . .', declaration said by Jewish people each morning, thanking God for permitting them to wake up to a new day

Moed (*Mo'ed*)   'Festival', the second division of the Mishnah

Mohel (*Mo'hel*)   A person who carries out circumcision

Moshav (*Mos'hav*)   Settlement or village where people own their own property. Opposite of kibbutz

Moshavim (*Mo'sha'vim*)   Plural of Moshav

Moshe (*Mo'sheh*)   Moses

Moshe Rabbenu (*Mo'sheh Ra'bey'noo*)   Our teacher Moses

Musaf (*Mu'saf*)   The additional service

Musar movement (*Mu'sar*, often pronounced **Mu'***sar*)   A movement which sought to improve the character training of Jews

Musar shteibel (**Mu'***sur shti'bel*)   'Ethics room', an idea of Rabbi Israel Lipkin of Salant who set up 'ethic rooms' as places where businessmen could spend time studying ethical works and reflecting on their lives

Nashim (*Na'shim*)   'Women', the third section of the Mishnah

Neilah (*Ne'i'lah*)   'Closing the gates', the concluding service of the Day of Atonement

Ner Tamid (*Ner' Ta 'mid*)   'Continual light', the light which is always kept burning in the synagogue

Nevi'im (*Ne'vi'im*)   'Prophets', Hebrew name for the second section of the Hebrew Bible

Nezikin (*Ne'zi'kim*)   'Damages', the fourth section of the Mishnah

Nidah (*Ni'dah*)   A woman who is menstruating

Nisan (*Ni'san*)   First month of the Jewish year, roughly corresponding with March/April

Nistarim (*Nis'ta'rim*) 'Hidden ones', name given to mystics who, during the seventeenth century, travelled about the east European Jewish villages teaching and encouraging

Noachide Laws Code of law given to Noah in the Bible and consisting of seven principles which Jews regard as the basic code of morality for all human beings

Omer (**O**'*mer*) A measure of barley; the name given to the period between Pesach and Shavuot

Onan (**O**'**nan**) A mourner up until the time of the burial

Parev or **Parve** (*Par'ev*, *Par've*) Food that may be eaten either with meat or dairy foods

Pasul (*Pa*'**sul**) Not kosher. Pasul refers to articles such as mezuzot or Torah scrolls that are unfit for use. Food that is not kosher is called treifah

Pesach (**Pe**'*sach*) Passover

Pidyan haben (*Pid '***yan** *ha*'**ben**) Redemption of a first-born son

Purim (*Pu*'**rim**) Festival commmemorating the Jews' deliverance from threat of extermination in the time of Xerxes 1, King of Persia

Pushkes (**Push**'*kes*) (Yiddish) Collection boxes

Rabbi 'My master', the spiritual leader of a Jewish community

Rashi (**Ra**'*shi*) Rabbi Shlomoh Yitzchaki (1040–1105) important Bible and Talmud commentator

Rebbe (**Re**'*be*) Leader of Hassidic group or movement

Rebbeim (*Re*'**bei**'*im*) Plural of rebbe

Rosh Chodesh (**Rosh Cho**'*desh*) 'Head of the month', the first day of a Jewish month

Rosh Chodesh (**Rosh Cho**'*desh*) 'Head of the month', the first day of a Jewish month

Rosh Hashanah (**Rosh** *Ha*'*sha*'**nah**) 'Head of the year', the Jewish New Year

Ruach hakodesh (**Ru**'*ach ha*'**ko**'*desh*) The holy spirit, a form of divine inspiration on a lower level than prophecy

Sandek (*San*'**dek**) The man who holds the child during circumcision

Sanhedrin (*San*'*hed*'**rin**) Supreme rabbinical court

Sarah Imenu Our mother Sarah

Seder (**Se**'*der*, usually rhymes with 'raider') 'Order', the Passover meal

Sefer Torah (*Se*'**fer** *Tor*'**rah**) 'Scroll of the Torah'

Selichot (*Se*'*lich*'**ot**) 'Pardons', prayers for forgiveness

Semichah (*Se*'*mi*'**cha**) Certificate certifying that a person has qualified as a rabbi

Sephardim (*Se*'*far*'**dim**) Oriental Jews

Shabbat (*Sha*'**bat**) Sabbath

Shabbat Mevarchim (*Sha*'**bat** *Me*'*var*'**chim**) 'Sabbath of blessing', the Sabbath preceding a new month

Shabbat shalom (*Sha*'**bat** *sha*'**lom**) 'Sabbath of peace', a Hebrew greeting used on the Sabbath

Shabbat Shuvah (*Sha*'**bat** *shu*'**vah**) 'Sabbath of returning', the Sabbath between the New Year and the Day of Atonement

Shabbos (**Sha**'*bos*) Western pronunciation of Shabbat

Shacharit (*Sha*'*char*'**it**) The morning service

Shalom (*Sha*'**lom**) Peace

Shamash (*Sha*'**mash**) 'Servant', the person responsible for seeing that the synagogue is in order, also the candle used to light up the other candles or oil lights in the Hanukkah lamp

Shatnez (*Shat*'**nez**) 'Mixed stuff', mixtures of linen and woollen fibres which may not be worn in the same garment

Shavuot (*Sha*'*vu*'**ot**) 'Weeks', the festival of Pentecost

Shechitah (*She*'*chi*'**tah**) Jewish method of animal slaughter

Shekel (**She**'*kel*) A Jewish coin

Sheloshim (*She*'*lo*'**shim**) Lit. thirty i.e. the month of mourning

Shema (*She*'**ma**) 'Hear', Jewish prayer declaring the oneness of God

Shemini Atzeret (*She*'*mi*'**ni** *Atz*'*er*'*et*) 'Assembly of the eighth day', a one-day festival occurring at the end of Sukkot

Shemitta (*She*'*mit*'**ta**) The year when the soil of Israel is to remain fallow

Shemot (*She*'**mot**) 'Names', the Hebrew name for the second Book of the Bible

Shemuel (*She*'*mu*'**el**) The Biblical Book of Samuel

Shevarim (*She*'*va*'**rim**) A note blown on the shofar (see Shofar)

Shevat (*She*'**vat**) Eleventh month of the Jewish year, roughly corresponding with January/February

Shir Hashirim (*Shir ha*'*shir*'**im**) The Biblical Book Songs of Songs

Shiva (*Shi*'**vah**) 'Seven', the first seven days after a funeral

Shiva brachot (**Shi**'*va bra*'**chot**) 'Seven blessings', blessings recited at a Jewish wedding and at the conclusion of each feast during the first seven days after a marriage

Shloshim (*Sh'lo'***shim**) 'Thirty', the first month after a funeral

Shmuesen (*Shmu'sen*) Yiddish for 'talks'

Shoah (*Sho'uh*) Lit. destruction, the Holocaust

Shochet (*Sho'***chet**) Slaughterer of animals

Shofar (*Sho'***far**) Ram's horn hollowed out and used to produce musical notes

Shteibel (*Shtee'bel*) Yiddish for 'room'

Shul (rhymes with 'fool') Yiddish for 'synagogue'

Shulchan Aruch (*Shul'***chan** *Ar'***ruch**) 'Table prepared', the code of Jewish law compiled by Rabbi Joseph Caro in the sixteenth century

Shushan Purim (*Shu'***shan** *Pu'***rim**) The day after Purim, celebrated as Purim in some places

Sidra (*Si'***drah**) A portion of the Torah read in the synagogue on Sabbath mornings

Siddur (*Si'***dur**) Prayer book

Siddurim (*Si'dur'***im**) Plural of Siddur

Simchat Torah (*Sim'***chat** *To'***rah**) Rejoicing of the law

Sivan (*Si'***van**) The third month of the Jewish year (starting from Nisan)

Sofer (*So'***fer**) A scribe. Plural soferim

Sukkah (*Su'***kah**) 'Covering', the temporary shelter covered with leaves that Jewish people live in during the festival of Sukkot

Sukkot (*Su'***kot**) Plural of Sukkah; also the name for the festival commemorating the trek of the ancient Israelites through the desert

Taharah (*Ta'ha'***rah**) Usually translated as 'purity'; for a full explanation of this term see page 82

Taharat hamishpacha (*Ta'ha'***rat** *ha'mish'pa'***chah**) 'Family purity', Jewish laws regulating sexual relations

Taharot (*Ta'ha'***rot**) Fifth section of the Mishnah

Takanah (*Ta'ka'***nah**) A rule instituted by the rabbis for the benefit of the community

Takanot (*Ta'ka'***not**) Plural of takanah

Tallit (*Ta'***lit**) 'Robe', woollen or silk robe worn by Jewish males during morning prayers

Tallit gadol (*Ta'***lit** *ga'***dol**) 'Large robe', full name for Tallit

Tallit katan (*Ta'lit ka'***tan**) 'Small robe', smaller version of the Tallit gadol worn by Jewish males during the daytime

Tallitot (*Ta'li'***tot**) Plural of Tallit

Talmud (*Tal'***mud**) Collection of writings of Jewish law and ethical teachings compiled about the year 500

Talmud Torah (*Tal'***mud** *To'***rah**, Ashkenazi pronunciation) Jewish religion classes

Tammuz (*Ta'***muz**) Fourth month of the Jewish year, roughly corresponding to June/July

Tashlich (*Tash'***lich**) 'Casting away', a service recited near a river at the Jewish New Year

Tefillah (*Te'fi'***lah**) 'Prayer'; also one of the leather boxes worn on the head and arm by Jewish males during morning prayers

Tefillah shel rosh (*Te'fi'***lah** *shel'***rosh**) Tefillah for the head (see Tefillin)

Tefillah shel yad (*Te'fi'***lah** *shel'***yad**) Tefillah for the arm (lit. hand)

Tefillin (*Te'fi'***lin**) Plural of Tefillah, the two leather boxes containing Biblical passages written on parchment scrolls that Jewish males wear at morning prayers during the week

Tehillim (*Te'hi'***lim**) Psalms, the Biblical Book of Psalms

Tekiah (*Te'ki'***yah**) One of the notes blown on the Shofar

Tenakh (*Te'***nakh**) Hebrew name for the Bible

Teruah (*Te'ru'***ah**) One of the notes blown on the Shofar

Tevet (*Te'***vet**) Tenth month of the Jewish year, roughly corresponding to December/January

Tikun (*Ti'***kun**) Improvement

Tikkun Olam (*Ti'***kun** *O'***lam**) Correcting the world i.e. improving society

Tisha b'Av (*Ti'***sha** *Be'***Av**) Ninth of Av, a fast day commemorating the destruction of the Temple and other tragedies

Tishrei (*Tish'***rey**) Seventh month of the Jewish year, roughly corresponding to September/October

Torah (*To'***rah**) 'Instruction', name by which Jews call the first five Books of the Bible, sometimes the whole of the Bible and sometimes the whole of rabbinic literature

Torah im dereth eretz (*To'***rah** *im de'***rech** **er**'*etz*) Torah study combined with an occupation; used by Rabbi Samson Raphael Hirsch to mean Torah study combined with secular study

Tosafot (*To'so'***fat**) Additions; Talmud commentaries

Tosefta (*To'sef'***ta**) 'Addition', a collection of those rabbinic opinions omitted from the Mishnah

Treifah (*Trey'***fah**) 'Torn', the opposite of kosher

Tumah (*Tu'***mah**) Often translated 'impurity'; for a full explanation see p. 82

Tzedaka (*Tze'dah'***kah**) 'Righteousness', act of giving money to a worthy cause (see also Gemilat hassadim)

Tzizit (*Tzi'***tzit**) 'Fringes', the tassels attached to each corner of the Tallit gadol and Tallit katan

Vayikra (*Va'yik'***rah**) 'And he called', Hebrew name for the third Book of the Bible

Yad Vashem (**Yad Va'***shem*) The Holocaust Memorial Centre, including exhibition and archives, in Jerusalem

Yamim neraim (*Yam'***im** *ne'ra'***im**) 'Days of Awe', Hebrew for the period beginning on New Year and concluding with the Day of Atonement

Yarmulke (**Yar'***mul'ke*) (Yiddish) a headcovering worn by religious males; also called a kippah or kupple

Yarzheit (**Yar'***tzite*) Yiddish term for the anniversary of a death

Yehoshua (*Ye'ho'***shu***'ah*) Biblical Book of Joshua

Yeshiva (*Ye'shi'***vah**) 'Place of sitting', a Talmudic academy

Yeshivot (*Ye'shi'***vot**) Plural of Yeshivah

Yichud (*Yi'***chud**) 'Togetherness', the moments following a wedding when bride and groom are together in private

Yiddish (**Yid'***dish*) Language spoken by some Western Jews, similar to German

Yom Ha'atzmaut (**Yom** Ha'atz'ma'**ut**) Israel Independence Day

Yom Hadin (**Yom** *Ha'***din**) Day of Judgement, one of the names of the Jewish New Year

Yom Hashoah (**Yom** *Ha'***sho***'ah*) Holocaust Remembrance Day

Yom Kippur (**Yom** *Ki'***pur**) Day of Atonement

Yom Yerushalayim (*Yom Ye'ru'sh'***lai***'im*) Jerusalem Day

Zeraim (*Ze'rn'***im**) the first section of the Mishnah

Zeved habat (**Ze'***ved ha'***bat**) 'the gift of a daughter', a naming ceremony for girls in Sephardi communities

Zion (*Tzi'***on**) Originally one of the names of Jerusalem, also used as a name for the Holy Land

Zohar (*Zo'***har**) The most important work of Jewish mysticism

INDEX